THE PAN ~~BOOK~~
OF
ORCHESTRAL MUSIC

Arthur Jacobs was born in Manchester in 1922 and educated at Oxford. He has been a music critic for various newspapers, principally the *Financial Times*, and since 1961 has been on the editorial board of the magazine *Opera*. Formerly a professor at the Royal Academy of Music and head of the music department at Huddersfield Polytechnic, he is well known as a translator of French, German, Italian and Russian operas and has also written an original libretto for an opera, *One Man Show*, by Nicholas Maw. He is the author of *A New Dictionary of Music* and of *Arthur Sullivan, a Victorian Musician*, and co-author of *The Pan Book of Opera*.

Also by Arthur Jacobs and Stanley Sadie in Pan Books:

THE PAN BOOK OF OPERA

Arthur Jacobs

The Pan Book of Orchestral Music

Pan Original
Pan Books London, Sydney and Auckland

First published 1987 by Pan Books Ltd, Cavaye Place,
London SW10 9PG
9 8 7 6 5 4 3 2 1
© Arthur Jacobs 1987
ISBN 0 330 30962 5
Photoset by Rowland Phototypesetting Ltd
Bury St Edmunds, Suffolk
Printed by Richard Clay Ltd Bungay, Suffolk

CONTENTS

AUTHOR'S PREFACE

Tastes change and preferences vary, but a companion to orchestral music starts by recognizing a core of favourites in the orchestral repertory. That repertory, corresponding to the musical inclinations of most of its listeners, is conservative. No apology is needed, therefore, that in selecting works for this book I have given particular attention to such composers as Beethoven, Haydn, Mozart and Tchaikovsky. But the list goes as far back as Corelli, Vivaldi and Bach, and far enough forward to include not only such twentieth-century giants as Shostakovich and Britten but also living composers of the stature of Boulez and Ligeti. The list is necessarily selective: it will, I hope, whet appetites even when not completely satisfying them.

What do we seek to know from the printed page before listening to the music in the concert-hall, on radio, or on recordings? My experiences as an avid listener to orchestral music since my earliest musical years, and later as a professional critic, have been my guides here. The information is intended to lead the listener towards a keener, more pleasurable experience in hearing the music itself. The listing of the orchestration for each work will, I hope, contribute to that. Particularly when the visual stimulus of the live concert is missing, and the music comes via loudspeaker, the listener is not always made aware of the range of sounds available.

Analysis, with indication of how the composer presents and uses his themes, may enable the listener to arrive sooner at the deeper stage of musical appreciation – not merely basking in sound, but relishing its succession of events. Historical details pertaining to the composers' lives and periods can also illuminate the present musical experience. By such means the listener may be brought closer to the world of the composer's own imagination and purpose.

A special remark should be made here about *keys* ('the first theme is in D minor, the second in F major', etc.). Readers with small technical knowledge of music may suppose that such information must be redundant for them, impossible to relate to their own listening experience. But in fact the change which every listener feels at Beethoven's famous transition to the finale of the Fifth Symphony, bursting from gloom to sunlight, is a change from C minor to C major; and, at the beginning of that symphony, the sensation of being lifted to 'somewhere different' by the entry of the horn-call is the change from C minor to E flat major. The listener's awareness is there already: it is hoped that the identification of the key-structure will sharpen that response.

ARTHUR JACOBS
1987

INTRODUCTION: HOW TO USE THIS BOOK

This book discusses 211 orchestral works by 75 composers. The composers are listed alphabetically, and there is a brief general introduction to their orchestral music. Under each composer, individual works are grouped in the following order:

> symphonies
> concertos
> other works (descriptive pieces, overtures, suites from the ballet, etc.)

Where more than one symphony or concerto by a given composer is to be discussed, there is a preliminary discussion of 'the symphonies' or 'the concertos' as well.

  Thus the order of reference is:

> Schumann –
>   The symphonies –
>   Symphony no. 1 in C

For each individual work the following information is given:

> Duration: an approximate duration of performance
> The historical background, with details of the first performance
> The orchestration, with any special features noted
> Analytical comment

Preceding this principal part of the book are two historical essays, *The Forms of Orchestral Music* and, dealing with musical instruments, *The Evolving Orchestra*.

  After the listing of composers and their works there is a *Glossary* in which an explanation is given of:

> Technical terms used, e.g., *recapitulation, rondo*
> Foreign (mainly Italian) words and phrases used by composers

> in movement-headings or in other contexts within the main
> body of the book
> The naming of instruments of the orchestra.

Finally, an *Index* lists not only the composers in their main place in
the book but also:

> References to incidental namings of composers elsewhere
> (e.g., the reference to Wagner in the discussion of Bruckner)
> Performers and other individuals mentioned
> Names and nicknames of musical works – so that a reader
> looking up *Bartered Bride, The* or *Resurrection* Symphony
> will be led to the appropriate page in entries under their
> respective composers, Smetana and Mahler.

THE FORMS OF ORCHESTRAL MUSIC

Even such apparently standard terms as *symphony* and *overture* have varied in meaning over the centuries, and a knowledge of different historical meanings can alert the present-day listener on what to expect.

The concerto: baroque and classical

In the earliest period covered by this book (up to and including Bach and Handel), the orchestral form most often encountered is the **concerto**. A varied, developed piece in several movements is implied, often but not necessarily with a soloist or a group of soloists standing out against the orchestra. The term **concerto grosso** (Handel's English equivalents were called **grand concertos**) is used for such works; but in a work with a group of soloists, concerto grosso may also indicate 'the full orchestra' as distinct from the **concertino** (soloists' group).

Vivaldi's concertos, widely influential, usually have three movements, fast–slow–fast, with the first (and sometimes the last) in **ritornello** form. In this form, the opening thematic material *returns* in different keys, always in the full orchestra, in the course of the movement. Sometimes the 'return' may be abbreviated. Thus the **baroque concerto** invites the listener to recognize the reappearance of the main theme in *several* different keys, and finally the home key again.

By Mozart's time (late eighteenth century) the modern standard use of concerto is established; it is nearly always a work for *one* solo instrument and orchestra and nearly always in *three* movements. In Mozart's and later use (the **classical concerto**), the first movement still follows the ritornello principle (the opening material later returning) but now with a changed emphasis, as follows.

The classical concerto strongly polarizes the *first* ritornello (normally the orchestra's opening of the work, without soloist) and the *second* or *central* ritornello. This arrives in the new key with a big sense of achievement by the orchestra – after a long, climactic trill by the solo instrument. After the central ritornello, a section akin to symphonic **development** (see below) takes place, and after that the opening of the movement is reasserted in a more unified sequence of key, like a symphonic **recapitulation** (see below).

For its slow movement, the classical concerto often adopts a simple twofold form giving the feeling of departure and return. The finale, always on the fast side, is often a set of **variations** – a straightforward tune subjected to a succession of new guises – or a **rondo**. In the latter, a principal theme returns periodically, always in the *same* key (unlike a ritornello).

The symphony and its first movement

Whereas English retained the Italian word *concerto*, it translated *sinfonia* as **symphony**. In Bach's and Handel's time the word was chiefly used to denote an introductory movement, or an instrumental interlude, in a vocal work. Hence the 'Pastoral Symphony' in Handel's *Messiah*. In Italian opera, *sinfonia* meant the overture, in the sequence of movements fast–slow–fast. This type of operatic overture, independently performed in concerts (and from the second half of the eighteenth century often extended to four movements by the interpolation of a minuet) became the symphony we know.

Just as the classical concerto is distinguished by a special form in its first movement, so is the **classical symphony**. This first-movement symphonic form corresponds to that of the first movement of an instrumental sonata of the same period, so the title **sonata-form** is often used. It is the most common form of fast orchestral movements from Haydn's period to such twentieth-century symphonists as Vaughan Williams and Shostakovich. It balances three main, obligatory sections of a movement, with or without optional sections at the front and back. Thus the sequence is: (optional slow introduction) – **exposition** – **development** – **recapitulation** – (optional coda).

The **exposition** first asserts an opening or 'home' key and then passes to a new 'complementary' key, normally by presenting a new theme in that key. The **development** 'plays with' these themes. The

recapitulation (a term which in music does not mean a simple repetition) brings a unity of key where the exposition had provided a contrast. The recapitulation gives to the home key not only its original material but the material that had conspicuously identified the *other* key.

The term *coda* (Italian for 'tail') is used to indicate any music that is heard after this new key-ordering of the old material is complete. Beethoven often extended this part beyond 'tail-like' proportions!

In the classical symphony, if the home key is major, its complementary key is the dominant, e.g. C major moves to G major; if the home key is minor, the complementary key is the relative major, e.g. D minor moves to F major. In the later nineteenth century, composers operated in a wider field of keys and their themes grow in number and complexity: such terms as 'first subject group' are often used to replace the simple 'first theme', etc.

Other symphonic movements

Other movements of the symphony follow in a contrast of tempos. The minuet, the only movement in a dance-rhythm in a Haydn or Mozart symphony, was speeded up by Beethoven into a more vigorous movement, often with touches of suddenness and surprise – hence the new term *scherzo*, literally a joke. Later composers (and, in the *Pastoral* symphony, Beethoven himself) sometimes expanded the symphony to five movements or more; or, much less often, reduced it to two movements (Nielsen, Symphony no. 5) or one (Sibelius, Symphony no. 7).

The **minuet** in its classical sense is characterized not only by its three-to-a-bar rhythm but by a particular form with literally repeated sections: A, A, B, A. The central contrasting section B is called a **trio**: early in its evolution it *was* played only by a threesome of instruments (see the Bach example, p. 35) and many later examples hint at this by allotting a reduced instrumentation to the trio. When the minuet became the **scherzo** and maintained the AABA form, the name trio was kept. A central contrasting section in a **march** is also sometimes called a trio.

The finale may be in the rondo or variation form already mentioned, but composers often wrote another movement in sonata-form as a finale.

Overture, rhapsody, symphonic poem

The **overture** (derived from the French *ouverture*, an opening) is in
baroque times specifically the **French overture**: a slow, stately
introduction leads to a main fast section and *may* end with a
resumption of slow tempo. Among works covered in this book,
only Handel used *overture* in this specific way. Later composers in
writing the overture to an opera or a play generally used sonata-
form, usually (e.g. Beethoven's *Egmont* and Weber's *Oberon*, both in
this book) with a slow introduction.

In the nineteenth century overture acquired a new meaning, away
from the theatre – a one-movement work, generally descriptive, of
which Mendelssohn's *The Hebrides* is the most famous example.
Sonata-form is generally used. A survival of the nomenclature is
found when Tchaikovsky calls his *Romeo and Juliet* not just a **fantasia**
(which could imply a free use of themes, to no pre-existent pattern)
but **overture-fantasia**. The term **rhapsody** can mean just such a
free form, especially one with some special local colour (Liszt's
Hungarian Rhapsodies, Gershwin's *Rhapsody in Blue*) but sometimes
denotes a set of variations as in Delius's *Brigg Fair*.

For a descriptive work of the nineteenth century a common
general term is **symphonic poem** – meaning something like a
narrative in music with the themes subjected to the close-knit
working characteristic of a symphony. An alternative name is
tone-poem, an approximation of the German *Tondichtung*, literally
a poem made with notes instead of words. The term *poem* has been
appropriated in other musical contexts without specific formal
meaning – as when Ravel called *La Valse* a **choreographic poem**,
i.e. a work for ballet with a narrative thread.

Some other forms

Suite (literally a 'following') has no specific meaning except a
succession of separate movements, often of dances and often with
the implication of light, uncomplicated forms. A set of extracts from
an opera or ballet (sometimes compiled by a hand other than the
composer's) is so called.

The **serenade**, literally an evening song and in ordinary use a song
addressed to the beloved, has a special meaning in Viennese–classical
musical usage; for example, in Mozart it is a set of movements for
orchestra (or a smaller ensemble), designed for social entertainment.

Marches and minuets but not long symphonic movements are included. The German **Nachtmusik** translates this sense, so Mozart's *Eine Kleine Nachtmusik* is *A little serenade*.

The Romantics and after

The composers of what is loosely called the Romantic period (1830–1910) tended to appropriate the older formal titles such as symphony and concerto and to reinterpret them. In particular, the former separate movements were often linked together – either by requiring no break between movements or by having themes in common (as in symphonies by Dvořák, Saint-Saëns and Tchaikovsky, in very different ways) or both. Beethoven is the progenitor of such an approach, his *Choral Symphony* inspiring the fusion of symphony and cantata so powerfully achieved by Mahler.

The twentieth century, conspicuous for the freedom with which composers have thrown over the past conventions of harmony, rhythm, and even tonality (the major/minor key system), has not been prodigal of new fixed forms. In Debussy and Ravel there are clear elements of recurrence and contrast in patterns of rather free design. Bartók, however, laid out many movements in what is called **arch-form** leading to a central point and back (e.g. ABCDEDCBA), but not adhering to a strict correspondence between sections.

Works written by Schoenberg in the 12-note method notably keep a reference to the contrasts, developments and recapitulation characteristics of classical sonata-form. Radical composers achieving prominence in the 1960s such as Pierre Boulez and Karlheinz Stockhausen largely abandoned the use of 'themes' (recognizably recurring units of music), which is one reason why most of the forms described here cannot be applied to their works. But they have notably developed the idea of leaving some decisions to the performer and to the occasion – for instance, decisions on the order of a sequence of notes or a sequence of sections of music.

THE EVOLVING ORCHESTRA

During a very recent period, less than two decades, something new has happened to the orchestra. Previously, for almost three centuries, new instruments had been adopted and old ones discarded, as composers altered their demands and listeners their preferences, and as musical performances changed their location. Louder sounds and faster articulation became available. Mechanical improvements to instruments (as well as an increase in numbers of performers) served to multiply the physical stimulations offered to the listener's ear. The word 'evolution' could be used of the orchestra almost in parallel to its meaning in biology.

But in recent years the 'early music' movement has arrested that process. In order to perform music of previous centuries in a spirit as close as possible to the original, instruments of the relevant period have been revived, re-manufactured and re-studied. Such a revivalist spirit had already been applied to music for solo instruments, particularly the cultivation of harpsichord, lute and viols. But that whole orchestras could be assembled to play Bach and Handel, and even a Monteverdi opera, on 'original' instruments – this was new, and depends not only on fresh attitudes of musicians to their task but also on the new artistic and marketing relationships in the era of compact discs and broadcasting.

Accordingly, our modern age is sensitive to the fact that not only music has a history, but musical *performance* as well. Even as we play Bach on our modern piano, for domestic delight or in the concert-hall, we are aware of 'translating' into our instrument's tone what was written for a harpsichord. Orchestral sounds have also changed. The one-keyed wooden flute of Bach's or Mozart's time was less powerful in sound, less able to cope fluently with keys remote from C major, than our modern instrument. Orchestral horns and trumpets remained without valves (generally, therefore, unable to negotiate scales) until the mid-nineteenth century. Only from about 1880

– from the time of late Wagner and Verdi – can an orchestra as heard by the composer be considered approximately the same as that which we hear today.

So, in the comments on individual works which constitute the main part of this book, the very *names* of the instruments have to be understood in a historical sense. The audience to whom Handel proclaimed 'The trumpet shall sound', the audience for whom Mozart made Tamino play his 'magic flute', did not hear what we normally hear as trumpet or flute. Our modern instruments serve the purpose, and may even play the original music more powerfully and with less liability to human error. But it is interesting, occasionally at least, to hear as nearly as possible the sounds the composer must have envisaged.

Up to this recent, deliberate historical reversion, however, the story of the orchestra pursued a linear development. The orchestra as we know it, a regular grouping of instruments playing its own concert repertory (apart from what it might do to serve the dance, worship or the theatre), has existed only from the mid-seventeenth century. Its basis is the string section – that is, the instruments of the violin family, the only such 'family' that could present a more or less homogeneous sound from top to bottom and could articulate the notes with a great dynamic (loud/soft) range and with a rich variety of expression. Orchestral sound distributed between first violins, second violins, violas and 'basses' (that is, cellos and double-basses, generally playing the same line at an octave distance) enabled Corelli in Italy to display brilliance and pathos in concertos which captured the cultivated taste of western Europe about 1700.

Such a string group, generally with a supporting keyboard instrument playing a *continuo* part (see Glossary), was preserved by early eighteenth-century Italian composers such as Vivaldi, who heightened the brilliance of string writing. The Italian-trained Handel delighted his British patrons with concertos on Corelli's model. Though composers in France showed some partiality to a five-part string group, other countries inclined to the Italian four-part grouping (counting all the 'basses' as one line). Other instruments regularly appeared as reinforcement in larger works (Handel's oratorios, Bach's Passions), or as soloists in concertos: they included flutes, recorders, oboes, horns and trumpets. Such were the typical orchestral sounds of the so-called 'high baroque' or 'late baroque'.

The change of taste between the era of Handel and that of Haydn (between 'late baroque' and 'classical' or from early to late eighteenth century) went with a proliferation of orchestras at courts, in theatres and in the first public orchestral concerts. The 'classical' orchestra, from the mid-eighteenth century, has a pair of oboes conspicuously standing out from the strings and a pair of horns thickening or binding the sound: other instruments often added, in a way familiar today from Haydn's and Mozart's symphonies, include one or two flutes and (in pairs) bassoons, trumpets and kettledrums (two drums, one player). The newly invented clarinet also joined the orchestra – likewise in pairs.

Descriptions, pictures and other historical evidence make it clear that the keyboard-player was also a regular participant in orchestral performances of Haydn's day as he had been in Handel's. Indeed he served to control the orchestra, sharing the function with the leader of the first violins. But the fuller orchestral scoring had removed the musical need for a keyboard player in a *continuo* role, so modern performances generally omit the keyboard participation altogether.

The invention of the conductor in the modern sense in the early nineteenth century was one of the things that transformed orchestral performance at that time. Weber, Mendelssohn, Berlioz and the now almost-forgotten Spohr were among the first composers to direct their works this way. By this time, the assembly of instruments needed for, say, Beethoven's late orchestral music had become standard everywhere. Local considerations would determine the number of stringed instruments, but the component of two each of basic woodwind (flutes, oboes, clarinets, bassoons), four horns, two trumpets, three trombones and kettledrums could be assumed. The piccolo, double-bassoon and, from the 1830s, the tuba might be added, as also harp and the supplementary percussion of snare drum, bass drum, cymbals and triangle.

The growth of public concert-going and opera-going in the nineteenth century gave financial encouragement to the enlargement of orchestral sound. New technical methods in constructing wood-wind and brass instruments increased their carrying power. Larger halls came into use. Around 1800, a total orchestra of forty would generally have been considered more than adequate; in 1880, the strings of an orchestra on their own might exceed that number. Composers could now more easily resort to *divided* strings: the first violins, for instance, might be split into sub-groups, so that between them more notes of a chord could be sounded.

A similar demand was made by composers for more players of each woodwind instrument – three flutes, for instance, instead of two, which could all be put to different notes as an alternative to reinforcing one another. Such extra instruments as piccolo and double-bassoon became the rule rather than exceptional. Such resources, serving to increase the weight of sound, were likewise available to heighten the orchestra's brilliance – with high cascading notes from multiple violins, or rapidly tongued exclamations from trumpets made newly agile by the invention of valves.

In the nineteenth-century opera house, composers sought to match scenic grandeur with largeness and unusualness of sound. French, Italian and German composers were all participants in this process – Meyerbeer, Verdi (the special effects of the extra trumpets for the Grand March in *Aida*) as well as Wagner. For *Das Rheingold*, Wagner demanded six harps each playing a different part. A quartet of the newly invented 'Wagner tubas', a kind of cross-breed between horn and tuba, was used in *The Ring* and was afterwards brought by Bruckner into the world of the symphony.

In the early twentieth century the growth of the orchestra in size and power was not yet finished. Demands for four or more of each woodwind instrument, demands for six or even eight horns (Mahler's Symphony No. 8, Skryabin's *Poem of Ecstasy*), and other brass, implies a very large and powerful string section to match. Stravinsky's *The Rite of Spring* is a famous example of very large orchestral scoring (see p. 326). But it is remarkable that composers such as Mahler, Strauss and Stravinsky, masters of the gigantic, also wrote other works with a new cultivation of small orchestral forces. Works for string orchestras alone, or even for orchestras composed of only one player for each separate instrument (Schoenberg's Chamber Symphony No. 1) are also a feature of the first half of the century.

The concept remained of a basic fixed orchestra in its four main sections of strings, woodwind, brass and percussion, plus an occasional harp – everything else being considered as an extra. Such extras were occasionally required by nineteenth-century composers, usually to convey a picturesque or regional flavour: examples are found in Bizet's employment of an alto saxophone in *The Woman of Arles* (L'Arlésienne) and in Tchaikovsky's use of the celesta for his sugar-plum fairy in *The Nutcracker*. Mahler's mandolin in the Symphony no. 8 provides a similar extension of sound. Rather different is the reinforcement of the general body of tone by the importation of a piano – by Stravinsky, Prokofiev and Copland, among others.

The widening of the range of orchestral tone-colour has not been expressed only in additions of instruments. Composers have also stimulated greater and greater technical skills on the part of the players. There has been an exploration of new extremes of high and low, from Berlioz's deep notes of the trombone, previously unheard, to Stravinsky's famous high bassoon at the beginning of *The Rite of Spring*. New methods of attacking a note have ranged from 'flutter-tonguing' of woodwind and brass (as in Schoenberg) to Bartók's hard *pizzicato* where the string bounces back against the fingerboard of the instrument. Mutes of different sorts alter the tone of strings and brass; a choice of many kinds of stick affects the sound of drums, cymbals and other instruments of percussion.

The innovations of the twentieth century include one completely new 'family' of instruments, those of electronic tone-generation (mostly outside the range of this book, except for the ondes Martenot, as in Messiaen's *Turangalîla*). Of wider application has been a vast expansion in the types and numbers of percussion instruments and in the technical virtuosity expected of their players. The increased *melodic* (or otherwise independent) role allotted to percussion, in many different ways from Bartók to Boulez, has been a significant feature of nearly every concert-goer's musical experience.

Note: titles of movements, indications of tempo, durations, etc

For works in more than one movement, the heading for each movement is given. Usually, such a heading is simply an indication of tempo in conventional Italian, e.g. *Allegro* – for an explanation of such terms, see the Glossary, p.367. Tempo indications in other languages, such as when a German composer writes directions in German, are here given in English.

Where a tempo direction is found enclosed in square brackets, it has been supplied editorially. In works before 1800 such a direction was often omitted by the composer because it would be inferred as a matter of course from what was customary.

Where a composer gives a heading in terms of musical form, e.g. 'scherzo', 'rondo', this is followed by a colon and then by the tempo indication beginning with a small letter, e.g. 'Rondo: allegro'. But where two or more successive tempos occur within a movement, a dash and an ensuing capital letter are used, e.g. 'Adagio – Allegro molto'.

Dance-forms are given in the language used by the composer, e.g. *menuet* (French) or *minuetto* (Italian) for 'minuet'. The incorrect *menuetto* as used by Haydn and some German-speaking contemporaries has been replaced by the correct Italian term. The sub-heading 'Trio', as an indication of the middle part of a 'Minuetto' or 'Scherzo' movement, is omitted from the headings here unless (as sometimes happens) it carries a new tempo indication of its own.

The indication 'Finale', which composers or their publishers appear to have used or omitted in a quite arbitrary manner, is not used here.

Durations of works are given in approximate times and in minutes, with information drawn from various listings used in concerts, broadcasting and recording. Even 'authorized' timings as given by composers or their publishers have been treated with caution, as different performances under a composer's auspices have been known to vary. An apparently very large range (e.g. 25–31 minutes) for a given work may be based not merely on conductors' differences of speed but on whether or not they observe repetitions indicated in the score.

COMPOSERS AND THEIR MUSIC

BACH

1685–1750

Johann Sebastian Bach never knew in his busy life the unsurpassed international admiration which posterity would grant him. His last twenty-seven years he spent at Leipzig, where he was employed by the city council as *cantor* of the St Thomas School (not, as often said in English writings, of the St Thomas church). His duties included teaching as well as choral direction in church. He was also *director musices* or musical director to the city.

But neither post gave him the direct responsibility for an orchestra which he had enjoyed in his previous post at Köthen (then spelt Cöthen), a small German town where he served as *Kapellmeister*, or head of the musical establishment, to the reigning prince. The princely orchestra was very small by modern standards: about a dozen players. Most of Bach's orchestral works are best thought of as a slightly inflated form of chamber music. Their performance by a modern, larger orchestra may demand an adjustment of attitude on the part of both performers and listeners.

Of those orchestral works, it is Bach's concertos which are most often heard. Others sometimes included in modern orchestral concerts are the Suite in B minor for flute and strings, attributed to his Leipzig period, and two suites in D, both exceptionally with three trumpets.

'BWV' numbers (*Bach Werke-Verzeichnis* = Bach Work Index, compiled by Wolfgang Schmieder) are used to index and define Bach's works.

The concertos

Bach took over an Italian style of composition, making it his own and adding a characteristic German solidity. For Bach as for Vivaldi the word *concerto* indicates a work of several movements, usually with a contrast between a soloist (or several soloists) and the whole ensemble. But not always so. No two of the six 'Brandenburg' concertos are alike in their instrumentation, and in nos. 3 and 6 there is no contrast of soloists versus the rest, but only an assembly of stringed instruments in busy interplay.

All the concertos are based on the three–movement form, fast–slow–fast, but in the Brandenburg Concerto no. 3 the expected second movement is omitted – or left to be supplied in performance (see below) – and in no. 1 a combination of minuet and polonaise is added as a concluding fourth movement. A feature common to the opening movements (as with Vivaldi) is the use of *ritornello* form, in which the opening material makes a complete or partial reappearance in other keys during the movement and finally in its original key.

Bach was apparently the first composer to use a keyboard instrument (the harpsichord) as soloist with orchestra. Its customary role in ensemble was as a supplier of the bass line with accompanying chords (see *continuo* as explained in the Glossary). In the Brandenburg Concerto no. 5, Bach gave it the novel role of soloist, and in Leipzig he proceeded to write further concertos for one or more harpsichords, most but not all adapted from works originally written with another solo instrument.

Brandenburg Concertos, BWV 1046–51

While at Köthen Bach completed his most celebrated set of orchestral works (though he may have worked earlier on some of them.) They are so named because they were printed in 1721 with a dedication to the Margrave of Brandenburg, a powerful nobleman whom Bach is presumed to have met on a visit to Berlin two years before. Whether the Margrave ever had them performed is unknown! Four of the concertos also survive in a manuscript copy with slightly different scoring – this presumably being a previous version, for performance by the orchestra at Köthen itself.

In the final 'Brandenburg' version some unfamiliar or non-standard instruments will be noted. In Concerto no. 1 Bach called for the *violino piccolo* or small violin, tuned a minor third higher than the usual instrument (bottom string therefore B flat), but the part is usually played today on the standard violin. In Concerto no. 6, *bass viol* indicates a member of the *viola da gamba* family, approximately of cello size. The recorder required in the Concertos nos. 2 and 4 is the treble size, or in Continental nomenclature the alto. Although in some modern performances the flute will be found taking over these recorder parts, Bach made a clear distinction between the instruments, requiring the flute in Concerto no. 5.

No.1 in F for 2 horns, oboe, and violino piccolo, with orchestra of 2 oboes, bassoon, strings, and continuo

> [Allegro]
> Adagio
> Allegro
> Minuet and Polonaise
> Duration: 21–23 minutes

The horns make themselves conspicuous right away, with figures which have been shown to be 'greeting calls', drawn from the hunting field. They also share in an exchange of phrases with other instruments. The opening section, complete with the 'greeting calls', returns at the end.

In the second movement (in D minor) the horns are silent, allowing a long contemplative melody to wander from a solo oboe to *violino piccolo*. The bass-line (bassoon, cello, double-bass) soon shares in the melody too. A formal close is followed by a questioning cadence which is resolved in the opening of . . .

. . . the third movement, in cheerful mood. Here the horns rejoin, helping to frame a piece which puts the *violino piccolo* in the role of a concerto soloist. As in the opening movement, the opening section returns as a conclusion.

Exceptionally, the combined dance-movements follow. They are extrovert and uncomplicated. The minuet, embracing all the instruments, is followed by a trio (contrasting section) in D minor which is literally written for a trio (two oboes and bassoon). After a repetition of the minuet there is a polonaise for strings only, in F; then a second trio for the two horns individually and all the oboes in unison) which breaks from the prevailing 3/4 into 2/4; and finally the minuet is presented yet again.

No.2 in F for trumpet, recorder, oboe and violin, with orchestra of strings and continuo

[Allegro]
Andante
Allegro assai
Duration: 13 minutes

Bach's choice of instruments for his quartet of soloists is unique. But will not a trumpet unreasonably dominate the others? If the valve-less, narrow-bored trumpet of Bach's own time is used in preference to the modern trumpet, this predominance is not so acute. But even so, there has been scholarly discussion on whether Bach really preferred a trumpet or a horn for this part, which would play the part an octave lower than a trumpet does.

Following the model of the time, *all* the performers including the soloists join in the *tutti* passages, first of all announcing the strongly formed main theme which will recur in various keys (*ritornello*). The solo instruments now show themselves successively on their own (violin, then oboe, recorder and trumpet) in a tiny snatch of theme which belongs to them alone. Later, they will re-enter in a different order. Increasingly, they also join with the orchestral strings in an expansion of the opening music. The mood continues cheerful to the end.

The slow middle movement brings a change of key to D minor and a complete change of texture. The trumpet is silent and so are the orchestral strings; recorder, oboe and violin form a trio against the bass-line played by a cello and harpsichord as *continuo*. The quiet melody seems to be spun out from the opening phrase.

The third movement brings back the key and the cheerful mood of the first, but this time it is the quartet of soloists who begin. A *continuo* line plies busily beneath, but the orchestral strings delay their entry; and later still they announce their own counter-theme. The soloists' opening theme, starting with a rising pair of notes and sometimes a trill, cannot fail to be recognized whenever it reappears. As the trumpet first announced it, so the trumpet briefly and emphatically asserts it at the end of the movement.

No.3 in G for 3 violins, 3 violas, 3 cellos with continuo

[Allegro]
(missing ?)
Allegro
Duration: 10–13 minutes

Though restricted to strings, plus a reinforcing harpsichord on the
continuo line, this concerto does not lack contrast. From time to time,
solo textures (each of the nine instruments playing its own part)
emerge from the solid texture of the united ensemble. The opening
ensemble passage, ending with a downward scale and a pronounced
'finishing' cadence, recurs in various keys throughout the first
movement – finally back in its original key. The movement's
cheerful swing is maintained throughout.

But what follows? Bach writes down two chords in slow time –
the same chords, in E minor, which in the Concerto no.4 will be
found at the end of a slow middle movement in that key. The
implication is that perhaps here also a movement in E minor, of the
performers' choice, was to be inserted; or that the chords were
indeed to be played without a middle movement, but embellished
with a cadenza by the leading violinist (or another player). To
perform these chords just by themselves would not be in the style of
the period.

The finale returns to G and, as usual, brings an air of lightness.
Though written in 12/8 time, it comes over as a *Ländler* (an ancestor
of the waltz) with three quick beats in the bar. The movement
divides into two – the first half proceeds to the dominant (D major)
and is then literally repeated; the second part takes the contrary
direction and it, too, is repeated. A special feature during the second
part is the rise of the first viola to a difficult florid passage out-soaring
the violins – it is believed that Bach himself would play this viola
part.

No.4 in G for violin and 2 recorders, with orchestra of strings and continuo

> Allegro
> Andante
> Presto
> Duration: 15 minutes

A gently lilting first movement begins with a prominent theme for the two recorders, who often proceed in sweetly linked thirds or sixths. The theme recurs in various keys throughout the movement. The violin takes a varied role, sometimes joining with the recorders and sometimes weaving its own tracery.

The slow second movement, in E minor, likewise displays combination and contrast for the paired recorders and the partly independent violin. A flourish for one of the recorders, ending like a question on the dominant chord, leads us to await . . .

. . . the final movement. The pace is fast and the texture is fugal, as the theme with its rising pair of opening notes enters four times in succession on the strings of the orchestra, the violin soloist joining in. Still higher, a fifth entry is made by the two recorders in unison. The recorders divide and reunite, and the violin later breaks into brilliant display.

No.5 in D for flute, violin and harpsichord, with orchestra of strings and continuo

> Allegro
> Affettuoso
> Presto
> Duration: 21–23 minutes

The vigorous opening *ritornello* begins by marching up the chord of D major and then down its scale – an unmistakable, oft-returning figure. The solo flute and solo violin follow immediately with a smoother, overlapping figure over the harpsichord's busy accompaniment. After a substantial time this balance is broken: the harpsichord takes command with a parade of display-figures against only the lightest accompaniment, and then with no accompaniment at all. Only for the last eight bars do the other performers re-enter, restating the *ritornello*.

A short central movement has the unusual direction *Affettuoso*, 'with feeling'. In the contrasting key of B minor, it is confined to the three solo instruments – but the two hands of the harpsichordist keep separate lines, so the effect is often of a quartet. Finally the opening bars return.

The merry 6/8 rhythm of a jig enlivens the final movement in D major. The texture builds up engagingly: the violin is pursued hot-foot by the flute, and the harpsichord takes up the same theme in the left hand followed by the right. Then the violas begin an orchestral participation. The music flows imperceptibly into a middle section in B minor which continues the contrast between the threesome of soloists and the full ensemble, or sometimes between the keyboard instrument and the rest. The whole of the opening section returns to end the movement with unabated cheerfulness.

No.6 in B flat for two violas, two bass viols, cello and continuo

[Allegro]
Adagio ma non tanto
Allegro
Duration: 19 minutes

Here is a work with a characteristic seldom found in classical orchestral music: it has no violin parts. The leading (top) voice is that of the first viola, which Bach himself is supposed to have played. In fact the work seems to have been designed as a sextet for soloists: two players of the viola, two of the bass viol (otherwise viola da gamba), a cello and a violone (ancestor of the double bass). With these six the participation of a keyboard *continuo* player is assumed.

The viol family, whose instruments are bowed like those of the violin but fretted like a guitar, was not quite obsolete in Bach's time, the strongest survivor being the 'bass' (approximately cello size). Bach's prince at Köthen played it, which gives a reason for the instrument's presence here. Unusual sonorities are therefore a feature of this concerto.

The spirited first movement opens with another unusual feature: instead of a combined attack, the two violas make their melodious entrance one just behind the other. The recurrence of that feature helps to unify the movement.

In the slow movement the bass viols are silent and the two violas utter the tender, melancholy theme which is to dominate the music.

The movement opened in E flat but moves away and ends in the key of G minor with a chord of D – setting up the same expectancy as precedes the finale of the Concertos nos. 3 and 4.

In the present finale Bach resolves matters with one of his most lively dance rhythms. It is a jig in 12/8 time, with strong syncopations. Later, the violas dash away in duet. The patterns of recurrence are strong and the cheerful impetus continues to the end.

Concerto in D minor for harpsichord and orchestra, BWV 1052

> Allegro
> Adagio
> Allegro
> Duration: 24 minutes

The first composer to designate a keyboard instrument as concerto soloist, Bach sometimes used as his starting-point a work by another composer. But the present work is a Bach original, probably written for the performances of the *collegium musicum* or music society which Bach directed at Leipzig from 1729. The two outer movements of the concerto had already been used as instrumental pieces (with organ solo) in Cantata no. 146, written in fulfilment of Bach's church duties a few years before. The keyboard player would be expected to play throughout – that is, supplying the *continuo* in the orchestral passages as well as being the soloist.

The first movement follows the *ritornello* principle: that is, the orchestra's initial theme is due to return in different keys at important points later. But in this case the very opening phrase, with its determined upward push, inserts itself frequently in supporting guise. The soloist supplies a contrast of tone and the most arresting, most brilliant musical ideas. Eventually a passage of increasing excitement leads to the return of the main theme in its original key and the original bare octaves.

A slow movement enclosed between two minor-key fast movements might well be in a contrasting major, but Bach finds contrast enough in G minor. An orchestral tune in bare octaves advances in slow tread and continues as the bass against which the soloist delivers its eloquently ornamented, plaintive melody. This melody expands and reaches its end, on which the unaltered bare octaves of the introduction return and close the movement.

The finale is the longest movement, growing out of two main themes – the swift descent of the opening and the chain of little repetitive motives which the soloist soon presents in a miniature dialogue with the orchestra. After exploring various keys, soloist and orchestra return to D minor for an emphatic re-assertion of the original descent. Then, unaccompanied (and fulfilling the function of a cadenza in the later Mozartian concerto), the soloist launches a display of heavy chords and rapid runs. There is a dramatic halt, then a resumption of the impetus as the concerto is rounded off.

Concerto in D minor for two violins and orchestra, BWV 1043

> Vivace
> Largo ma non tanto
> Allegro
> Duration: 16 minutes

Familiarly called 'Bach's Double Concerto', this was composed and presumably first performed during Bach's years at Köthen (1717–23). It is the best-known and much-loved example of that special musical texture in which the two violins interweave their strands in a way which may now suggest a raptly poised balance, now a vigorous game of follow-my-leader. The soloists are equals: the first to be heard in a solo role, after the opening orchestral *tutti*, is in fact the player of the second violin – meaning the second line as Bach writes the music on the page. The other player follows immediately.

But in fact the two players are supposed to play *with* the orchestra from the outset – an orchestra simply of strings plus the keyboard *continuo*. The soloists lead their colleagues, the first and second violins, throughout the work, breaking out on their own for intermittent display. Characteristically, the theme of the opening bars acts as *ritornello*, heard later in the orchestra in other keys and then in the original key to end the first movement.

The central movement brings the contrast of a gently rocking rhythm and a major key (F), with the soloists now floating in a more detached way above the rest. Vigorous energy returns with the original minor key in the finale: here again the opening subject returns in different guises, and the two soloists seem to compete in athletic beauty.

BARBER

1910–81

Opera, songs, symphonies and concertos all helped to give Samuel Barber his high reputation among American composers. But the music most closely associated with his name is the following youthful work. Barber's fellow-Americans adopted it as a musical token of public solemnity, rather as 'Nimrod' from Elgar's *Enigma Variations* had been adopted in British use. On 14 April 1945 it was performed after the radio announcement of President Roosevelt's death.

Adagio for Strings, opus 11

Duration: 7–8 minutes

Taken originally from a string quartet, this work had its first orchestral performance when Arturo Toscanini conducted the orchestra of the National Broadcasting Corporation (New York) on 5 November 1938.

The piece opens softly. A yearning phrase on the first violins passes to other instruments. As the music's passion increases, the entire texture moves very high, the double-basses falling silent and the cellos ascending to the top of the treble stave. There is an emotional pause on a loud chord, followed by a descent to a soft ending. Throughout, the sense of solemnity, as in a church chant, is enhanced by the 'modal' harmony. The ordinary sense of key would suggest an ending in B flat minor but the music closes on a chord of F major.

BARTÓK

1881–1945

Between the two World Wars, Béla Bartók established a leading reputation among European composers. With Kodály and Dohnányi he gave Hungary a strong profile in the picture of modern music. He was himself the soloist in the first performance of his first two piano concertos. While the six string quartets unfolded webs of intense and sometimes difficult musical thought, the orchestral *Dance Suite* of 1923 adopted a lively, accessible style indebted to Hungarian and Romanian folk-music. The second and third of the works discussed below represent the Bartók of this period.

In 1940, in the wake of the physical and cultural destruction brought on Continental Europe by the Nazis, he settled in New York. In the five years that remained to him before his death he remained active despite ill-health and personal anxieties. He composed a third piano concerto (all but the final 16 bars) and an unaccompanied violin sonata (for Yehudi Menuhin) as well as the Concerto for Orchestra, treated below, which has continued to be widely enjoyed.

Concerto for Orchestra

Introduction: Andante non troppo – Allegro vivace
Play of the couples: Allegro scherzando
Elegy: Andante non troppo
Interrupted Intermezzo: Allegretto
Presto
Duration: 37 minutes

Boston (and not New York, as stated in the printed score) heard the first performance of this work on 1 December 1944. It had been commissioned by Serge Koussevitzky, the eminent conductor of the Boston Symphony Orchestra and the patron of many composers. In using the term 'concerto' for a purely orchestral work the composer seemed to be reviving a usage of the eighteenth century (see p. 11): the formal expectations of a 'symphony' are avoided, and the functions of showmanship now associated with the word 'concerto' are fulfilled not by a single soloist but by members of the orchestra in turn. The forces required are 3 each of flutes, oboes, clarinets and bassoons; 4 horns, 3 trumpets, 3 trombones and tuba; kettledrums, snare drum, bass drum, cymbals, triangle, tam-tam; 2 harps and strings.

Four of the five movements have titles (in Italian in the original). The first, itself called 'Introduction', has a brief slow opening, less than one minute long: the main, faster section follows with a leaping theme for violins, a strident phrase for trombone, and a quietly undulating theme for oboe. Eventually the oboe's theme re-emerges on a solo horn, after which the leaping theme and the assertive trombone conclude the movement.

A tapping side-drum, without snares, begins the second movement: couples of bassoons, oboes, clarinets, flutes and muted trumpets appear in turn. A hymn-like strain for brass ensues – perhaps a wedding hymn, since the bassoons now reappear as a threesome! New colours are heard, including those of two harps. The side-drum taps a receding farewell.

The mournful third movement ('Elegy') forms a single span, proceeding from a low, regular tread to misty visions and then to more definite themes, ending with the low tread again.

The fourth movement ('Interrupted intermezzo') presents a gentle, ingratiating theme in subtly irregular rhythm. With comically noisy effect, a march bursts in – said to be the parody of an 'heroic' theme in Shostakovich's *Leningrad* (seventh) symphony. The gentle tune is resumed, decorated with a flute cadenza.

Seven heavy (*pesante*) bars begin the finale, after which an exhilarating chase follows. There are interruptions, one of them a long fugue begun by violins. The original end to this work being rather sudden and unceremonious, the composer provided an optional extension with trumpet-call and cymbal-clash.

Concerto no.2 for violin and orchestra

Allegro non troppo
Andante tranquillo
Allegro molto
Duration: 32 minutes

This is *the* Bartók violin concerto which, during his lifetime, was published and performed without being described as 'no.2'. Bartók's violinist friend and fellow-Hungarian, Zoltán Székely, gave the first performance on 23 April 1939 with the Concertgebouw Orchestra of Amsterdam, conducted by Willem Mengelberg. Only after the composer's death was an earlier, two-movement concerto made known and inevitably called 'no.1': some dissatisfaction with it had led the composer to keep it unperformed.

The present concerto is in B major (though not so labelled) and each movement is based on a traditional form. It was published with two alternative endings, one of which is for orchestra alone, the other (at Székely's prompting) allowing the soloist to participate to the end in a more traditional manner. The orchestration calls for 2 flutes (second doubling piccolo), 2 oboes (second doubling english horn), 2 clarinets (second doubling bass clarinet), and 2 bassoons (second doubling double-bassoon), 4 horns, 2 trumpets, 3 trombones, kettledrums and an array of extra percussion (including tam-tam and, unusually, *two* snare drums), harp, celesta and strings. Some specifically modern effects are used, including a very strong, *pizzicato* so that the string snaps back against the finger-board – as heard from the complete string section almost at the end of the first movement.

The first movement is based on the classical sonata form. The harp sets up a rhythmical background of chords in B major against which the solo violin delivers a 'singing', wide-spanning theme. Violin and orchestra move to a passage marked *risoluto* (decisively). A calmer theme now delivered by the soloist comprises all the twelve available notes – although this is not a 'twelve-note' construction in Schoenberg's sense. It has a continuation in which trills are prominent. After a climax, the thrumming of the harp is again heard as an accompaniment to a version of the first theme, now in F major and beginning the middle or development section of the movement. During this, a striking passage displays the theme upside-down high on the violin, against an accompaniment of celesta and harp. After a climax the first theme returns, again in B major but without its harp accompaniment and an octave higher than originally. Other material is also recapitulated. The long solo cadenza was supplied by Bartók himself.

The second movement in G major is a series of variations on a theme of a rhapsodical nature. The solo violin takes the lead in announcing it, with two closing bars for orchestra. In Variation 1, more florid, the solo instrument is at first accompanied only by isolated beats on kettledrums, reinforced by double-basses. Variation 2 begins with repeated sustained notes on the flutes, against which solo violin, harp and then celesta are prominent. Variation 3 is marked 'roughly' – horns and solo violin prominent. In Variation 4, trills and rapid figurations for the solo instrument accompany a melody on cellos and double-basses. Triangle and snare drum enter into the lightly moving Variation 5 (scherzando). In Variation 6, strings and drums have a feathery accompaniment from the solo instrument. Then, as the drums cease, the soloist comes slowly down an expressive scale and continues into the conclusion of the movement – a varied restatement of the theme itself, tapering off to the single high note G.

The final movement is a rondo, centred on the keynote B. After an energetic few bars for the orchestra, the violin delivers the main theme – itself derived from the main theme of the first movement. There are abrupt changes of pace and expression, and formidable demands continue to be made on the virtuosity of the soloist. After a decisive but short cadenza, the main theme holds attention until the end of the work – whichever ending is played. The ending *without* the soloist (see above) has some sensational *glissando* display for the brass.

Music for strings, percussion and celesta

> Andante tranquillo
> Allegro
> Adagio
> Allegro molto
> Duration: 24 minutes

To call a piece simply 'Music . . .', rather than using one of the usual formal titles (symphony, suite, etc.) was a practice favoured by several mid-twentieth-century composers, notably Hindemith. In this case four contrasted movements are unified by being based on the same thematic figure. A sonata-form movement comes second rather than first, as almost invariably in a symphony. Unity also comes from the sharing of A as key-centre of both first and last movements; the key-centre of the second is C, and of the third movement F sharp.

Written for one of the most progressive and influential orchestras of its period, Paul Sacher's Basle Chamber Orchestra, it received its first performance from that orchestra and conductor on 21 January 1937, at Basle. The orchestration is unique. There are two equally balanced string sections; a celesta used with unusual prominence, and a percussion section under which Bartók includes piano and harp (often used in a percussive manner) as well as kettledrums, snare drum, bass drum, cymbals, tam-tam and xylophone.

Quietly, on the violas, the fugal design of the first movement takes shape. At first all the stringed instruments are muted. The successive 'entries' each reproduce the opening melodic curve, at a pitch a fifth higher or a fifth lower. There is a gradual *crescendo*; percussion joins in, and a bass-drum stroke marks the climax of sound which occurs on a chord of E flat, the tonal point furthest from the initial A. The music then spirals downward, the celesta adding a misty halo to the string sound.

The piano, silent in the first movement, thrusts itself forward in the second. It is the strings, however, which announce the first and second subjects of the sonata-form – the second occurring after a climax and two bars' silence. A substantial development brings contrasts of both colour and rhythm. Then a recapitulation is begun by the unified string force plus kettledrums, with the original pulse of 2/4 now transformed to a lively 3/8.

The slow third movement begins with the tapping of a high F on the xylophone. An eerie contrast is added in repetitive figures from strings and kettledrums, the latter being heard in a sliding effect, produced by a pedal which slackens or tightens the drum after it is struck. A new section presents a smooth melody on high violins and celesta; another section cumulates the up-and-down effects of piano, celesta and harp; yet another section, offering maximum sound, forms the centre of the movement. Then, with modifications, the music of the various sections returns in reverse order, and finally the xylophone taps out its high F almost to vanishing-point.

The vigorous finale employs a different sectional construction. After a brisk opening drum-tap followed by heavy plucked chords (the composer stipulates an unusual downward *pizzicato*), the main flow starts with an up-and-down scale-theme carrying dance-like stresses. It will recur in varied treatment towards the end. At an earlier point in the movement, against tinkling octaves from the celesta, the lower strings reassert the fugue theme from the opening movement, altered to fit the finale's more optimistic temper.

BEETHOVEN

1770–1827

Born in Bonn in the German Rhineland, Ludwig van Beethoven settled in Vienna and built an international reputation which has remained dominant and undisturbed since his day. His nine symphonies and five piano concertos stand alongside his string quartets and piano sonatas as forming, in themselves, massive continents of musical sound, with striking contrasts of landscape and scale.

Because his early works pursue the paths established by Haydn and Mozart, and even his later works retain links with the formal structures and melodic shapes used by those composers, historians have put Beethoven with them as one of the 'Vienna classics'. But concert-goers have never seen Beethoven that way. The early pieces apart, his music is characerically more forceful, less polite; less smooth, more challenging. He produced symphonic movements longer than before (the Third, *Eroica* Symphony being a milestone); he broke precedent by adding trombones to the Fifth Symphony and all but one of its successors, and then fused symphony with cantata in the ninth. The Fourth and Fifth Piano Concertos seem to present a bigger, more powerful kind of music than the idea of concerto had offered before.

In one sense, we ourselves make it bigger. The pianos used in Beethoven's day were wooden framed and not capable of the volume of modern instruments. The orchestral sounds were also not quite the same: horns and trumpets, for instance, having no valves, were of a narrower bore and a less full tone than those favoured today. Orchestras, playing in smaller halls, were themselves customarily smaller. Some modern ventures into reconstructing an 'original' Beethoven orchestra have alerted us to the differences.

The symphonies

Beethoven's nine symphonies are rooted in two inheritances from Haydn and Mozart: the four-movement form (of which the first movement is an allegro, with or without a slow introduction) and the 'classical' orchestra, in which the strings are supplemented by woodwind instruments in pairs (but sometimes only one flute), two horns, two trumpets and kettledrums (two drums, one player).

The older type of third movement, a minuet in fairly sedate mood and in moderate time, is changed by Beethoven to the more energetic scherzo. Four movements remain standard: where there are more, in the sixth (*Pastoral*) symphony, this is felt to be a deliberate departure; and it is surely no coincidence that this occurs in a symphony which abandons the usual abstraction to introduce a 'programme'.

Any departure from the wind–instrument norm is also significant. The pairs of normal woodwind are flutes, oboes, clarinets (now standard; they had been irregular for Haydn and Mozart) and bassoons. The importation of the piccolo and double-bassoon gives the fifth symphony a special characteristic. Likewise a trio of trombones in that symphony: trombones do not occur in symphonies by Haydn and Mozart, though they might be used in opera (Mozart's *Don Giovanni*) or oratorio (Haydn's *The Creation*).

The ninth (*Choral*) symphony, exceptional in concept, is also exceptional in orchestral demands. Its 'march of freedom' is appropriately reinforced by 'military' percussion, the same as in Haydn's *Military* Symphony (see p. 183).

Symphony no. 1 in C, opus 21

> Adagio molto – Allegro con brio
> Andante cantabile con moto
> Minuetto: allegro molto e vivace
> Adagio – Allegro molto e vivace
> Duration: 26 minutes

With this work, at a concert in Vienna on 2 April 1800, the twenty-nine-year-old Beethoven first offered himself as a symphonist. The orchestra is 'classical': 2 each of flutes, oboes, clarinets, bassoons, horns, trumpets, with kettledrums and strings. But the musical content, characteristically of its composer, has its surprises.

A playful touch opens the first movement. Instead of establishing its key immediately, it adds to the chord of C major the note B flat, requiring most of the twelve-bar slow introduction to fix the true key. The main *Allegro* follows, very downright in tone. A lighter texture brings the second subject as an oboe solo, in dialogue with flute. Development is based on the first subject, which returns in its original shape and key, *fortissimo* on the full orchestra, for the recapitulation. Beethoven extends the form, making the coda (literally a tail) into almost a second development: this was to be his way.

The second (slow) movement, in F, applies 'first-movement' form (exposition, development, recapitulation) to gracious melodic material. But the recapitulation comes not with a bang but with the main theme stealing in on the violas while the cellos play a countermelody. Later the theme comes back yet again (violins) to begin a substantial coda.

A third movement (in C) retains the old heading of minuet but quickens the beat to one-in-a-bar – the pace and vigour of the new scherzo. A central trio is lighter, without trumpets and drums, after which the opening section returns.

Beethoven is in humorous vein as the fourth movement opens: the violins apparently need several attempts to launch their scale. The scheme of exposition–development–recapitulation ('first-movement' form) is again followed. On recapitulation, the first theme has shed its original false start and is inserted gracefully by the violins beneath the piping of the woodwind. A surprise comes when material which was expected in the home key of C now turns up in F. From there the music takes on a further extension, with an eventual reminder of that original false start. A joyful finish is assured.

Symphony no.2 in D, opus 36

> Adagio molto – Allegro con brio
> Larghetto
> Scherzo
> Allegro molto
> Duration: 33 minutes

The concert in Vienna at which this symphony was launched (5 April 1803) also saw the première of Beethoven's Piano Concerto no.3. The symphony, using the same orchestration as no.1, is altogether bigger in conception. Passages of unusual abruptness puzzled some music-lovers of the day, and Beethoven's characteristic sudden contrasts of loud and soft are present in the mysterious slow introduction to the first movement. The violins dash down the scale to begin the main *Allegro* which has a cheerful march-tune on clarinets, bassoons and horns for its second subject. Sonata-form is followed.

The second movement overflows with Beethoven's gift for serene, expansive melody. Typically he introduces a smooth phrase and then, without losing the smoothness, makes it flower with additional notes.

In the third movement the title *Scherzo* is introduced to the symphony for the first time. The tempo is faster, the mood more breezy, than in the older minuet. The central section, with contrasting tone for wind instruments alone, starts off more sedately but soon takes part in the general explosiveness of the symphony.

The fourth movement begins with a terse, downward-leaping figure on the violins: it recurs through the movement and its component parts are thrown hither and thither. A passage of sustained soft notes is the deceptive pointer to a boisterous ending.

Symphony no.3 in E flat (Eroica), opus 55

Allegro con brio
Marcia funebre: adagio assai
Scherzo: allegro vivace
Allegro molto
Duration: 49 minutes

'Heroic symphony, composed to celebrate the memory of a great man': that was Beethoven's own inscription for this symphony, of which the composer himself conducted the first public performance on 7 April 1805 in Vienna. (There had been previous private performances at the house of one of his patrons, Prince Lobkowitz.) The original designation, 'Grand Symphony entitled *Bonaparte*', had been removed when the revolutionary conqueror disgraced himself in the composer's eyes by accepting an emperor's crown.

The symphony's fame rests on its grandeur and the surprises and violence of its expression – with an unusually wide traversal of keys and an unusually long span. The second movement, a funeral march, pays its direct 'military' tribute to the original subject. The athletic and joyous strains of the last movement might suggest some kind of victory games: Beethoven presumably found significance in employing here a theme from his ballet *Prometheus*, after the legendary figure who is associated with fire and creativity. The emphasis on emotional intensity is helped by the use of three horns instead of two; otherwise the orchestration is as for the previous two symphonies.

Two sharply pronounced chords, like a call to order, precede the cellos' opening theme. The theme is later put through waves of evolving tension, in which violent off-beat chords make a typical Beethoven gesture. The formal pattern involves the expected 're-capitulation' for which the harmony would have been expected to settle down into the home key: it has nearly settled, but not quite, when the horn enters with the opening theme before the violins have quitted the two softly held notes. Our present conditioning through later, more discordant music, makes it difficult to feel the force of this once famous, purposely 'wrong' entry.

The Funeral March makes its own point, with a slurred figure before the beats (cellos and double-basses) surely representing a military drum marking the step. The emotional revelation of the movement comes from the ascent (out of the original C-minor gloom) of the oboe's tune in C major. Finally the march-theme disintegrates: an obvious metaphor.

The third movement's bustling, playful vigour is indicated in the heading *Scherzo*, the term likewise introduced in the previous symphony. The form retains its inheritance from the minuet: A (repeated), B, A, coda.

After an introductory flourish, the fourth movement announces a theme on plucked strings. This (the *Prometheus* theme) becomes the subject of a set of free variations, among them a sort of rough march. . The moods vary but the 'heroic symphony' ends with assertion and command.

Symphony no.4 in B flat, opus 60

> Adagio: allegro vivace
> Adagio
> Allegro vivace; (Trio) Un poco meno allegro
> Allegro ma non troppo
> Duration: 34 minutes

On 5 March 1807 Beethoven directed a performance of his new symphony 'at the house of Prince L.' according to a Vienna journal's report – the initial now being understood to refer to his patron Prince Lobkowitz. Standing between the two 'titans' of the *Eroica* and the Fifth, it differs from them in not going beyond the classical orchestra of double wind instruments, kettledrums and strings.

This is a cheerful symphony. The deceptive gloom of the introduction (in the key of B flat minor, not major) is swept away when the main section begins. In contrast with the full orchestral sound, a quieter theme in F major later arises from the woodwind. The music gathers force again before arriving at the end of the exposition (which is repeated in the normal 'classical' manner). Development now proceeds to a point where wisps of themes and soft kettledrum rolls create an uncertainty. It is decisively resolved with a *crescendo* over an ever more insistent beat, arriving *fortissimo* at the recapitulation of the principal material. The exuberant music is extended in a coda.

The second movement, in E flat, presents a 'rocking' accompaniment on the second violins over which a singing melody is heard from the first violins. This melody, tenderly varied as it periodically returns, forms the main material of the movement; also notable is a more static theme, first heard on two bassoons. The end of the movement is remarkable – a whole bar in which the 'rocking' figure is taken up softly by the kettledrums, capped by two soft chords and two loud ones from the rest of the orchestra.

The third movement, returning to the home key of B flat, plunges into a musical whirlwind, with sudden changes between loud and soft in Beethoven's energetic manner. Each half of this initial part (the scherzo proper) is repeated. A marked change arrives with the trio: smooth and slower, it is begun by the oboes, clarinets, bassoons and horns alone, but soon swells to an energetic climax. The faster tempo is now resumed with a repeat of the scherzo, extended to a conclusion with prominent horns.

A perpetual-motion figure rather than a definite theme opens the finale. Sonata-form is followed, the first part (exposition) being repeated. The development brings forceful alternations of loud and soft, as in the previous movement. Expectancy builds up for the return of the main theme – which arrives, surprisingly, on a solo bassoon. This itself seems part of the merry spirit of this work, since at this pace the tune is very difficult for the bassoon to play, quite apart from the instruction to achieve it *dolce*, that is, 'gently'! The music eventually comes to rest after a long kettledrum roll, then starts to gather pace again, with further playful pauses before the boisterous conclusion.

Symphony no.5 in C minor, opus 67

Allegro con brio
Andante con moto
Allegro
Allegro
Duration: 32 minutes

Few symphonies have exerted such compulsion over audiences. The opening theme has been called (not by Beethoven) a 'Fate' theme, and an unmistakable quality of urgency and assertiveness pervades the first, third and fourth movements. Even the second movement cannot escape from it. An extra-large orchestra assists: in addition to 'classical' forces (as in nos. 1, 2 and 4) Beethoven imports the piccolo, double-bassoon and three trombones – instruments which had their occasional place in opera and other music, but had remained outside the symphony's domain. To make the maximum effect, Beethoven strategically reserves their entry until the last movement. But he did not go beyond the conventional two kettledrums: as he put it, the music is 'not for three drums, but it will make more noise and better noise than if there were six'.

A concert in Vienna on 22 December 1808 unveiled both this work and the Symphony no.6 (below) as well as the Piano Concerto No.4 and other new works. At the rehearsal the irascible Beethoven appears to have insulted the orchestra. The accounts of the concert itself leave doubts whether he actually conducted these two symphonies or not.

The first movement conveys an extraordinary power – partly from being so concise in the way it sets out the themes, but partly in the coiled-spring tension of the initial theme itself, today so well known that its originality goes unremarked. A four-note 'summons to attention' with a pause on the final note, it is repeated one step lower. Soon a *fortissimo* horn-call retains the rhythm but dramatically widens the gap between the notes. The smooth second subject is given by the strings, joined by solo clarinet and solo flute. The exposition is repeated; a development and recapitulation (notice the returning horn-call) preserve the tension; a coda brings a deceptive hush but in a moment the former force breaks out again.

As the second movement (in A flat) begins, one of Beethoven's serenely flowing slow melodies is heard from the lower strings. It is shortly followed, without a break, by another theme on clarinets and bassoons which becomes assertive with the entry of trumpets and drums. The movement gives variations on both these, the first theme flowering expressively but finally borrowing the assertive vein of its companion.

The third movement is a scherzo in C minor, starting mysteriously, then erupting in a *fortissimo* horn-call which bears a rhythmical reminder of the opening theme of the first movement. In a contrasting Trio, a whirling figure rises from the cellos and double-basses. The 'mysterious' scherzo-theme restarts but never reaches the horn-call. Instead a drum solo begins to tap out three-in-a-bar in a *crescendo* in which the other instruments join – leading to the symphony's most dramatic moment . . .

With piccolo, double-bassoon and three trombones joining in, the Finale begins like a march of triumph. Horns and woodwind add a second theme in similar vein. A third theme moves to G and ends the exposition (marked to be repeated). The development maintains the impetus and the mood but is suddenly interrupted for a ghostly reminiscence of the scherzo. But not for long. With a *crescendo*, it vanishes: the march of the Finale is triumphantly recapitulated. Bassoons alone lead off a coda which uses an increase of speed for a further and final excitement.

Symphony no.6 in F (Pastoral), opus 68

Awakening of cheerful feelings on arrival in the country:
  Allegro ma non troppo
Scene by the brook: *Andante molto mosso*
Merry gathering of countryfolk: *Allegro*, leading to
Thunderstorm – tempest: *Allegro*, leading to
Shepherd's song – glad and grateful feelings after the storm:
  Allegretto
Duration: 42 minutes

'Pastoral symphony, or Recollections of country life: an expression of feeling rather than tone-painting' – this was Beethoven's own heading for his work. But since the titles he gave to the movements *do* suggest scenic tone-painting, and since the end of the second movement enshrines three named bird-calls, Beethoven's disclaimer must be understood as warning the listener against too much seeking for descriptive detail.

The orchestral depiction of birdsong, thunder and other sounds had long been common (chiefly in opera), and the 6/8 'rocking' rhythm was an accepted symbol for pastoral peace. An early example from Corelli may be noted on p.132. But to incorporate a whole series of such things on a narrative basis into a fully worked-out Viennese symphony – this was new. Beethoven departs from his norm here and writes five rather than four movements, the last three played without a break.

The symphony was first given on the same occasion as the Fifth Symphony (see above). The basic classical orchestra is used for the first three movements; but because the prevailing mood is gentle, no trumpets are called for until the third movement and no drums until the fourth. In that fourth movement Beethoven bursts out of the classical frame: the storm calls for the extra excitement of a piccolo (in addition to the two flutes) and for the extra weight of two trombones (an exception to the general orchestral rule that trombones go in threes). The trombones remain for the finale.

The 'happy feelings' make the first movement more serene, less assertive than Beethoven's first movements generally are. After the exposition (repeated), a little falling phrase will be passed with particular charm from instrument to instrument. The first *fortissimo* for all participating instruments does not arrive until the recapitulation (return of the first tune in its original key). A coda makes a brief visit to another key before a quiet ending.

The second movement (in B flat) depicts the murmuring brook by a close-moving, undulating motion in the strings. Two cellos join in this effect while the others align themselves with the double-basses. Above the murmur, a smooth melody unfolds. Eventually, after an enriched return of the opening, Beethoven briefly lets the birds sing (overlappingly): a nightingale (flute), quail (oboe) and cuckoo (clarinet).

The third movement (returning to F major) shows the expected lively 3/4 rhythm of a scherzo but applies it to a humorous evocation of clumsy, countrified music making. An oboe tune is accompanied by a bassoonist who is apparently restricted to three 'safe' notes. A central section changes to a rough dance-rhythm; the scherzo returns, but there is a quickening and then an interruption . . .

. . . Storm! Not a drum-roll, but a trembling single note on cellos and double-basses, indicates distant thunder. The full tempest eventually arrives. The music is in F minor, but as the storm abates there is a turn to a happier F major, confirmed by a simple rising scale on a solo flute . . .

. . . which passes straight into the 'thanksgiving' of the fifth (final) movement. It begins with warmly held chords over which the shepherd's call is heard from a solo clarinet, then a solo horn – this anticipating the 'true' principal theme of the movement which now rises from the violins. Beethoven dwells on the theme, expanding it with florid melody and hardly leaving it for a single bar. A muted horn gives a last echo of it as the symphony quietly closes.

Symphony no. 7 in A, opus 92

> Poco sostenuto – Vivace
> Allegretto
> Presto – Assai meno presto
> Allegro con brio
> Duration: 38 minutes

With his Russian campaign in ruins, Napoleon's power was sinking in 1812–13, but Europe still felt the ravages of war. A benefit concert held in the hall of Vienna University in aid of wounded Austrian and Bavarian soldiers was the occasion of the first performance of this symphony on 8 December 1813, which Beethoven himself directed. Highly successful from the first, it is a work which conveys great energy, particularly in its first and last movements. It is equally famous for the stillness and inwardness of its slow movement, with its 'melody' dwelling for so long on one repeated note. A classical orchestra is used: two each of flutes, oboes, clarinets, bassoons, horns and trumpets, with kettledrums and strings.

A long, slow introduction in 4/4 time rises to a climax, and the main faster section in 6/8 begins quietly with a repeated rhythmical figure on the woodwind from which a confident, cheerful melody develops. The rhythm persists even when the music turns to E major to close the exposition with a heavy ascent on the strings followed by two empty bars like a question-mark. The exposition is repeated, and the development puts a new urgency into the music without losing its onward flow, leading to a recapitulation. When that ends (again with the ascent and the question-mark) the cellos and double-basses begin a quieter diversion which soon switches to full-orchestral vigour again as a conclusion of the movement.

A new key of A minor is announced by a chord on woodwind and horns. The lower strings now set up a kind of solemn dance, subdued at first but then gathering force and richness. A contrasting section in A major brings an easeful melody on clarinets and bassoons. The A-minor dance melody returns, varied: the contrasting melody also makes a second appearance; but it is the 'solemn dance' which concludes the movement in a stripped-down bleakness, with a woodwind chord of A minor (like that of the opening) to seal the final bars.

The third movement, in A major, is a scherzo which begins in the usual vigorous 3/4 (in two parts, each repeated) but with a surprise in store. The central contrasting section or trio turns out to be in 2/4 and is marked 'much less fast' (*Assai meno presto*): its smooth tune in D major on clarinets, bassoons and horns is worked up to a forceful climax. The main section (*Presto*) returns. The trio also is heard again in full; then again the main section. A snatch of the trio is *again* heard (not now in D major, however): is there to be a *third* statement? No, the faster music briskly dismisses it and the movement ends.

A brief call to attention, with trumpets and drums prominent, launches the finale on its whirlwind of a dance. The trumpet-and-drum rhythm takes part in it. A quieter strain moves into C sharp minor, and then there is an emphatic close in E major. A repetition of all the previous material is marked. Beethoven is in fact using the framework of a traditional sonata-form movement, but the effect of the formal divisions is less striking than the succession of whirling or stamping figures, interrupted by silent bars of expectation. Cumulative repetition keeps up the vigour to the end.

Symphony no.8 in F, opus 93

> Allegro vivace e con brio
> Allegretto scherzando
> Tempo di minuetto
> Allegro vivace
> Duration: 26 minutes

Standing between the heavyweight Seventh and Ninth, this is a 'little' symphony, shorter in span, more lightly scored, and reverting to the traditional minuet tempo in the third movement. Its second movement has not the traditional pathos. But in itself it is every bit as typical of Beethoven, as full of his surprises and ingenuities, as those other works. Scored with minimal (double) woodwind, horns and trumpets, with a surprise in the two kettledrums (see below), it was first given in Vienna on 27 January 1814.

A lively, unproblematic first movement (without slow introduction) deploys its graceful tunes in the expected sonata form. The exposition is repeated, and development begins when a little phrase passes upwards from bassoon to clarinet to oboe to flute. Eventually after a loud and insistent climax, the music makes its way to an unexpected quiet ending.

The second movement (in B flat) carries the word *scherzando* in its title – 'jestingly'. The light toc-toc-toc of the repeated woodwind chords at the opening suggests mechanical counting, and indeed this is an imitation of the machine on which Beethoven's friend Maelzel was then working – to evolve, *after* this, into the metronome. Over this figure comes the delicate sound of the main tune.

Returning to the home key of F, the third movement 'rediscovers' the minuet (in place of the scherzo preferred in the previous symphonies). In the contrasting middle section comes a gently melodious strain for two horns.

In the fourth movement a humorous, impudent vein takes over. The opening theme starts off with what seems to be simple robustness but drops almost immediately on to an intrusive note (it is a C sharp in the key of F). Each time that the theme comes round, the intrusive note is differently treated: that is, a different harmony comes to ignore it or take it up. The kettledrums, with an unusual tuning (both are tuned to the note F, an octave apart), help to maintain the music's good humour to the end.

Symphony no.9 in D minor (Choral), opus 125

Allegro ma non troppo, un poco maestoso
Molto vivace – (Trio) Presto
Adagio molto e cantabile – Andante moderato (alternating)
Presto – Allegro assai (and other tempos)
Duration: 69 minutes

The place held by Beethoven's Ninth Symphony is unique. Some later composers followed its example in importing voices into the finale of an otherwise orchestral work – notably Mendelssohn with the *Hymn of Praise* (Symphony no.2) and Liszt with his *Faust Symphony*. But these, more rarely heard, do not exert the strong spiritual pull of Beethoven's chosen text and the music written for it.

The text of this final movement is Schiller's 'Ode to Joy' which makes little sense without the realization that it is really an ode to freedom. Such a title gives meaning to couplets like 'All mankind are brothers plighted/ Where thy gentle wings abide', as an English translation put it. The topic was politically too dangerous for exposure at its original period, but it is odd that modern perform- ances (whether in German or in translation) have not generally restored the 'forbidden' word.

Not only the inclusion of a choral finale (or, to be exact, a finale incorporating four solo voices and chorus) makes the symphony remarkable. It is very long – over an hour. Its slow movement employs a scheme of double variations (unique in the symphonies) which represents one of the peaks of Beethoven's late manner. The finale itself takes on a unique role of summing up the whole work, since it starts by bringing back (and then, as it were, rejecting) themes from the previous movements. The orchestral forces include the reinforcements of the Fifth Symphony (piccolo, double-bassoon, trombones) but also, as an appropriately military accompani- ment to the 'freedom march' of the finale, the bass drum, cymbals and triangle. The horn section is expanded to four.

By the time of the first performance of the symphony (Vienna, 7 May 1824), Beethoven had become too deaf to conduct. He apparently indicated the beat at the start of the movements, but another musician, Michael Umlauf, then took over (with Beethoven's friend Ignaz Schuppanzigh as violinist–leader). The composer sat among the orchestra and apparently went on beating time even when the applause, unheard by him, burst in.

The first movement opens softly, with expectation and hints of a theme. The theme itself bursts out in D minor from the full orchestra; a more lyrical section ensues. The opening returns, now leading to a development section. The recapitulation (the main theme itself, without its preliminaries) arrives with thunderously rolling drums. As usual with Beethoven, this section is vastly extended: among the memorable features is the transformation of part of the original D-minor theme into a gentle D-major call on the horns. But the minor-key stress returns to end the movement.

The scherzo movement is placed second, not third, and follows an entirely traditional pattern: main section (in two 'halves', each repeated), intermediate section (so-called *Trio*); exact repetition of main section; coda. The fast tempo and the insistent, driving rhythm with prominent kettledrums likewise fulfil our expectations of a Beethoven scherzo, but with even greater tension than usual. The intermediate section quite unexpectedly shifts from 3/4 to 4/4 and from D minor to D major: a smooth melody on the woodwind brings relief from the explosiveness which has gone before and which will return with the repetition of the main section. The coda briefly brings back the D-major smoothness but with a heavily explosive end.

The third movement, after an introductory phrase from clarinets and bassoons, presents a long, slow melody in B flat on the first violins, eventually taken over by the woodwind. It merges into a new, lower-pitched and more flowing theme announced on second violins and violas with a change of rhythm (from 4/4 to 3/4) and a new key (D). The first of the sections re-enters in varied form; then the second in varied form and a new key (G). Thereafter (from a point where the first theme is strikingly heard in E flat from woodwind and horns alone), the music remains dominated by the tempo and character of the first section, but with the material of the second section absorbed in it. Even the occasional solemn fanfare does not seem to interrupt the grandly solemn stream of music.

But the fourth movement does indeed bring an interruption: it opens with a din, a chord containing an obvious wrong note, a seeming denial of any sense of harmony. Cellos and double-basses take it on themselves to 'answer' this with a curious, almost vocal melody: Beethoven wanted it played 'like a recitative'. The din recurs; so does a snatch of the 'recitative'. The orchestra offers quotations from the openings of the preceding movements, which successively fail to silence the objections of the 'recitative'. Then the woodwind and horns try a new tune: the cellos and basses show a disposition to accept it and indeed take over and expand the tune themselves, the rest of the orchestra eventually joining in.

This is the celebrated 'Joy' tune, in D, on which the rest of the movement is founded. The following pattern ensues:

'Din' (recurrence)

Baritone solo (echoing previous orchestral 'recitative'), asking for 'more pleasant, more joyful sounds'

Baritone, chorus and orchestra: 'Joy' tune: 'Hail to thee, Joy (Freedom), daughter of the gods, uniter of mankind'

Long, loud choral pause on the phrase 'Before God' (*Vor Gott*)

March in B flat, begun by bassoons and bass drum, other wind and military percussion joining in, then tenor and male chorus: 'Brothers, advance like a hero towards victory'

Orchestral continuation of march

Chorus: 'Joy' tune, always in D

Slower section, in G, then B flat: chorus, initially with promi-

nent trombone accompaniment: 'Ye millions, be embraced!
In heaven a loving father dwells.'

Chorus: 'Joy' tune, more energetic and elaborate, taking over
material from preceding section

Soprano, contralto, tenor and bass solos, with chorus: further
elaboration of 'Joy' tune, ending quietly and slowly (soloists
only)

(*Prestissimo*) Noisy re-entry of military percussion and other
instruments; final choral version of 'Joy' tune, with one
dramatic holding-back of tempo just before the on-rushing
end.

The concertos

Beethoven was a virtuoso pianist whose concerts in Vienna were a
substantial contribution to his income. He himself gave the first
performances of his first four piano concertos (by the time of the
fifth, his deafness penalized him) and did not publish them until he
had enjoyed their exclusive initial use. As with the symphonies,
Beethoven uses a received, 'classical' concerto form: Mozart's piano
concertos were the most successful examples. Lacking a minuet or
scherzo, the concertos are in three movements as opposed to the
basic four of the symphony. Following his predecessors, Beethoven
assists the prominence of the soloist in a concerto by keeping the
orchestra light: wind instruments are in pairs only, and include
neither trombones nor other 'extras'.

The opening movements of the concertos may seem a little like
their counterparts in the symphony, making use of one main assertive subject and one more lyrical, but in fact the construction is
different. The concerto normally opens with a long orchestral
presentation, the soloist then entering with his own presentation
with the incorporation of some new material. The musical discussion settles into the new territory of the complementary key (see
p.12), and the arrival at this point is always marked with a long trill
on the solo instrument. It is in the quality of this musical discussion,
throughout the movements, that we feel the essential Beethoven –
now strong in expression to the point of violence, now on the most
rarefied heights of contemplation.

As with the symphony, Beethoven's departures from the norm
(see, particularly, the Piano Concerto no.4) are intended to be
striking.

The slow movements give the opportunity for clear, melodious dialogue between soloist and orchestra, after which a finale (always in rondo form, another traditional inheritance) keeps a cheerful bustle. Whereas in the symphony the finale may sometimes seem even weightier than the first movement, in the concerto it never does.

Beethoven follows his predecessors in normally marking a place for a cadenza of the soloist's choice to be played in the first and last movement of each concerto (at the end of the last main thematic statement, to be followed by a coda). Beethoven, himself the most masterful of pianists, wrote several cadenzas for his first four piano concertos but they were not considered, nor printed, as part of the score itself. In the fifth Beethoven integrates a cadenza-substitute into the whole, requiring no interpolation by the pianist; in the Triple Concerto he similarly leaves nothing to be added.

Concerto no.1 in C for piano and orchestra, opus 15

Allegro con brio
Largo
Rondo: allegro scherzando
Duration: 38 minutes

At a concert in Vienna organized by Haydn, on 18 December 1795, the young Beethoven played a concerto – which, it is believed, was this one. Though called no.1, it was actually composed after the so-called no.2. Like this work, it is 'good-mannered' music, not unsuitable for a concert involving Haydn and without the forceful surprises of later Beethoven.

Beethoven left one very long cadenza for the first movement and two shorter alternatives (one of them incomplete); he also left a single short cadenza for insertion at one point in the third movement – but, as will be seen, two fully written-out cadenzas follow in the score a few bars later. The orchestra is a conventional one of the Viennese–classical style: 1 flute, 2 each of oboes, clarinets, bassoons, horns and trumpets; kettledrums and strings.

A soft orchestral opening is soon emphatically expanded; a second theme, in E flat, is confined to the strings. The music returns to C major for the piano's entrance – announcing new material before alluding to the original opening theme. The secondary theme, originally in E flat, makes a new appearance in G, first in the orchestra and then on the piano. The solo instrument displays its paces in consolidating the new key, showing off with a complex trill before handing over to the orchestra. A central development leads to a headlong downward scale for the piano and a very emphatic restatement of the opening, the secondary (original E flat) theme falling into place in the home key of C major. The cadenza allows the soloist further expansion and a short, affirmative coda ends the movement.

The slow movement is located in the recognizably remote key-area of A flat major. The passionate arabesques of the soloist are set against characteristic figures for orchestral strings, woodwind and horns. A solo clarinet is used with particular eloquence – early in the movement and again at the end.

A chuckling rondo theme in C major, given out by piano alone, sets the mood for the finale. The orchestra boisterously follows. Recurrences and contrasts succeed one another in a clear pattern. After the cadenza the composer plays a humorous trick: an apparently conventional trill on the piano pushes itself upwards and a snatch of earlier themes is heard in a 'wrong' key (B major); then, after a new short cadenza which begins very shortly and ends very loudly, the whole orchestra jumps in with the rondo theme in its home key of C. Beethoven has yet another surprise – another, even shorter, cadenza and a slow, suspended phrase for the two oboes, after which the orchestra ends the concerto briskly.

Concerto no.2 in B flat for piano and orchestra, opus 19

> Allegro con brio
> Adagio
> Rondo: molto allegro
> Duration: 29 minutes

Second in order of publication (and therefore bearing a later opus number, and called 'no.2'), this was the first piano concerto that Beethoven composed. The date of the first performance, with Beethoven as soloist, is fixed by modern authorities as 29 March 1795. Beethoven revised the work in 1798. With a smaller orchestra than any of the concertos that followed, it employs no clarinets, trumpets or drums.

Like no.1, it has something of the regularity and the polite modesty of a Mozart concerto. The first movement immediately displays two contrasting ideas: a call to attention, like a fanfare, for full orchestra, and a smoothly folded phrase for strings only. The piano enters as if feeling the way, then delivers the 'fanfare' with lively extension. After the pianist's 'signal trill' provides the expectation of the original thematic material redirected into the new key, Beethoven insists we listen carefully for it: the 'fanfare' theme is on the *lower* strings!

The serenity of the second movement is achieved by Beethoven's characteristically flowering kind of melody, spanning a two-part structure. Beginning in E flat, the music moves to the complementary B flat, then restarts in the home key and finishes in it.

The cheerful third movement has an impudent syncopation in its main theme. After this theme has twice returned, the piano produces the surprise of a smoothed-out, *un*-syncopated version in a remote key (G major) before a final return of the original. The sudden loud–soft contrast in the closing bars is another characteristic of Beethoven's youthfully energetic style.

Concerto no.3 in C minor for piano and orchestra, opus 37

Allegro con brio
Largo
Rondo: allegro
Duration: 36 minutes

This piano concerto is the first to display Beethoven's bigger, more heroic manner. The manuscript score bears the date 1800, and has some solo passages not fully written out, which would have been filled in by the composer himself as soloist at the first performance, in Vienna on 5 April 1803. At some other points the piano part as given in manuscript is cramped in the right hand because it had to fit within the restricted upper range of the piano at that period. But by the time the piano part was engraved for printing, in 1804, the keyboard had been extended (though not as fully as in today's pianos) and Beethoven rewrote with use of the extra notes.

The key-relation between the movements (slow movement in E major between two in C minor) is striking to the listener who can sustain the feeling of the transitions. Another special feature is the role of the cadenza: in the first movement Beethoven follows tradition in simply indicating the place, leaving the soloist to supply the music; but in the second movement there is a short, fully written-out cadenza and in the third *two* short flourishes, one in the usual cadenza place towards the end and one as an unexpected occurrence soon after the movement opens.

The opening theme of the first movement is of an assertive character, but starts softly. After its climax, a lyrical, contrasting theme is offered. (Ears attuned to 'classical' procedures will prick up at this point: the new theme is in E flat, the 'complementary' key, which is usually held in reserve until after the soloist has entered.) The soloist arrives with thundering scales and then the main theme. Towards the end, after the cadenza, there is a remarkable passage where the theme is recalled in dialogue between two kettledrums and the piano.

In the central movement the piano proposes melodies, decorates them, 'listens' while the orchestra makes its leisurely reply, and provides a harp-like accompaniment for the melodic interchange of bassoon and flute.

The final *Rondo*, though lively, has a rather stern recurring theme, lightened by the episodes in between. Only at the end (after the piano's cadenza–substitute) does the theme take on a merry, major-key shape with a new, 6/8 rhythm.

Concerto no.4 in G for piano and orchestra, opus 58

> Allegro moderato
> Andante con moto, *leading to*
> Rondo: vivace . . . Presto
> Duration: 35 minutes

The concert in Vienna at which Beethoven launched his Fifth and Sixth Symphonies – on 22 December 1808 – was also that at which he played the first performance of this concerto. The relation between the keyboard instrument and the orchestra still seems remarkably original: the first movement contradicts expectation by beginning on the piano, and the second movement is a kind of dialogue between soloist and the strings of the orchestra which Liszt compared to Orpheus taming the power of the wild beasts with the soothing magic of his lyre.

A 'classical' orchestra is used (but with only one flute), but differently for each movement. Apart from the restriction to strings only in the second movement, trumpets and drums do not appear in the first movement either, the full forces thus being effectively reserved until the vigorous finale.

The first movement opens on the piano alone, but this is something of a double deception: it is a surprise to hear the soloist so early, but the solo entry turns out to last for a mere five bars, after which the orchestra has a normal first section to itself. Later the piano has *its* normal entry and proceeds to add something new to what the orchestra has presented. A development takes the music not only into remote keys but into what seems a remote atmosphere; firm ground is regained by the pianist's assertive statement of the very opening theme, beginning a recapitulation. A cadenza is then required, and is followed by a short coda.

In the second movement the key is E minor and the atmosphere one of stillness. The quietly persuasive piano, using the soft pedal except at the climax, subdues the stark gestures of the unison strings. The piano's final phrase is tender and prolonged, carrying over the E minor chord to . . .

. . . a chord of C major which begins the third movement on the strings. The theme which they tap is in fact the cheerful rondo theme. The piano varies it with the unusual accompaniment of a single cello, and then the theme is stated more loudly – the first entry of the full orchestra! The piano sets out on various adventures before the rondo theme returns, again on quietly tapping strings, again followed by the piano-plus-cello and the loud statement of the theme. After further new material, the rondo theme arrives in broken form on the piano and is restored to healthy shape by the orchestra. A cadenza (Beethoven instructs that it should be short) is followed by piano trills, and finally a quickened pace ends the concerto.

Concerto no.5 in E flat for piano and orchestra (Emperor), opus 73

> Allegro
> Adagio un poco mosso, *leading to*
> Rondo: allegro
> Duration: 38 minutes

Who gave this work the nickname of 'Emperor' is uncertain, but it was not the composer. This being the longest of Beethoven's

concertos and the most forceful, it is no wonder that the name has
stuck. It was composed in 1809, when the victorious army of
Napoleon occupied Vienna. But before the end of the year France
and Austria had signed a peace treaty, so the war cannot explain the
curious fact that the concerto was not heard in Vienna till 1812
(Beethoven's favourite pupil Carl Czerny being the soloist). The
first performance apparently took place at Leipzig on 28 November
1811 with Friedrich Schneider as soloist.

Uniquely in Beethoven's piano concertos, a gradual, suspenseful
transition connects the second movement to the finale – a dramatic
effect like the link between the last two movements of the Fifth
Symphony. The orchestration, however, remains within 'classical'
limits, using the same doubled woodwind as the first and third
concertos.

The opening movement immediately proclaims the concerto's air
of command. As in the Concerto no. 4, a 'double deceit' is used in the
unexpected beginning with the solo instrument. It makes only a kind
of extended flourish: continuous musical argument begins only
when the piano falls silent and the orchestra gives out a march theme
in E flat major. Soon follows a softer (but still march-like) theme in E
flat minor, sliding into major as the two horns put forward their own
smoother version of the tune. This orchestral exposition is considerably prolonged before the piano re-enters, this time to join in fully.
Eventually the pianist's scales in contrary directions produce a
climax in the key of B flat, a key seized by the orchestra to remind us
of what it stated at the beginning.

The piano joins in again, taking the music into remoter regions
and accompanying various orchestral soloists. The piano strides
loudly in octaves, then quietens. A huge climax ushers in the
recapitulation with the soloist's flourish made grander and more
exciting. Now, instead of settling and concluding, the pianist takes
to new fields: against strings *pizzicato*, the remote E major is
reached, the piano softly evoking the two-horn tune from early in
the movement. After such a detour, a further recapitulation in more
powerful sound re-establishes the home key. At a point where the
soloist might expect to insert a cadenza, Beethoven explicitly forbids
one, and the music now proceeds massively but more directly to the
end.

The very long first movement (about half the concerto's length) is
followed by the compressed, intense second movement – which
comes with a vivid change of key from E flat major to B major.

Strings, of which the violins are muted, give out a hymn-like melody; rippling figures high in the piano keyboard help to provide a meditation on it. On its conclusion, the music sinks to the note B on a bassoon, then further to a sustained, expectant B flat on the horns. Over that note the piano, in successive, hesitant phrases, begins to build a theme . . .

. . . which turns out to be the choppy, powerful rondo theme of the third movement. Its recurrences are unmistakable and are separated by highly inventive new material (at one point going to E major, as in the first movement). Eventually the piano reminisces over drum-taps: the music nearly halts, re-animates, and the initial choppy syncopations make a forceful end.

Concerto in D for violin and orchestra, opus 61

> Allegro ma non troppo
> Larghetto, *leading to*
> Rondo [Allegro]
> Duration: 44 minutes

Universally admired, and considered by not a few music-lovers the greatest of violin concertos, Beethoven's was written for a twenty-six-year-old violinist, Franz Clement. Already at that age so prominent in Vienna's musical life as to be 'first violinist and conductor' at the Theater an der Wien, he gave the first performance on 23 December 1806.

The concerto is not fiercely assertive like the Fourth and Fifth Piano Concertos, or like Brahms's future Violin Concerto: its first movement is of haunting intensity, its second contemplative, its third joyous, all the moods taking expression in musical phrasing which lies so well for the solo violin. (Curiously, however, Beethoven also prepared a version of this work as a piano concerto – now very rarely performed.)

Its most striking feature is at the very opening: five soft, even beats on the solo kettledrum, on the fifth of which the orchestra gives out the principal melody. The solo violin, after introducing itself with a rhapsodic passage, etherealizes the orchestra's opening melody in a very high register. When the soloist arrives at the long trill which would normally settle the music into the complementary key, scales intervene and lead temporarily into a surprising, different key. The 'five even beats' (from the opening) become important. After this figure has been heard in quiet, insistent octaves on the trumpets, the

solo violin mounts ecstatically to the point of a *fortissimo* for the full
orchestra. Here the five beats proclaim the arrival at the final section,
with the home key of D now triumphant.

The orchestra's muted violins pronounce the theme of the slow
movement, in G: the soloist's first response is to provide a gentle
decoration. To be noted, later, is a reprise of this theme in outline
form (yet unmistakable) on *pizzicato* strings in the orchestra, against
a still more decorated solo line. A short cadenza directly links this
movement to the finale . . .

The finale is launched in a swinging rhythm by the solo violin.
The player delivers its theme (it is the rondo theme and will recur
constantly) wholly on the G string – that is, the lowest string of the
instrument, giving a particularly full, vibrant effect. Some merry
play for the orchestra's pair of horns is heard, and recurs later.
Eventually, a cadenza for the soloist leads to an additional section
(coda) in which the rhythm of the rondo theme is turned to a phrase
of graceful charm: but the end is loudly affirmative.

Concerto in C major for piano, violin, cello and orchestra ('Triple Concerto'), opus 56

> Allegro
> Largo, *leading to*
> Rondo alla polacca
> Duration: 35 minutes

This unusual combination of three solo instruments with orchestra
tempts us to seek parallels – perhaps with Bach's fifth 'Brandenburg'
(see p.38), or the concerto that Mozart wrote for three pianos, or
even Michael Tippett's 'triple' for the different combination of
violin, viola and cello. But these are less relevant than the music
which Beethoven wrote (as did Haydn and Mozart) for the 'piano
trio' – that is, piano, violin and cello on their own. Indeed
Beethoven's patron, Archduke Rudolf of Austria, who gives his
name to Beethoven's so-called *Archduke Trio*, was the amateur
performer for whom Beethoven also designed the piano part of this
concerto. It was first performed in May 1808 in Vienna.

There are no cadenzas. The uninterrupted transition from slow
movement to finale is notable: not so dramatically presented as in the
Fifth Piano Concerto, the *Emperor*, but more so than in the Violin
Concerto.

The soloists enter one by one (cello, violin, piano) after a full orchestral introduction. Shortly after occurs the strong impression of a *four*-voiced climax, each of the pianist's hands plus the two string-players joining in triplet figures running up and down: a new theme in A major (surprising in a C-major movement) follows, the cello again leading. In this lively first movement the two stringed instruments are more often paired than firmly separated. A final excitement is provided by stamping chords, and by scales and trills which unite all the soloists.

At the start of the second movement, the muted violins of the orchestra introduce the cello in a melody full of pathos, the effect accentuated on this instrument by the high register. The music flowers in a delicately complex tracery of notes but the movement is soon over: 53 bars, compared with 531 of the opening movement! When the solo violin has disappeared in the heights, the cello's throbbing grows in intensity and passes directly to the finale . . .

The cello solo continues, opening the finale in the *polacca* rhythm (the dance-rhythm otherwise called *polonaise*, both terms meaning Polish) which persists throughout. Towards the end of the movement the solo violin initiates a more lightly treated, scampering version of the theme in a changed rhythm (2/4). Combined trills on all instruments lead to a final return of the theme in its original *polacca* rhythm.

Overture, Coriolanus, *opus 62*

Duration: 7–8 minutes

The Greek chronicler Plutarch tells of Coriolanus, a proud general exiled by the Roman senate, who joined Rome's enemies and led an attack on the city. Only a plea from his wife Volumnia was able to persuade him to mercy. The story forms the basis of both Shakespeare's play *Coriolanus*, and also a play by Beethoven's Austrian contemporary, Heinrich Joseph von Collin, entitled *Coriolan* (1802). This German form is sometimes found also in English-speaking references to the overture which Beethoven composed five years later.

The overture was presumably used for a Viennese production of the play in April 1807, but Beethoven directed its first performance during the previous month (exact day uncertain) at a concert in the Vienna house of one of his patrons, Prince Lichnowsky. The 'classical' orchestra with paired wind instruments is used. The overture is in C minor, a key which Beethoven favoured for suggestions of heroic defiance – the key of the Fifth Symphony, and of the funeral march in the *Eroica*.

For a representation of the drama Beethoven found a suitable musical form in the traditional sonata-form. In this case the first subject (in C minor) with its defiant gestures must be taken as representing the hero himself, and the softer theme (in E flat) represents Volumnia. The exposition is not repeated, so the music flows with an uninterrupted flow: the 'defiant' theme makes its eventual return in F minor instead of C minor, and the 'broken' ending has an obvious symbolism in the hero's downfall: in Collin's play (though not in Shakespeare's) he commits suicide.

Overture, Egmont, *opus 84*

Duration: 10 minutes

In the period when Spain ruled Flanders, Egmont (Count Egmont, 1522–68) was a Flemish nobleman who had given distinguished service to the Spanish king. Later, standing for a more liberal attitude to the people, he incurred the enmity of the Duke of Alba, the repressive Spanish captain-general who executed about 18,000 people. Egmont, himself executed in Brussels and remembered as a national hero, is the central figure of Goethe's play, *Egmont* (1788). Admiring Goethe, Beethoven responded to the anti-tyrant theme. The play itself is now chiefly immortalized by the incidental music which Beethoven contributed to a Vienna production in 1810.

There are nine numbers including two songs and this overture. Not yet completed when the play opened (24 May), Beethoven's music was first heard at the performance on 15 June 1810. The score uses two each of flutes, oboes, clarinets, bassoons and trumpets, along with kettledrums and strings; but four horns are used instead of two, and the second flute is required to change to piccolo for a dramatic purpose at the end.

Unlike the *Coriolanus* overture which is in one continuous tempo, the *Egmont* (in F minor) has a solemn slow introduction. The main Allegro has an agitated main theme, descending on the cellos, and a second theme beginning in chords on the strings: a 'knocking' or 'destiny' figure as definite as the one which opens the Fifth Symphony. The exposition is not repeated, but merges into a short development; at the recapitulation, the cellos again take the main theme. The destiny theme is followed by an expectant pause and an evidently feeble reply. The cause of liberty has failed for the moment; but a swelling coda, in F major, with the piccolo adding a new note of excitement, signifies its coming triumph.

Overture, Leonora (no.3), *opus 72b*

Beethoven laboured with some difficulty over his only opera, *Fidelio*, which now holds the repertory in his third and final version of 1814. For this production he composed a fairly short overture in E major, now naturally known as the *Fidelio overture*, which breathes a vigorous, confident spirit and does not anticipate the tensions of the opera itself. It makes a highly effective work in the concert-hall.

But Beethoven produced three previous overtures, all of which are now called by the name of the heroine, Leonora (or, in the German form, Leonore). All quote from the opera itself. The most celebrated is the third, used for an interim version of the opera first heard on 29 March 1806. Weighty and intense, it seems almost to sum up the drama in orchestral form. Beethoven's decision *not* to use it in his final version of the opera must stem from a feeling that it is out of scale in the theatre – though some later conductors of the opera have improperly reinserted it between the two acts, or between the two scenes of the second act.

In the concert-hall the *Leonora no.3* remains self-sufficient, immensely powerful, and additionally effective if the story which it represents is known. The use of a trumpet *off-stage*, representing the distant trumpet-call in the opera which heralds the arrival of the liberating Minister of State, is a unique gesture. (Mahler and other later composers would follow it with other off-stage instruments in their concert works.) Beethoven's scoring has double woodwind, four horns instead of the two most commonly used at the time, two trumpets, and the significant extra weight of three trombones as well as the usual kettledrums and strings.

BERG

1885–1935

Schoenberg was the pioneer, Webern the most extreme, in breaking from the established patterns of musical composition. But of all three major figures in the twentieth-century innovation known as '12-note music', Alban Berg is the one who retained the strongest, most convincing link with late-Romantic music. He made the listener feel the emotional pull of major and minor keys even when the music obeyed 12-note principles – which, in theory, had dethroned the hierarchical key-system in favour of an equality between the notes. More than this, the curves of his melodies seem to plead, console or agonize in the traditional Romantic way.

Born in Vienna, Berg pursued his career there as composer and teacher. He died without quite finishing his second opera, *Lulu*, but had arranged from it a concert suite for soprano and orchestra which powerfully displays his expressive qualities. Another orchestral work which is in fact an arrangement is the *Three movements from the Lyric Suite*, stemming from an original six-movement composition for string quartet. A late and an early piece are discussed below, the earlier using the concept of a 'chamber orchestra'. This is a specifically twentieth-century concept which may be seen as a polar opposite to the very large, apparently ever-increasing orchestra of the time.

Concerto for violin and orchestra

> Andante – Allegretto
> Allegro – Adagio
> Duration: 27 minutes

The dedication, 'To the memory of an angel', and the story behind it no doubt promoted the public acceptance of this concerto. The 'angel' was the eighteen-year-old Manon Gropius (daughter of the architect Walter Gropius and the former Alma Mahler) who had died of polio. But a deeper musical appeal is the use of a Bach quotation, a chorale (hymn) which seems to sum up the spirit of elegy and resignation which goes through the work.

Berg had already received a commission for a concerto from the American violinist Louis Krasner, and the news of the young woman's death moved him to interrupt the composition of his opera *Lulu* and compose this concerto. The composer himself died, however, too soon to hear the first performance, given by Krasner in Barcelona (at a festival of the International Society for Contemporary Music), with Hermann Scherchen conducting, on 19 April 1936.

A large and distinctive orchestra is used: 2 flutes, both doubling 2 piccolo; 2 oboes, one doubling 1 english horn, 2 clarinets and bass clarinet, 1 alto saxophone (doubling as third clarinet), 2 bassoons and double-bassoon, 4 horns and 2 trumpets, 2 (not 3) trombones and tuba, various percussion including high-pitched gong and low-pitched tam-tam, harp and strings.

The concerto is divided into two parts, each with an initial first movement flowing into a contrasted second movement. Given the nature of the dedication it would not be unreasonable to take this as:

I: a pensive introduction followed by a scherzo-like movement evoking through its dance-rhythms the gaiety of youth,
II: a wild cry and a stormy emotion, as in grief, leading to a consoling slow final movement based on a traditional hymn – itself to be interrupted by a reminiscence of gaiety from the first part.

But this sequence is not compiled in a free and rhapsodic way. It is tightly constructed, with due prominence for the soloist, who enters (after ten opening orchestral bars) with an ascending theme which states the 12-note 'row'. The soloist's descent which follows is an 'inversion' of the row (the intervals between the successive notes being the same as before, but not heard in downward order). These slow up-and-down figures return, after a more animated section, then slacken off with long-held notes for the soloist, leading to . . .

. . . the Allegretto, starting with a 'dancing' theme for two clarinets which is immediately interchanged with the soloist (on two strings!) After a long solo passage, new energy comes with a section in which the cellos divide into two and strike the strings with the back of the bow (*col legno*) while the other stringed instruments play normally. A slower section follows. Towards the end of the movement, under the soloist's high notes, a solo horn and then a solo trumpet give out what might be a fragment of a folk-tune – and is in fact just that.

The stormy second movement leads the soloist to a long central cadenza. Brass and percussion are subsequently prominent in a drive to a mighty climax of emphatic rhythms. There follows a rapid 'collapse': the dark tones of trombones, tuba, bass drum and double-basses form a sombre background as the soloist arrives at . . .

. . . the Adagio, in which the violin announces in slow notes the *chorale* or hymn-tune, 'Es ist genug' ('It is enough'). Though the indication is plainly 'peace after the storm', the hymn is made strange by the harmonization. But the tune is repeated by three clarinets and bass clarinet, sounding like an organ, in the harmonization which Bach gave to it – an evocation of a traditional church context. The alternation between the Berg and the Bach harmonies continues. A varied treatment of this material rises to its own huge climax (with tam-tam). As the music subsides, the folk-tune of the previous movement is recalled by the orchestral violins, bringing a hint of waltz-rhythm before the 4/4 hymn-tune reasserts its presence for a brief coda. As the final long-held chord is heard, with a single high note softly sustained by the soloist, a typical touch of Berg is found: the very opening of the concerto is quoted in a distant figure on first violins and double-basses.

Chamber concerto for piano and violin, with 13 wind instruments

> Tema scherzoso con variazioni, *leading to*
> Adagio, *leading to*
> Rondo ritmico con introduzione ('Cadenza')
> Duration: 38 minutes

Intended by Berg as a 50th birthday present for Schoenberg in 1924, this work was not completed until a year later and received its first performance on 20 March 1927, when Hermann Scherchen conducted it in Berlin. On the model of Schoenberg's own *Chamber Symphony* (1906), Berg used a small group of 'orchestral' wind instruments as individuals, without massed effects: piccolo, flute, oboe, english horn, high clarinet in E flat, clarinet in A, bass clarinet, trumpet, 2 horns and trombone. In contrast with them, the piano is soloist in the first movement, the violin in the second, and both in the third.

At the head of the score, the composer placed a 'motto' – five bars of music to be played first. The motto presents three simultaneous musical cryptograms (based on an association of letters with notes). The piano's set of notes corresponds to 'Arnold Schönberg' (as that name was then spelt), the horn's to 'Alban Berg', the violin's to 'Anton Webern'. All these enter the fabric of the concerto. This is atonal music but not systematized in the twelve-note method which Berg later used in the Violin Concerto and other works. The pattern of parallels and recurrences, inherited from Berg's Viennese predecessors, becomes elusive in the absence of conventional melodies and conventional key-structures.

The first movement is a set of variations intended, according to the composer, to have a scherzo character. The long 'theme' unfolds in three distinct parts – the first rather stolid, on english horn and 2 clarinets; the second entering as an animated, waltz-like tune on a solo clarinet; the third slower again (low notes on the flute, with sustained accompaniment on bass clarinet, bassoon and one horn). The piano enters to deliver the first variation, observing the same three-part division, and four further variations follow.

Without a break, the solo violin enters on a high note to begin the second, which has the traditional slow and intense character but an unusual form. Starting with an eloquent violin solo over the brass instruments, it unfolds for about six minutes (in several distinct tempos, like the first movement) until a soft high harmonic on the violin is heard against repetitions of a low note on the piano. Then the material is restated backwards – at first by a complete mirror-image, note for note, then more freely.

The second movement was considerably longer than the first; the third is longer still. After sharing a long, passionate cadenza, the two soloists launch what the composer calls a 'rhythmical rondo': it is not a main *tune* that comes round, but a main *rhythm* (with other sections in contrast). This main rhythm is heard first in the jumpy melody of the violins, later in a similarly jumpy but not identical melody on the trumpet. A strong sense of onward movement and of contrasting instrumental textures continues until, rather suddenly, the music splits into fragments and vanishes on the *pizzicato* of the solo violin.

BERIO

b. 1925

Among his contemporaries in exploring new musical directions, including those of electronic sound, Luciano Berio has shown a special fondness for the voice, whether solo or in ensemble. It is perhaps too easy to say that this fondness is 'natural' for an Italian. His work entitled *Coro* (Italian for *Chorus*), 1974–6, calls on forty individual voices and forty instruments to perform a text in a multiplicity of languages. His celebrated series of virtuoso (indeed, exhibitionistic) solo pieces, each called *Sequenza*, includes one for female voice.

But his output over more than thirty years has included various pieces for normal full orchestra or chamber orchestra, with or without soloists. A concerto for two pianos and orchestra, 1973, was followed by a remarkably titled work for cello and orchestra: *Ritorno degli Snovidenie* (Italian-plus-Russian, 'Return of dreams'). Berio's style is sometimes transparently lyrical and sometimes rather dense, but very rarely harsh.

Sinfonia for eight voices and orchestra

> Five movements, without conventional tempo-headings, the
> second bearing the title *O King* and the third movement
> running into the fourth without pause
> Duration: 33 minutes

Sinfonia, the Italian form of symphony, has been retained in English use for this singular work by an Italian composer. Berio himself was the conductor when it was originally produced in four movements in New York on 10 October 1968; a fifth movement was added in the following year. The use of eight microphoned voices makes it unique, and was made possible by the virtuosity of the Swingle Singers (a Europe-based ensemble led by an American, Ward

Swingle) who participated in the opening performances. Likewise unqiue is the way in which the third movement is built on the scherzo of Mahler's Symphony no. 2 (*Resurrection*).

Many other composers (including Bach, Wagner, Debussy and Berio himself!) are more fleetingly quoted in that movement, though the composer was at pains to reject the word 'collage' for his process. There are further external allusions in other movements. Performance requires three percussion groups, placed 'as far apart as possible':

1 kettledrums, low-pitched tam-tam, snare drum, bongos, glockenspiel
2 marimba, triangle, guiro, medium-pitched tam-tam, handbells, 3 wood-blocks, snare drum, bongos, suspended cymbals, tambourine, bass drum, whip
3 vibraphone, snare drum, handbells, guiro, small tam-tam, tambourine, 2 triangles, castanets

A string section of precisely 46 players is specified (with violins divided into three – compare Shostakovich's Symphony no. 5!) The rest of the orchestra includes a piano and both an electric organ and an electric harpsichord, as well as 3 flutes and piccolo, 3 clarinets and high clarinet, 2 oboes and english horn, alto and tenor saxophone, 2 bassoons and double-bassoon, 4 horns, 4 trumpets, 3 trombones and tuba.

The first movement displays the eight-voice ensemble in three ways – vocalizing according to symbols of the phonetic alphabet; singing actual words, usually in fragmentary phrases; and speaking. The text (in French) is excerpted from one of the most famous books of modern anthropology, *Le cru et le cuit* (The raw and the cooked), by Claude Lévi-Strauss. Vocal and orchestral sound combine in agitated patterns which are presumably not to be followed for sense – but near the end of the first section come the significant words 'héros furieux . . . héros tué' (furious hero, slain hero). Voices and oppressive percussion suddenly cease; a sparse texture of piano, electric harpsichord and harp is heard, across which onslaughts are made by wind and percussion. The voices rejoin and end the movement with the word 'tué' (slain) as a high flute lingers on.

The second movement is a memorial to the American civil rights campaigner Martin Luther King, assassinated in 1968; the syllables of his name, separately and complete, are slowly and variously sung against spaced-out accompaniment. Strokes of the tam-tam perhaps symbolize a lamentation like a bell.

The third and longest movement is a kind of phantom performance of the third movement of Mahler's Symphony no.2 (see p.218). That being in dance-time (a *ländler* or early waltz), this movement in Berio's work also takes on a regular pulse which differentiates it from the rest. Of other works which are more briefly quoted, some are in waltz-time (Ravel's *La Valse*, one of Richard Strauss's waltzes from *Der Rosenkavalier*). At the very opening the voices pronounce the German word 'Peripetie', giving a clue to the quotation from Schoenberg's *Five Orchestral Pieces* (see p.285). Almost throughout, the microphoned voices keep up a chatter in English which is mainly based on Samuel Beckett's *The Unnameable* but takes in other material: a male voice finishes (while Mahler's dance-rhythm faintly persists) by introducing the other singers and thanking the conductor by name.

Immediately (during the resonance of the last chord of the previous movement) the unaccompanied voices in long-held chords begin the fourth movement. The effect, shortly reinforced by instruments, is of stability pivoted on the notes D flat and E flat – seemingly an allusion to the *fourth* movement of the Mahler symphony. Berio's text on the French words 'rose de sang' (blood rose) likewise connects with Mahler's text: see p.221.

The finale, added later to the score, is a long movement of powerful sound and jagged rhythms. It is intended to recapitulate some of the earlier material, and the singers add the rapid articulations of 'scat-singing' to their previous techniques. The French anthropological text of the first movement is recalled, and it may be in allusion to Martin Luther King also that the 'héros tué' occupies the final bars – along with the sustained high call of the flute which similarly ended the first movement.

BERLIOZ

1803–69

If the Romantic composer is thought of as the one whose art directly represents an outcome of unique personal emotion, it is no wonder that Hector Berlioz has come to incarnate that image. Coming to Paris from the French provinces, Berlioz at first followed his family's wish by studying medicine and did not take up formal musical study at the Conservatoire until he was twenty-two. His own lively *Memoirs* together with other literary works paint the portrait of a man as impatient of academics and pedants as of stupidity and hypocrisy in public life. His *Fantastic Symphony* represents a sort of wild, fictionalized autobiography, and in doing so bursts apart the conventional restrictions on the symphony orchestra.

The treatise on orchestration which Berlioz brought out in 1843 shows his delight in the emotional suggestiveness of the different instruments and in their power *en masse*. But, master of the grandiose though he is, he is equally skilful in the most delicate of colourings, as in the song cycle *Summer nights* (*Les Nuits d'été*) with accompanying small orchestra. *The Damnation of Faust*, a work which he styled a 'concert opera' but which is occasionally given in theatres also, yields three orchestral excerpts including the famous *Rákóczi March* or *Hungarian March*. His opera *The Trojans* includes an equally remarkable *Trojan March*, while two orchestral pieces linked to another opera are dealt with below.

Fantastic Symphony, *opus 14*

Reveries (*Largo*) – Passions (*Allegro agitato e appassionato assai*)
A Ball (Valse: *allegro non troppo*)
Scene in the fields (*Adagio*)
March to the Scaffold (*Allegretto non troppo*)
Dream of a Witches' Sabbath (*Larghetto* – Allegro – Ronde du Sabbat)
Duration: 55 minutes

Unveiled in Paris on 6 December 1830, this was by no means the first French symphony – but it was the first to show Beethoven's revolutionary impact and remains the most often played of French symphonies. Its conception is unique: five 'episodes in the life of an artist', all based on a recurring musical theme meant to denote a lover's obsession. It reflects Berlioz's own stormy relationship with the Irish actress Harriet Smithson, but the episodes cannot claim to be literally autobiographical.

Seeking the maximum force, expression and variety of tone-colour, the composer hoped for an orchestra of 220 players (the first performance had about 150). Among his demands were: high E flat clarinet as well as the usual clarinets; two cornets as well as two trumpets (in those days the trumpets still lacked valves, so could not play melodies as readily as the valved cornets); two tubas instead of one, and either piano or tubular bells to suggest the church bells in the finale. In the 'Scene in the fields' a distant thunderstorm is evoked by four-note rolled chords on the kettledrums, requiring four drummers.

The first movement is the only one that can be regarded as traditionally symphonic: a slow section (*Reveries*) leads to the main, faster section (*Passions*) which has an exposition clearly marked to be repeated and then what corresponds to development and recapitulation. But the impact is much more strongly of mood than of structure. The theme heard at the beginning of *Passions* on a solo clarinet, drawn out, first rising and then falling, is the so-called *idée fixe*, an obsessional phrase which will take various guises.

The second movement is in waltz-time: at a ball, the loved one is seen amid brilliance and festivity.

The scene in the countryside presents a dialogue between the pipes of two shepherds (one oboe, one english horn). Rural tranquillity cannot console the distressed lover, for *her* theme rises in his imagination. Finally the lack of an answer from the second shepherd signifies desolation in the thundery landscape.

The fourth movement is a nightmare march: the lover is being taken to the scaffold! The terrible moment arrives – the drums roll – the fatal theme is shrieked out by the high clarinet.

Finally, another nightmare – a witches' sabbath in which the beloved participates. The grotesque dance in 6/8 time is succeeded by the measured tread of the *Dies irae*, a church chant from the Mass for the dead; then both these themes are heard together.

Harold in Italy, *Symphony for orchestra with viola solo, opus 16*

Harold in the mountains: scenes of melancholy, happiness and joy (*Adagio – Allegro*)

March of the pilgrims singing their evening hymn (*Allegretto*)

Serenade of an Abruzzi mountaineer to his mistress (*Allegro assai – Allegretto*)

Orgy of the brigands: recollections of the preceding scenes (*Allegro frenetico*)

Duration: 42 minutes

'In fitting the viola into my poetical memories of my wanderings in the Abruzzi [mountains], I wanted to make the instrument into a sort of melancholy dreamer, in the style of Byron's *Childe Harold*.' Thus Berlioz paid tribute to one of the most admired poets of his time. Byron had published *Childe Harold's Pilgrimage* in instalments between 1812 and 1818 (the term 'Childe' indicating a young man of privileged position). The poem tells of adventurous journeys to various places, Italy being one of them – but Berlioz borrowed no incident from it, deciding instead to represent his own 'pilgrimage'.

According to the composer, the suggestion for a work had come from the great violinist Paganini, who had acquired a fine Stradivarius viola and needed music for it – but on seeing Berlioz's first movement, he rejected the work. It is indeed no showpiece in the way that Paganini's own violin concertos are. But it is, in conception and in the role given to that Cinderella of string instruments, a unique work in the orchestral repertory – though less forceful than the *Fantastic Symphony*.

As in that work, a fundamental theme (*idée fixe*) recurs in all four movements. In the finale, reminiscences occur of the three preceding movements, a procedure rather too readily recalling Beethoven's Ninth. Berlioz's 'Pilgrims' March' may similarly carry a reminder that Mendelssohn's *Italian* Symphony with a similar movement was first heard in 1833. Berlioz's *Harold* was composed in 1834 and first given on 23 November 1834 in Paris, Narcisse Girard conducting.

Most unusually, minimum numbers are specified for the strings: 15 first and 15 second violins, 10 violas, 12 cellos, 9 double-basses. Berlioz uses 2 cornets to supplement his (valveless) trumpets, plus the usual four horns, three trombones and (for the last movement only) tuba. The modest woodwind requirement is for two flutes (one doubling piccolo), two oboes (one doubling english horn), two clarinets and four bassoons (a conventional French strengthening). A harp lends its special expressiveness.

The first movement (in G) opens with a slow section in which the solo viola enters over harp accompaniment. It presents the fundamental theme – played twice over, the second time 'as quietly as possible'. The main faster section strikes up a lively orchestral 6/8; a sudden breaking-off leads to a second theme (in D) on the solo instrument. This part of the movement is now repeated. A development gives varied appearances of the fundamental theme to show Harold's straying thoughts, followed by a final section growing faster at the end.

The second movement, with a change to E major, presents a pilgrims' march. A picturesque effect of repeated bells is suggested by a high B (flute, oboe and harp) and middle C (horns and harp). Again the solo viola with its characteristic theme conveys Harold's presence, at one point furnishing an *arpeggio* (up-and-down) accompaniment to the march, which finally dies away.

In place of a symphonic scherzo comes the mountaineer's serenade. In C major, a rustic 6/8 dance-rhythm is first heard on piccolo and oboe against a bagpipe-like drone. The serenade proper is a smoother tune delivered by the english horn. The viola (Harold) contributes its own theme and later participates in the scene, taking over the former english horn tune.

The direction frenzied (*frenetico*) goes with the music that opens the fourth movement in G minor: this is the brigands' orgy, about which Berlioz gives us no particulars. Its violent strains are soon interrupted as Harold in his viola-self recalls his past adventures – that is, recalls the music from the first movement, the pilgrims' march, the serenade, and again the first movement. The brigands' rough celebrations are resumed, but they do not reach their end before two solo violins and a cello have again recalled, as from a distance, the pilgrims' march. The soloist also makes his farewell.

Overture, Benvenuto Cellini

Duration: 10–11 minutes

The opera *Benvenuto Cellini*, about the famous sixteenth-century Florentine sculptor and goldsmith, was 'hissed with admirable energy and unanimity', as Berlioz put it, when first produced in Paris

on 10 September 1838. It is now occasionally revived, either in its
original version or in an abbreviated version which Berlioz prepared
later. Irrespective of the opera, the overture has been and is one of the
most admired specimens of Berlioz's musical vigour. Its form is
original to the composer: not a slow introduction followed by a
faster main section, but a fast section followed by a slower and then
by a resumption of the faster material.

At a time when trumpets had no valves and so were restricted in
available notes, Berlioz achieved his required brilliance of sound by
using *four* trumpets each in a different key (i.e. with different notes
available) plus two cornets (which had valves). Modern orchestras
with valve-trumpets can reduce the number of players. A tuba,
replacing the original ophicleide, takes the lowest line of brass tone.
Two kettledrummers are required, who change from normal hard
sticks to softer sponge-headed ones for the slow section.

The vivacious opening theme (in G) is original to the overture,
but the slow section quotes from the opera itself – the first theme
(cellos and double-basses *pizzicato*) representing the Pope who has
power of life and death over Cellini; the high woodwind tune comes
from a harlequinade. The faster section resumes with its original
tune and key; a prominent later woodwind tune in D is a love-theme
from the opera. At the final climax of the overture, with both
timpanists thundering out the rhythm, the trombones requote the
Pope's theme. After a dramatic pause the cellos requote it softly,
unaccompanied, and within a few bars the piece is over.

Overture, The Roman Carnival

Duration: 9 minutes

From his failed opera *Benvenuto Cellini* (see immediately above)
Berlioz triumphantly re-worked some musical material to make this
concert overture. It was first performed, under the composer's
direction, in Paris on 3 February 1844. The orchestral requirement
differs slightly from that of the *Benvenuto Cellini* overture itself –
only one kettledrummer is used, the tuba (ophicleide) is absent, but
the second oboe is called on to change to english horn for a
prominent solo. Unusually, Berlioz specifies minimum numbers for
the strings, the same as for *Harold in Italy*.

The formal plan is as for the *Benvenuto Cellini* overture, but this
time the initial fast section is very short. The slower section follows

at considerable length, and then the faster section is resumed. The dominating rhythm of the first and last sections is that of the Italian dance-rhythm (a *salterello*) which characterizes the Roman Carnival in the opera – the scene not only of merrymaking but of an abduction and a fatal duel. The slow section has a lyrical tune (english horn solo, then viola solo) taken from the first-act love-duet of Cellini and Teresa. The faster section resumes with the dance. In a lull, the love-theme recurs. The end comes with brilliant exploitation of the brass.

BERNSTEIN

b. 1918

Leonard Bernstein is known as one of the leading conductors of his day (he was the first native-born American to be named as conductor of the New York Philharmonic Orchestra, 1958), as the composer of *West Side Story*, and as a brilliant expositor of music via the spoken word and television. But throughout his career he has also produced symphonic and chamber music, songs and solo pieces. His *Chichester Psalms*, a choral work with a Hebrew text (one of Bernstein's many musical allusions to his Jewish origin), was commissioned for performance in Chichester Cathedral.

As with Aaron Copland, a strong element of popular music is found in many of Bernstein's works. A jazz episode enters into his Symphony no. 2, subtitled *The Age of Anxiety* (after a poem by W. H. Auden), which has a solo piano part that was played by Bernstein himself at the première in Boston in 1949. Jazz style dominates the ballet score *Fancy Free* from which the musical *On the Town* was derived; it is prominent also in Bernstein's *Mass* (a theatre piece, not a liturgical mass) written for the opening of the Kennedy Center in Washington, 1971.

Overture, Candide

Duration: 4–5 minutes

Produced in New York on 1 December 1956, *Candide* was a failure on Broadway, no rival to the extraordinarily successful *West Side Story*. Unlike that work it was operatic in tone (sometimes mock-operatic) and ironically detached in feeling, with a libretto by Lillian Hellman based on the famous novel by Voltaire. The work re-emerged in 1974 with a new text by Hugh Wheeler, still falling short of success, as did an 'opera house version' produced in 1982.

Whatever the fate of the show, the brilliance and verve of the overture established it independently (and in full orchestral dress, not in reduced theatre orchestration). It had its first concert performance, under the composer's baton, in New York on 26 December 1957. Rhythmic zest is emphasized by a large percussion section (kettledrums, snare drum, tenor drum, triangle, cymbals, glockenspiel, xylophone), the remaining requirement being 2 flutes plus piccolo, 2 oboes, 2 clarinets plus high clarinet in E flat and bass clarinet, 2 bassoons and double-bassoon, 4 horns, 2 trumpets, 3 trombones, tuba, harp and strings.

It is in one rapid tempo, a brief fanfare leading to a pert, syncopated theme in E flat which is contrasted with a smoother theme in B flat: this classical key-relationship continues when both are eventually restated in E flat, followed by a headlong coda.

BIZET

1838–75

Carmen is often enough excerpted in orchestral concerts, but those who relish the composer's verve and melodic genius can find examples beyond that favourite opera. Georges Bizet was born in Paris, where *Carmen* was eventually produced only a few months before he died; nothing else brought him such notice, not even his opera *The Pearl Fishers* eight years before. As for his contribution to the orchestral repertory, it is ironic that we turn to an arrangement (not entirely by him) of his music to a play, and to a symphony which he himself never made public (see below). There is also an orchestral suite (the *Petite Suite d'orchestre*) which is the composer's scoring of five pieces from the longer suite *Children's Games* (*Jeux d'Enfants*) for piano duet.

Symphony in C

> Allegro vivo
> Adagio
> Allegro vivace
> Allegro vivace
> Duration: 29 minutes

Youthful works are not infrequently suppressed by composers who come, in maturity, to regard them as defective. But there is no more surprising case of repression than that of Bizet with this symphony – a light and lyrical work, full of tunes, based on the classical (Haydn–Mozart) type. He wrote it in 1855 at the age of seventeen, when he was a student at the Paris Conservatory, and never brought it to performance. He apparently thought it too much indebted to Gounod, a composer he reverenced. Today a stylistic link can be felt with Mendelssohn, who similarly freshened the classical model.

The manuscript was discovered in the library of the Paris Conservatory by Bizet's first English biographer, D. C. Parker, who brought it to the attention of the conductor Felix Weingartner. Under his baton the symphony had its long-delayed first performance on 26 February 1935. Its orchestration, apart from the requirement of four horns, is classical – 2 each of flutes, oboes, clarinets, bassoons and trumpets, with kettledrums and strings.

The first movement, in sonata form, dwells at some length on the vigorous opening subject. In contrast comes a smooth, singing melody in G on a solo oboe. The exposition is repeated; a development section makes attractive use of the horns; and the recapitulation begins *fortissimo*, the former oboe melody eventually recurring in the expected C major but in octaves on solo flute and clarinet.

The second movement is to be in A minor but does not move there immediately: an introductory passage makes a transition from the C major which ends the previous movement. Then the solo oboe begins its melody in A minor with a characteristic, swaying rhythm. The flow continues gracefully, with the four horns imaginatively used; after a mid-point in C major, the oboe melody is again heard but against a richer texture of accompanying sound.

The third movement is a scherzo, though not so named; in fact the composer, at the end of the usual contrasting section of trio, gives the instruction to repeat the 'minuet' (i.e. the opening section). But this is no minuet – its brisk one-in-a-bar music is scored with an outdoor vigour. In the central trio, a bagpipe-like drone sets up a quieter melodic strain.

The finale embarks on a whirling, spinning-top figure on the strings for its first subject; the wind instruments offer a different sort of jollity; then in due course the violins deliver the true contrasting second subject in G. (Mendelssohn is not far away.) Development shifts the music to E flat, then to other keys, leading to a *fortissimo*. It quietens, and the spinning-top theme begins the regular recapitulation.

Suites from The Woman of Arles (L'Arlésienne)

    Suite no. 1: Prelude
             Minuet
             Adagietto
             Carillon
             Duration: 18 minutes
    Suite no. 2 (arranged by Ernest Guiraud):
             Pastoral

Intermezzo
Minuet
Farandole
Duration: 18 minutes

Music to plays, including the use of *melodrama* in its original sense
(see below), could provide substantial commissions for nineteenth-
century composers from Beethoven to Sullivan. Such music does
not always successfully transfer to the concert stage, but fortunately
Bizet's music to Alphonse Daudet's *L'Arlésienne* has not shared the
oblivion which has enveloped the play. For the production of the
play (Paris, 1 October 1872) Bizet was restricted to twenty-six
musicians, but he used a full symphonic orchestra in making a
four-movement suite which was first heard under the conductorship
of Jules Pasdeloup at a Paris concert on 10 November 1872.

Bizet's suite is now known as the 'Suite no.1'. After his death a
second suite was compiled by Ernest Guiraud (who also composed
recitatives for the parts of *Carmen* which the composer had designed
for spoken dialogue). A 'Provençal drum' lends local colour to the
march (no.1) of the first suite and two numbers of the second suite,
and the alto saxophone retains the prominent role it enjoyed in the
original theatre score. The other instruments, besides the strings,
are: 2 flutes (one interchangeable with piccolo), 2 oboes (one interchangeable with english horn), 2 clarinets, 2 bassoons, 4 horns, 2
trumpets and 2 cornets, three trombones, harp and kettledrums. The
second suite only has also bass drum and cymbals.

Suite no.1

The prelude is really twofold in impact. At first comes a march-like
strain, melody bold and unharmonized which then becomes softly
harmonized by woodwind alone. After further restatement, the
tempo and mood change: a melody tenderly characterizing 'the
Simpleton' (the hero's younger brother) is delivered by the alto
saxophone, followed by the impassioned love-theme of the hero,
Frédéri.

The minuet is a piece played between two of the acts of the play. Its
sprightly first part is succeeded by a smoother, central section
(another solo for saxophone) after which the first section returns in a
modified form as if in farewell.

The slow and emotional third movement (*adagietto*) is scored only
for muted stringed instruments (without double-basses). It was used

for 'melodrama' in the strict sense – a spoken dramatic scene with musical accompaniment. On stage two people are seen who have long kept apart so as not to yield to a fatal attraction, and who now meet and embrace in old age.

Finally the famous movement entitled *Carillon* combines two movements from the play – an exultant *carillon* (bell) movement used as a prelude to Act 4, and music for another tender scene of 'melodrama'.

Suite no.2

The second suite, described as being 'arranged' by Guiraud, is largely of his own musical invention.

It opens with a *Pastorale* which has a wordless chorus in Bizet's original. The *Intermezzo* (wholly Bizet's) is music played between the scenes of Act 2. No.3 is not from Bizet's music to the Daudet play at all, but is an arrangement from his opera *The Fair Maid of Perth* with a flute-and-harp duet prominent at the beginning and end. No.4 begins by presenting the march from the opening of Bizet's own Suite no.1. There is a lively interruption on the Provençal drum as a traditional dance, the *farandole*, is heard; then Guiraud brilliantly sets the two together.

BLOCH

1880–1959

Ernest Bloch was born in Geneva and completed his first musical studies there. He is, indeed, the only Swiss composer represented in this book. He first travelled to the United States to conduct a dance company, later becoming an American citizen and a conservatory director in Cleveland, and then in San Francisco. He composed a considerable variety of orchestral and chamber music (including two piano quintets) of an abstract nature, but it was the works alluding to his Jewish origin which caught a special public attention. They include one of the very few concert settings of a Jewish service (*Avodath hakodesh*) and the 'rhapsody' discussed below.

Schelomo, *Hebrew Rhapsody for cello and orchestra*

Duration: 21 minutes

The name is that of Solomon – to be precise, a German spelling of the Hebrew form of the name which is today more usually transcribed 'Shlomo' in English-speaking countries. The sight of a statue of King Solomon made by the wife of the cellist Alexander Barjansky is said to have prompted Bloch to compose the work. Barjansky gave the first performance in New York on 3 May 1917, with Artur Bodanzky conducting.

Rhapsodical in style, this one-movement work makes the cello the voice of the king – imagined not as the mighty builder of the Temple, but as the meditator of Ecclesiastes who declared 'Vanity of vanities, all is vanity'. The composer's gift successfully exploits the cello's sonorities and sees that they are not obliterated by a larger orchestra than is found in most works featuring that solo instrument. The instrumentation is for 3 flutes (one doubling piccolo), 2 oboes and english horn, 2 clarinets and bass clarinet, 2 bassoons and double-bassoon, 4 horns, 3 trumpets, 3 trombones, tuba, a big percussion section (snare drum, tambourine, bass drum, cymbals and tam-tam, besides the kettledrums), two harps, celesta and strings.

An introduction launches the cello itself into a passionate statement, first with the orchestra and then in a solo cadenza. This anticipates the chief structural theme, delivered by the orchestral violas. It is continued by the soloist, with an oriental character in the rhythmic and harmonic inflexions of the melody. After a big climax and a brief cadenza, a slower section presents utterances from solo oboe and bassoon which seem almost like syllabic speech: these utterances too are taken up by the soloist. At a later point a similar rhythmical 'speech' issues from the kettledrums. The cello solo line continues, making an occasional use of quarter-tones. Solomon's meditations end, with agony of thought not quite soothed, in a long-sustained note on the cello's lowest string.

BORODIN

1833–87

The regular, salaried occupation of Alexander Borodin was that of
an academic, his subject being not music but chemistry, in which he
published some important papers. Only in his leisure, therefore,
could he release that creative gift which makes him one of the most
important of Russian composers. His total musical output was
understandably small, and several of his works were left unfinished.
Not only his opera *Prince Igor* but his third symphony were completed after his death by his colleagues Nikolai Rimsky-Korsakov
(see p.276) and Alexander Glazunov.

Like Rimsky-Korsakov, he came under the influence of the composer Mily Balakirev (1837–1910), the determined advocate of
musical nationalism. Borodin's music associates itself with Russian
history and landscape, taking melodic and rhythmic vigour from
both Slav–Russian and Russian–oriental sources. In his tone-poem
In Central Asia (better known in the West as *In the Steppes of Central
Asia*), composed in 1880, Borodin wove this inspiration into a work
which won the admiration of Liszt. Orientalism also adds to the
attractiveness of the 'Polovtsian Dances' from *Prince Igor*, which
properly require choral as well as orchestral performance.

Symphony no.2 in B minor

Allegro
Prestissimo
Andante, leading to
Allegro
Duration: 28 minutes

Suddenly learning that the Russian Music Society in St Petersburg
wished to perform the symphony on which he had worked for
several years, Borodin was unable to find all his material and, though

ill in bed, had to write out again the orchestration of the first and last movements. Under the baton of Eduard Napravnik on 10 March 1877 the work was not counted much of a success. The composer lightened the scoring for a performance under Rimsky-Korsakov two years later and the work eventually took its place among the most admired of Russian symphonies.

The actual publication was delayed till after the composer's death, so Rimsky-Korsakov helped his friend's score through the press (but did not meddle in the composition). Forceful in expression, with touches of harmony and melody which still seem exotically appealing, it uses a large orchestra with that flair for instrumental colour which characterizes the Russian nineteenth-century masters. The first movement has the rather conservative orchestration of 2 flutes (one interchangeable with piccolo), 2 oboes (one interchangeable with english horn), 2 clarinets, 2 bassoons, 4 horns, 2 trumpets, 3 trombones, tuba, kettledrums and strings. The second movement adds harp and triangle. Only in the finale are *four* extra percussionists used, with parts for triangle, tambourine, cymbals and bass drum.

The forceful 'elemental' element which forms such an attraction in this as in other Russian works is encapsulated in the opening phrase, like some fierce slogan several times declaimed. Not only is this utterance short, loud, incisive; it also makes use of an 'irregular' musical scale. It becomes the movement's main theme in B minor, gaining a more flowing counter-theme on the high woodwind. Later at a slightly slower tempo the cellos deliver a tranquil melody in D, related to Russian folk song. There is no cut-off end to this exposition, and no repetition of it as on the classical model. Instead, a vigorous new section in D minor begins, built from an unaccompanied rhythmical figure on a kettledrum. A full recapitulation begins in the original key (B minor) and the 'elemental' theme – with its time-values slowed down to a majestic unison delivery – ends the movement.

A scherzo comes next – a long, diminishing brass chord serving as transition from the previous movement's B minor to the new F major. Unusually, this is a scherzo in 4/4 time, not 3/4. The first theme rises in detached notes on cellos and double-basses; a smoother but also more impassioned theme in D flat later comes from the violins, violas and cellos together. A contrasting trio in D major is slightly slower (Allegretto) a languid oboe melody sways to an accompaniment of triangle and harp. The scherzo proper is then repeated, but with a changed ending.

The third movement, by turns both dreamy and impassioned, is in D flat. After the briefest introduction on clarinet and harp, the horn delivers a rising-and-falling theme against a warm background of strings and harp. Later the oboe adds a drooping theme. The music grows more urgent. After the fullest orchestral sonorities the texture is finally reduced to clarinet and harp as at the opening, which leads directly to . . .

. . . the finale, which is vigorous throughout, in B major. After some introductory hints, the boisterous main theme, heard on the full orchestra, intermingles bars of 3/4 and 2/4. A new, smoother tune in D major, on a solo clarinet, leads to a fading-out, then a dramatic interjection as trombones and tuba issue a reminder of the main theme. A development drives the music to C major, with a full force of percussion, and then an instantaneous shift of harmony produces B major at the moment when the opening material is recapitulated. The 'smoother' tune, more richly accompanied, returns in B major. The course is set for an ending which speeds to a final flourish with trilling strings and woodwind and the jingle of triangle and tambourine.

Overture, Prince Igor

Duration: 11 minutes

After Borodin's death, his friends Rimsky-Korsakov and Glazunov were obliged to orchestrate about half the score of his opera *Prince Igor* in order to finish it and bring it to production – at St Petersburg on 16 November 1890. Like so many Russian operas of its century it is strongly national in feeling, telling of the medieval Russian prince who successfully combats the Asian invaders on his borders and the intriguers who menace from within.

The overture was completed by Glazunov, using the composer's sketches and his own memories of hearing Borodin play it on the piano. Quoting as it does from the opera itself, the overture stands on its song-like melodies and strong rhythms. Doubled woodwind is used (plus piccolo), 4 horns, 2 trumpets, three trombones, tuba, kettledrums and strings.

The brass scoring is particularly exciting, as in the cumulative fanfares which (after a slow, sombre introduction in D minor) begin the main part of the overture in D major. There is a winding, graceful tune on a solo clarinet followed by a broadly sweeping tune from the massed orchestra: it comes from the hero's patriotic song when in captivity to his enemies. It is heard at this point in B flat, then recurs in D major when this uninterruptedly vigorous, melodious overture is nearing its end.

BOULEZ

b.1925

Most composers acquire sufficient competence in conducting to direct performances of their own work if need arises; few do it with the brilliance of Benjamin Britten, and fewer still acquire an independent recognition as masterly conductors of others' music. Mahler did so, however, and Richard Strauss likewise; and among the moderns, Pierre Boulez graduated from early experience with a theatre company in Paris to take posts of authority with the BBC Symphony Orchestra, the New York Philharmonic and the Bayreuth Festival.

He also showed himself a planner, organizer and inspirer of others, particularly as founder-director of the Paris institute which explores advanced methods of electronic and other composition (IRCAM – Institut de recherche et de co-ordination acoustique/ musique). His conducting skill has been of immense service to the presentation of his own music. His process of composition is such that he often releases a work for performance but later produces another version, sometimes combined with other works.

In sound, the music of Boulez often seems aggressive in impact, jagged in outline, but displays (even to those unconvinced by his structures) an obvious mastery in reconciling and balancing unusual sonorities.

Fold upon fold (Pli selon pli) for soprano and orchestra

> Gift ('Don')
> Improvisations on Mallarmé:
>   1: 'Le vierge, le vivace et le bel aujourd'hui'
>   2: 'Une dentelle s'abolit'
>   3: 'A la nue accablante tu'
> Tomb ('Tombeau')
> Duration: 75 minutes

The French poet Stéphane Mallarmé (1842–98), whose mark on musical history was already assured with Debussy (see p. 134), has much influenced Boulez. In the present work, settings of three sonnets under the name of *Improvisations on Mallarmé* are encased between two other, longer movements to become the composite entity called *Fold upon fold* (Pli selon pli). That phrase comes from a poem by Mallarmé which is not actually set: the poet had used it to describe the way the lifting mist reveals the buildings of Bruges, and the composer uses it for a gradual revealing of a 'portrait of Mallarmé'.

The complete work was first given, under the composer's baton, on 20 October 1962 at Donaueschingen (the German town which has been a nursery of advanced modern music). Eva-Maria Rogner was the soprano soloist. It combines, as do many other modern works sharing a similar aesthetic approach, two apparently opposite features – the most exact and detailed marks of expression for each instrument, and the provision for major variables in performance. Conductor and performers are made responsible for choosing between different sequences of small inner sections, and for exercising other options.

An unusual and very large orchestra is used for the two outer pieces, and a smaller but eclectic choice of instruments for the three inner pieces. The total requirement is: 3 flutes (2 doubling piccolo), alto flute, oboe (doubling english horn), 1 clarinet, 1 high clarinet in E flat, 1 bass clarinet, 2 alto saxophones, 1 bassoon, 4 horns, 2 trumpets, 3 trombones, piano, 3 harps, celesta, mandolin, guitar and strings, plus 7 percussionists playing vibraphones, xylophones, kettledrums, bass drum, snare drum, cymbals, glockenspiel, tubular bells, cowbells, gongs, crotales, bongos, claves and maracas.

An explosive, full orchestral chord opens the first piece and a similar chord closes the work. The two pieces complement each other: the title of the first, 'Gift' ('Don'), evidently stands for the poet's initial 'gift' or inspiration, while 'Tomb' ('Tombeau') conveys a remembrance of him. The voice in the first number enters immediately and is confined to a single line, 'I bring you the child of an Idumaean night!', plus fragmentary phrases from the texts of the three inner numbers; in the concluding number the voice enters only in the final moments.

The opening movement displays a great diversity of texture from the extreme sparsity of the opening (piano, joined successively by one or two notes from harp, celesta, vibraphone and guitar) to extreme complexity. The soprano's eventual 'pre-quotations' (from the coming 'Improvisations', in the reverse order) are not exact nor intended to be literally comprehended. After the orchestra has for some time been playing in two semi-independent groups, one following the conductor's left hand and one the right hand, they unite for the movement's abrupt end.

There follow the three 'Improvisations'. Though the vocal line is seeming irregular and 'jumpy', the musical form in fact corresponds to the poetic. The first four lines of each sonnet are quoted below. The poet uses a highly concentrated construction to balance sound and sense.

Improvisation I

Two alto saxophones (unique to this movement) join the flutes, clarinets, horns, celesta, mandolin, guitar, multiple percussion, 3 harps, violas and double-basses. After an introductory chord the soloist begins immediately, not pausing until after the four-line stanza. The poem later develops the image of a swan frozen in ice: 'cygne' ('swan') is the last word to be sung.

> Le vierge, le vivace et le bel aujourd'hui
> Va-t-il nous déchirer avec un coup d'aile ivre
> Ce lac oublié que hante sous le givre
> Le transparent glacier des vols qui n'ont pas fui!
>
> Will the virginal, lively and beautiful today
> Tear for us with a drunken flap of the wing
> This hard forgotten lake haunted under the ice
> By the transparent glacier of flights never flown?

Improvisation II

This movement, at the centre of the work, is the most restricted in sound, accompanying the voice with harp, piano, celesta and percussion only – nine instrumentalists in all. A short complete section precedes the singer's entry, and similarly at the end there is a short decisive instrumental flourish led by piano and the shuffling sound of maracas. The hidden imagery of the poem is apparently sexual.

> Une dentelle s'abolit
> Dans le doute du Jeu suprême
> A n'entr'ouvrir comme un blasphème
> Qu'absence éternelle de lit.

A lace is abolished
In the doubt of the supreme Game,
Revealing as a blasphemy
Only the eternal absence of a bed.

Improvisation III

Two of the three harps used in this number are tuned in quarter-tones. With them are four flutes, a trombone, guitar, mandolin, a large percussion group, cellos and double-basses. This is the longest of the three Improvisations but the least 'verbal'. Only the first three lines of the sonnet are set (in the latter half of the piece). The imagery of the unsung lines, presumably interpreted instrumentally, deals with shipwreck and drowning.

A la nue accablante tu
Basse de basalte et de laves
A même les echos esclaves
Par une trompe sans vertu . . .

Silenced under the overwhelming cloud
Base of basalt and lava
Even with the servile echoes
Of an ineffective trumpet . . .

The long concluding section of the work, 'Tomb' ('Tombeau') reassembles the large orchestra for a very dense and complicated web of sound dominated by the piano. A violent climax is reached, suddenly cut off. Finally the soprano enters with the last line of a sonnet in which Mallarmé commemorated another poet ('Tombeau de Verlaine'): 'Un peu profond ruisseau calomnié la mort' (A hardly deep rivulet slandered – death). Each syllable is separate and prolonged, with a dramatic gap before the final two – the word 'la' being sung on a low note, 'mort' being *spoken*. The final explosive chord follows.

BRAHMS

1833–97

Born in Hamburg but choosing from his thirties to make Vienna his home, Johannes Brahms established – and has kept – the role of successor to Beethoven. In one direction he was the more conservative of the two: he did not depart from the traditional four-movement pattern of the symphony, nor did he encourage non-musical associations by affixing a name to a symphony or by incorporating a sung text. His work has a stern rigour in developing its themes, and despises the more colourful allurements of orchestral tone. Compared to Schumann, who stood as his musical and personal mentor, Brahms breathes a lofty, less genial air.

He wrote no story-telling orchestral music and no opera or other work for the theatre. But his contribution to the orchestral repertory is substantial: besides his four symphonies with their own different musical atmospheres, four concertos and a set of orchestral variations bear the stamp of his mastery, as does a popular festive overture. His friendship with the Hungarian violinist Joseph Joachim (two years older than he, and a celebrity long before Brahms was) had a firm musical foundation: apart from his virtuosity as a performer, Joachim was a composer whose views Brahms respected, and a conductor on whose understanding he could rely.

The symphonies

Brahms's symphonies – a series which he delayed launching until he was over forty – are 'classical' in the context of his time. They inherit the structures and melody-types bequeathed by Beethoven, and they move cautiously forward from Beethoven's and Schubert's harmonies, not making the big jump into chromatic language with Liszt and Wagner. The Beethoven legacy may have not been without its burden: challenged on the resemblance of the main theme of the finale of his first symphony to the 'Joy' theme of the finale of

Beethoven's Ninth, he is said to have replied: 'Any ass can see that'. Brahms's symphonies do, however, avoid the Viennese minuet or its successor, the scherzo in 3/4 time: he seeks some other light contrast to set between slow second movement and weighty finale.

Symphony no.1 in C minor, opus 68

> Un poco sostenuto – Allegro
> Andante sostenuto
> Un poco allegretto e grazioso
> Adagio – Più andante – Allegro non troppo, ma con brio
> Duration: 46 minutes

Brahms was in the audience at Karlsruhe when his symphony had its first performance on 4 November 1876: Otto Dessoff conducted. It was introduced to Vienna in the following year. A new, authoritative composer of the most imposing of orchestral forms had arrived. The double-bassoon and three trombones are added to the orchestral force, following Beethoven's example, and four horns are used; but otherwise, the double wind instruments suffice, with kettledrums and strings. The movements of the symphony are related in an unusual way: the successive keys are a third apart, C (minor/major), E (major), A flat (major), C (minor/major).

The pounding beat of kettledrums opens a slow introduction which does not, like a Haydn or Beethoven symphonic introduction, simply disappear: this music will recur to close the movement. Between comes the main, faster section in a surging, stormy vein. A moment of hushed dialogue in E flat between a clarinet and horn is soon quitted as the exposition sweeps onward (and is repeated). Development follows; in the recapitulation the hushed dialogue is in C major, and it is with the major chord that the movement ends.

The slow, meditative second movement begins with a solemn, uplifting strain. A middle section is followed by a varied repetition of the first part in which a solo violin (for the only time in a Brahms symphony!) seems to add a consolatory note of its own.

In the third movement, a display of graceful but subtle melody is led by a prominent clarinet solo. Though the energetic feeling of a scherzo is avoided, the scherzo form is followed, with a contrasting middle section. The varied return of the first part carries the tiniest hint of the big theme which is to come in the finale.

So far, the three trombones have sat silent in the orchestral ranks.

Like Beethoven in his Fifth Symphony, Brahms has reserved their weight for the last movement, which opens sombrely in the symphony's original minor key. The long slow introduction includes two striking themes, first a horn-call and then a hymn-like utterance on bassoons, double-bassoon, and trombones. The main section bursts into C major with its swinging march-like tune on the violins. Both horn-call and hymn reappear during the development and final triumph.

Symphony no.2 in D, opus 73

> Allegro non troppo
> Adagio non troppo
> Allegretto grazioso, quasi andantino
> Allegro con spirito
> Duration: 39 minutes

After delaying until his mid-career to launch his first symphony, Brahms was sufficiently confident to begin writing his second immediately after. On 30 December 1877 it received, under Hans Richter's baton in Vienna, its successful first performance. Away from the gravity and even portentousness of no.1, this is a sunny work and there has even been the suggestion that it represents 'Brahms's *Pastoral* symphony'. A tuba is added to the orchestral force required in the previous symphony.

The first movement opens with a three-note phrase on the cellos and double-basses, D – C sharp – D, which appears merely introductory but in fact gives a pointer to much of what happens later in this close-packed music. A 'Romantic' horn-call follows as the principal theme, and later a tune emerges in F sharp minor for violas and cellos in thirds, a special warmth of tone being felt from the fact that the cellos take the upper line! Density of texture and continuity of flow are achieved within a sonata-form frame, with an unmistakable feeling of repose at the end (coda) in the smooth singing of horns and strings.

A subtle first movement is followed by a subtle second (in B major), begun by a slow, outpouring theme on the cellos. A later theme in lighter vein with syncopated accents moves on into a more stormy section, and finally a variant of the first part returns.

Not called a scherzo, the third movement in G major is nevertheless light, melodious and rhythmically engaging. A graceful section

in 3/4 time (oboe solo, with a notable *pizzicato* accompaniment for
the cellos) is succeeded by a contrasting section (trio) in 2/4 time; the
first section, varied, returns and is succeeded by a different trio in 3/8
and then by another varied return. But in *all* these sections a
permutation of the same musical germ may be found.

A sonata-form structure makes a powerful finale for the symphony, starting softly with a theme which uncurls towards mighty
deeds. The end with its exulting trumpets and powerful trombones
has more of sheer effectiveness than Brahms usually shows.

Symphony no.3 in F, opus 90

> Allegro con brio
> Andante
> Poco allegretto
> Allegro
> Duration: 36 minutes

Hans Richter was again the conductor when Brahms produced a
third symphony, giving the first performance on 2 December 1883.
The orchestration is as for the first symphony. No.3 is distinguished,
among other things, for the melting tune of its third movement, and
also for the fact that Brahms revealed a 'motto' for the work. He
apparently attached to himself the label 'frei aber froh' ('free but
happy', a curious indication of Brahms' outlook). This yields the
initials F, A, F, which Brahms presents as musical notes, sometimes
allowing the interpretation of 'A' to be A flat.

Indeed the major/minor ambiguity, characteristically a powerful
point of expression for Brahms, has an important role in this
symphony. Thus the first theme, exploding upwards, is in F minor
and passes to the stated key of the symphony, F major. A change of
pulse from 6/4 to 9/4 brings a winding, rather elusive new theme on
a clarinet. Sonata-form is followed through a wide range of keys to a
quiet ending.

The two middle movements impose silence on trumpets and
drums. The second, in C major, has an opening melody that is
sometimes felt to be 'folk-like': it returns, varied, after the passage of
gentle incidents. The third movement in C minor brings out the
song-making qualities of cellos and horn: there is a central section
and a return (with altered scoring) to the first.

The key of F minor opens the fourth movement, as it did the first:

the mood is stormy. Later, over a marching bass, a big and confident tune on the horns and cellos rings out in C major. That spirit returns later but is not allowed a triumphant conclusion. A coda re-establishes calm: the opening stormy subject has achieved tranquillity, and the motto (F-A-F) from the first movement gently inserts itself into the web of sound.

Symphony no.4 in E minor, opus 98

> Allegro non troppo
> Andante moderato
> Allegro giocoso
> Allegro energico e passionato
> Duration: 39 minutes

Brahms's final symphony, which reasserts the commanding mood of the first (with even a hint of tragedy), was the only one to receive its first performance under his own conductorship – at Meiningen (Germany) on 25 October 1885. The form of the last movement is unique in the symphony up to that time – a *passacaglia*, a set of variations built over a short recurring theme in the bass. The achievement of that structure is forecast in Brahms's *St Anthony* Variations (see below). The orchestration of the symphony is as for the first and third symphonies.

The first movement observes the usual sonata-form construction but opens with a captivating and unusual 'singing' melody. The exposition is repeated, and the development starts as if once again the music has returned to the opening. But the recapitulation, with subtlety, presents the opening tune not in singing form but in slow, solemn notes. The end comes in the minor key and with full orchestral sound – except for the trombones, reserved for the finale.

The second movement presents a gentle summons on the horns which turns the music to E major, and one of the composer's most fetching lyrical tunes as a second subject in B major on the cellos.

The third movement, opening with a rollicking tune in C major, has all the energy and exhilaration expected of a scherzo but is in 2/4 and not 3/4 time. Moreover it is not in scherzo form but in a taut, small-scale sonata-form: the second subject (in G, on the violins), is almost as jolly as the first.

The finale unleashes the trombones (at last) to deliver the sequence of eight chords in E minor, remarkably harmonized, which is its theme. Thirty variations follow, merging one into the next so that the effect is of large symphonic periods, not small-scale piling of bricks. The melodic line of the theme, first heard as the upper notes of the successive chords, sometimes passes to the bass-line and sometimes is hidden in the middle. As the end approaches there is a turn towards an optimistic E major – but it is rejected, and the tragic E minor leaves its mark of destiny.

The concertos

Brahms's four concertos are all massive in feeling, making as much intellectual challenge as his symphonies do: they are not without their element of virtuoso display, but sheer exhilaration of the audience is never the aim. Symphonic argument is one of their chief qualities, and the second piano concerto takes the symphonic four-movement shape instead of following the usual three-movement plan. Nevertheless Brahms preserves his classical restraint, and at the same time avoids swamping his soloists, by confining the orchestra in all works to a dimension almost the same as Beethoven's: there are pairs only of woodwind, with two trumpets, kettledrums and strings – but with the thicker sound of four horns as against Beethoven's two.

Concerto no. 1 in D minor for piano and orchestra, opus 15

>Maestoso
>Adagio
>Rondo: allegro non troppo
>Duration: 45 minutes

The sophisticated concertgoers of Leipzig showed a cold indifference to this concerto on 27 January 1859, when the young Brahms was himself the soloist and his friend Joachim the conductor. (The two had given the work its first performance, apparently in not quite finished form, five days before at Hanover.) The music was considered too heavy, not pretty enough: no doubt the thick orchestration did not help, nor a certain lack of contrast because all movements are in D (whether minor or major). Evidently a taste for Brahms was yet to be formed.

The first movement starts menacingly: over a kettledrum-roll on the keynote an unexpected first chord crashes in (D, F, B flat). When the long orchestral exposition finally subsides, the piano enters with a new, rippling subject, following it shortly with a brighter and more positive subject in F major. A rhythmical horn-call sounds. A stormy octave passage on the piano now begins to develop this material, eventually leading to a drum-roll on the note D: the chord that thunders out is *not* that of the opening, but D, E, G sharp, B: it is on the recognition of that difference that the impact of this moment depends! Here the recapitulation of themes begins. Returning, the rhythmical horn-call affirms D major, but the minor-key sadness takes over as the kettledrums linger on the rhythm. No cadenza breaks the flow.

Above the phrase for muted violins which opens the second movement the composer's manuscript has the words 'Benedictus qui venit in nomine domini' (Blessed is he who cometh in the name of the Lord). It may be conjectured whether this quotation from the Roman Catholic mass had some personal association for Brahms (who was not a Catholic) or whether it is merely a remembered phrase which gave rise to the melody. This opening is extended by orchestra and piano. A more animated section is built on a new theme announced by clarinets; then a variation of the opening returns to which the soloist adds a meditative cadenza.

A vigorous syncopated tune from the piano is the rondo-theme on which the finale is pivoted. Between the recurrences of that theme are clearly identifiable contrasts – one of which (in B flat) provides, on the violins, an easy-going, placid tune as a relaxation of previous stress. After the pianist's cadenza, that 'placid' tune takes on a farewell quality in the horns in D major. The music gathers animation to finish in that key.

Concerto no.2 in B flat for piano and orchestra, opus 83

> Allegro non troppo
> Allegro appassionato
> Andante
> Allegretto grazioso
> Duration: 50 minutes

This is a 'heavyweight' among concertos – not only in having four movements instead of the usual three, but in its general gravity and the absence of brilliant display. Brahms himself was the soloist at the first performance – given in Budapest on 9 November 1881, conducted by Sandor Erkel. The orchestra comprises double woodwind, four horns, two trumpets, kettledrums and strings.

The meditative – almost dreamy – opening, shared by a solo horn and the piano, is deceptive, for the character of the movement as a whole is stormy; and the stormiest, or at any rate the most challenging, parts of it arise from the opening theme itself. The use made of the first three rising notes is particularly notable. Other themes present themselves, but this movement is not primarily a matter of contrast and nicely separated sections: the music is to be drained in a single draught, so to speak. After the brief introduction, orchestra alone and then piano and orchestra together present the thematic material; then for a moment the first theme resumes its original guise as a horn solo – but this time in a minor key – as 'development' unobtrusively, and plays its part also in the emphatic bars which close the movement.

Brahms, describing the second movement as 'a little scherzo' showed the same spirit of elephantine banter that led him to speak of the whole work as 'a little concerto', and to say that it was 'not for little girls' (to play). In fact the second movement is hefty at times, almost uncouth – although the initial lumbering in D minor is presently relieved by a more withdrawn theme initiated by the strings in unaccompanied octaves. The more passive mood then returns. A trio provides the contrast of the major key, and then the 'scherzo' material returns in a varied form, not in a literal reappearance.

The slow movement (in B flat) is dominated by the peaceful tune given forth in the opening bars by a solo cello: the cello, in fact, maintains its separate identity right up to the close of the movement. This is the 'singing' movement of the concerto. The cello theme indeed recalls Brahms's later song *Immer leiser wird mein Schlummer*; and the theme given by the clarinets, when the music has moved from B flat to F sharp, was also used by Brahms in the song *Todessehnen*.

Brahms follows the tradition whereby the last movement of a concerto is the lightest. Here the concluding rondo has, at the beginning of its second group of subjects, a dash of that Hungarian-gypsy style of which Brahms had made even more use in the Violin Concerto. After this group has come round for a second appearance, the piano by itself begins to chop up into cheerful triplets the theme with which the movement is opened. The orchestra joins in, and the work ends in high spirits.

Concerto in D for violin and orchestra, opus 77

Allegro ma non troppo
Adagio
Allegro giocoso, ma non troppo vivace
Duration: 41 minutes

Their friendship of twenty-five years made it natural that Brahms should dedicate his violin concerto to Joseph Joachim. Having been consulted on the practicability of the solo part, Joachim gave the first performance in Leipzig on 1 January 1879, with the composer conducting. Joachim also composed the original cadenza (only one is required, in the first movement); it is still the most often performed, though some alternatives have been written. The Hungarian–dance style of the finale is supposedly a tribute to the soloist, though this was not Brahms's only recourse to it.

Originally planned as a concerto in four movements, like the second piano concerto (see p. 109), it was recast in the usual three. It is a work of grandeur, even of severity – suggested by prominent minor-key sections which Brahms locates even within a major-key movement (as all these three are). Though demanding a formidable violin technique, it lacks the audience-catching kind of acrobatic feats, and the soloist has to suffer the allocation of the slow movement's beautiful theme to an oboe!

The concerto opens in classical style with a long exposition for orchestra alone, displaying several different themes – among them, a jagged theme in the minor key for strings alone. Immediately afterwards the soloist enters, also in the minor key, eventually arriving with some sense of achievement at the smooth, major-key theme of the opening. In contrast is the soloist's strenuous theme of chords in triple-stopping (see Glossary). A *fortissimo* climax with a drum-roll establishes A minor (instead of the expected A major), and a development follows. Further drum-rolls later lead to a recapitulation of themes, and finally to the soloist's cadenza and to a coda which starts tranquilly but gains in animation at the end.

As the second movement begins, the oboe delivers its memorable and peaceful tune against an ensemble of other woodwind and two horns – a highly distinctive sound. In contrasting tone, orchestral strings accompany the soloist in an elaboration of the tune. A marked shift of key (F major to F sharp minor) brings the more agitated middle section, after which yet another elaboration of the main tune ends the movement as peacefully as it began.

Again following a classical model, Brahms chooses a rondo pattern for his finale, letting the soloist launch without preliminaries into the 'Hungarian' theme. The final pages are brilliantly contrived: unaccompanied at first, then with the orchestra joining, the violin pursues a path of triplets, trills and rapidly flashing phrases. The 'Hungarian' theme then takes on a surprising, march-like jollity before the rather terse ending.

Concerto in A minor for violin, cello and orchestra, opus 102

> Allegro
> Andante
> Vivace non troppo
> Duration: 30 minutes

Brahms's 'Double Concerto', as it is usually called, is unique. Overcoming the fact that whereas the violin penetrates orchestral sound with ease, the cello does so with difficulty, Brahms created a work which shows off both instruments equally well. Moreover it does so without any compromise in the essential qualities of the composer's own musical style. There cannot be, of course, the sharply focused sense of 'one versus all' which contributes to the excitement of single-instrument concertos, but instead there is a subtle interrelationship of duo and full orchestral sound.

It is Brahms's last orchestral work. He had fallen out with Joachim, the great friend and collaborator of his youthful and maturing years, over the matter of Joachim's divorce; but after some years of silence he reapproached Joachim with a proposal for this concerto. Their warm relationship was renewed, and on 18 October 1887 at Cologne Brahms conducted the first public performance (a private performance having been given a little while before): in the solo roles, Joachim was partnered by Robert Hausmann, the cellist of Joachim's own string quartet.

The first movement begins by allowing the cello, then the violin, then both together, to meditate freely on the themes to come: it is like a double cadenza at the opposite end of the movement from where it might be expected. A vigorous full orchestral exposition follows, after which the soloists take the lead. After an intertwining of solo instruments, a falling figure on a clarinet leads to the cello's delivery of a gentle theme in C major. After the orchestra has eventually recapitulated its earlier material, this theme is heard high on the violin in A major against the cello's rippling accompaniment, and then with the instruments' roles reversed. But the music declines the comfort of a major-key ending and reverts to an energetic A minor.

The slow movement in D major presents one of Brahms's most memorable tunes, played by the two soloists an octave apart – a striking sonority. Typically of Brahms, its eventual return is not identical but takes a subtly varied form.

The cello's dance-like tune initiates a traditionally light-hearted concerto finale. It is the cello which also delivers (against orchestral cellos and double-basses only) a contrasting, solid, chordal subject in C major – which eventually comes back in A major, the same procedure as in the first movement. But this time the A major holds its place, embracing the dance-like opening tune in a transformed rhythm, and the concerto ends exuberantly.

Academic Festival Overture, *opus 80*

Duration: 10 minutes

The university at Breslau (then a German city, now Wrocław, Poland) conferred on Brahms an honorary doctorate of philosophy in 1879: with four symphonies and other major works to his credit, he was at the height of his fame. His response, when he was gently prodded to make one, was this concert overture built on student songs: Brahms himself conducted the first performance at Breslau in January 1881. With piccolo, double-bassoon, three trombones, tuba, bass drum, cymbals and triangle, the orchestra is unusually large for Brahms, resulting in a jollity which was doubtless intended to suit the festive occasion.

Brahms pretended to belittle the work as a pot-pourri, that is, merely a stringing together, but the music can be analysed in the usual symphonic first-movement form and is kept under Brahms's habitually restraining hand. The tunes (including an initiation song, 'The Foxes' Ride', as a duet for two bassoons) make their appearance and reappearance, with the climax reserved for the most famous of the songs, presented once only, at the end (in analytical terms, a coda). It is 'Gaudeamus igitur', the Latin words of which run:

> So let us rejoice while we are young . . .
> After joyful youth and troublesome age, the ground will have us!

St Anthony Variations, *opus 56a*

Duration: 19 minutes

In 1870 Brahms was shown the manuscript of an open-air suite for wind instruments composed nearly 100 years before by Haydn (as was then thought). Delighted with one tune, which in the manuscript was identified as 'St Anthony's Chorale', he based on it the present work of 1872, entitling it *Variations on a theme by Joseph Haydn*, and scoring it for modest orchestra without trombones. Brahms also made an alternative version for two pianos.

But the theme is now thought to be the work of 'Anon', though used by Haydn, and the preferred title for Brahms's work is as above. The theme, heard first, is in a clear doubled form, with each part repeated (A, A; B, B): the second part is the longer. Nine variations follow, not simply presenting variations of the melody but ingeniously transforming the harmony, rhythms and structure as well. *Variation 1* (starting with deliberate, 'mark time' beats on bassoons, double-bassoon and horns) retains the original major key; *Variation 2* is in the minor. The next variation, and the two that follow, make a structural change: instead of exact repetitions of the A and B sections, the repeats themselves make changes.

The last (ninth) variation is the longest, starting with a *passacaglia* over a sturdy bass theme, obviously taken from the main theme. When the main tune eventually returns as heard at the outset of the work, it is festively dressed with the notable addition of the triangle – a typical gesture for Brahms, who avoided flashy orchestration but knew how to make a point.

BRITTEN

1913–76

Benjamin Britten left hardly any area of music untouched. Never before had a British composer awakened a sustained international interest in his operas – a series that began with *Peter Grimes* in 1945. The *Sea Interludes* from that opera, treated below, are the sole example of an excerpt from his stage work which is regularly heard in the orchestral concert-hall. Britten's principal combinations of solo instrument and orchestra – the Piano Concerto (1938), Violin Concerto (1939) and the much later Cello Symphony (1963) – have not established themselves in the repertory. But for orchestra alone, both in its reduced size (chamber orchestra or string orchestra) and at full strength, he composed notably. The *Variations on a Theme of Frank Bridge*, written for the Boyd Neel String Orchestra to play at the Salzburg Festival in 1937, was the work which mainly launched him as a composer; the *Sinfonia da Requiem* of three years later stands, in today's retrospect, among Britten's strongest works of testimony (one should perhaps say 'political testimony'). Here, as in the *War Requiem* of 1962, in which the traditional text of the Catholic liturgy is matched with war poems of Wilfred Owen, Britten exercises the power of music both to warn and to reconcile through its images.

Sinfonia da Requiem, opus 20

> Lacrymosa
> Dies irae
> Requiem aeternam
> Duration: 23 minutes

A pacifist, Benjamin Britten chose on the outbreak of the Second World War in 1939 to leave Britain for the as yet unengaged United States. He was to return to war-torn England three years later. In March 1940 under the baton of another Englishman, John Barbirolli, this *Sinfonia da Requiem* was unveiled in New York by the New York Philharmonic Orchestra. Its title was unique, formed evidently on the analogy of Verdi's *Messa da Requiem*. Verdi's Italianized title was also unique, in preference to the usual *Missa pro defunctis*, the Latin mass for the dead. The influence of that work of Verdi's can be felt in Britten's actual score, even in such a detail as the doom-portending strokes on the bass drum.

As a symphony, the balance of the *Sinfonia da Requiem* is decidedly out of the ordinary: not four movements but three, and not two fast movements surrounding a slower, but a tense, fast middle movement (a 'dance of death' perhaps) between two slower ones. The Latin titles of the movements, from the Mass for the Dead itself, give the emotional clues. *Lacrymosa dies illa* ('That tearful day', or 'day of weeping') is one way of looking at the Last Judgement; *Dies irae* ('Day of anger') is another. For those who suffer, the Latin text offers the prayer 'Dona eis requiem' ('Grant them rest'). In Verdi's setting it is heard at both the beginning and end of the work, but in Britten's scheme it occurs only after the climax of violence.

At the opening of the work, the heavy, doom-like pounding of the drums may remind us of Verdi's *Requiem* itself. The drums are reinforced by double basses, two harps and, unusually, a piano. Later in the first movement an alto saxophone enters with a wailing theme; the instrument is prominent in the second movement too. But in the final movement Britten invokes the traditional peaceful sound of flutes (three of them, the lowest an alto flute), over a rocking figure on the harp. Their clear smooth sound, with major chords after so much agitation and dissonance, comes like a consolation or blessing: and, as if the blessing works immediately, the movement is short.

'Sea Interludes' from Peter Grimes, opus 33

    Dawn
    Sunday Morning
    Moonlight
    Storm
    Duration: 16 minutes

Peter Grimes, his first opera, not only made Benjamin Britten's reputation in that field but inaugurated the wave of native opera which thereafter marked the British musical scene. It was first given in London on 7 June 1945, conducted by Reginald Goodall. The strong characterization (Grimes himself being a brutal and socially ostracized fisherman) is one feature of the work; another is the young composer's evocative and powerful handling of the orchestra, which made possible the excerpting of these four musical numbers for concert performances. A fifth number (*Passacaglia*) is also sometimes excerpted.

The complete opera is set in a fishing village, and the dependence of all the action on the sea and sea-fishing gives rise to the name of 'Sea Interludes' for this selection. The first three numbers are heard in the concert-hall in their correct operatic order, but the *Storm* which ends the concert sequence powerfully is originally found in the opera's first act. Britten's orchestral force here, excluding certain other instruments used elsewhere in the opera, is of 2 flutes (inter-changeably with piccolos), 2 oboes, 2 clarinets, 2 bassoons and double-bassoon, four horns, 3 trumpets, 3 trombones, tuba, kettle-drums, other percussion (including bells, tam-tam, gong and xylophone), harp and strings.

After a court-room prologue, the interlude called *Dawn* is heard: the high calls on violins and flutes can hardly be taken for anything other than sea-birds, while the slow-moving brass chords suggest the superficially calm but in reality treacherous sea.

Sunday Morning is the prelude to the second act: the ringing of church bells is suggested, first by horns and woodwind.

The opera's third and final act brings Grimes's suicide as the price of his brutality. The prelude (*Moonlight*) is a representation of darkness and uncertainty – the harp's sounds flickering like moonbeams.

The rough energy of the *Storm*'s opening theme will recur, later, with counter-themes. Downpour as well as winds seem to be indicated in the headlong drive of the music.

The Young Person's Guide to the Orchestra, *opus 34*

Duration: 18 minutes

Receiving its first concert performance at Liverpool on 15 October 1946, conducted by Malcolm Sargent, Britten's *Guide* was com-missioned for a film of that year, *Instruments of the Orchestra*. In concert form, with or without a speaker to introduce the various

instruments or groups as they enter, it has remained popular among
the composer's works. It takes the form of variations and fugue on a
tune written by Henry Purcell (1659–95) as part of his incidental
music to the play *Abdelazer, or The Moor's Revenge*, produced in
London in the year of his death. The alternative title of the *Variations
and Fugue on a Theme of Purcell* is sometimes used for Britten's work.
Its orchestration will be clear from the description which follows.

First, Purcell's tune is played by the full orchestra. Then follow
four restatements of the tune – for woodwind alone; for brass alone;
for strings and harp; and for percussion. Then come the variations
themselves, displaying the instruments in this order:

> 2 flutes and piccolo
> 2 oboes
> 2 clarinets
> 2 bassoons
> violins – violas – cellos – double-basses
> harp
> 4 horns
> 3 trumpets
> 3 trombones and tuba
> kettledrums
> bass drum and cymbals
> tambourine and triangle
> snare drum and chinese block
> castanets and gong
> whip

This presentation concluded, all the instruments join in building up
the fugue, entering once more in the above order. At the height of
the busy fugue, Purcell's original tune peals forth majestically. The
end is loud and imposing, with every player occupied.

BRUCH

1838–1920

Two works perpetuate Max Bruch in the concert-hall. He was a prominent conductor as well as a composer, and it was while in charge of the Liverpool Philharmonic Orchestra (1880–3) that he composed for that city's Jewish community his *Kol nidrei* for cello and orchestra, an arrangement of a prayer-melody for the Day of Atonement. Not himself Jewish, he was born in Cologne and later spent almost 20 years as a professor of composition in Berlin.

Concerto No.1 in G minor for violin and orchestra, opus 26

Allegro moderato, *leading to*
Adagio
Allegro energico
Duration: 24–25 minutes

The first (and the only famous one) of Bruch's three violin concertos had its first hearing 24 April 1866 at Koblenz, a German city on the river Rhine, with the composer conducting and with a soloist not destined for historical celebrity, Otto von Koenigsloew. But in revising it, Bruch sought the assistance of Joachim, the famous associate of Brahms (see p. 103), who two years later gave the first performance of the work in the form now known. The composer was again the conductor.

Not to be found here is the spirit of mighty effort which goes into Brahms's concerto. Instead, there is brilliance with a tinge of melancholy, as in Mendelssohn's concerto: like that work, Bruch's is in a minor key with a major-key finale and, between them, a smoothly intense middle movement linked to the first without a break. Like Mendelssohn, Bruch hastens to introduce the soloist, without a prolonged orchestral *tutti*.

The first movement avoids 'strict' form altogether. Preluded by a little repeated phrase on the woodwind, the violin embarks on a long delivery, rhapsodic at first and then with an assertive theme. After a high trill, the soloist eventually yields to the orchestra. When the opening woodwind phrase returns, the soloist answers with a further rhapsodic cadenza. The music then falls away, leading to . . .

. . . the second movement. Here the intensity of the slow melody (E flat, after the G minor of the opening movement) is reinforced by the use of the solo violin's lower strings. The sustained line of the melody later blossoms into more decorated patterns, but the mood of serenity persists to the end.

The energetic finale centres on the decisive theme in G major given out in double-stopping technique by the soloist. Later, the soloist's series of rising trills lead to the re-entry of that theme on the surprising chord of E flat major: a brief, accelerated finish is not long delayed.

BRUCKNER

1824–96

An Austrian contemporary of Brahms's, Anton Bruckner has not achieved that universal recognition in symphonic music which attaches to Brahms's name. Yet Bruckner's nine symphonies (excluding two earlier symphonies which he did not recognize with the others) have their own special reputation – and are seen as marking a special path in harmony which comes from Liszt and Wagner and leads to Mahler and Schoenberg. Hence the interest in Bruckner has grown from the middle of the twentieth century, along with the cultivation of Mahler's music of a generation later.

Long active as a cathedral musician and organist, Bruckner's other principal compositions are of masses (some with full orchestral accompaniment) and other church music; he wrote no concertos, no opera.

The symphonies

Bruckner wrote Viennese music – his symphonies observing the traditional Austrian four-movement form and in particular recalling Schubert in their march and scherzo rhythms, song-like melodies, and 'heavenly length' (see the note on Schubert's Symphony no.9, p.291). A fervent admirer of Wagner, he dedicated his Symphony no.3 to that great innovator – 'the unattainable, world-famous and exalted master of poetry and music'. From Wagner's operas Bruckner derived an advanced harmonic language, and in the three last symphonies he embraced the special sonority of the 'Wagner tubas'. But compared to Liszt, or the Russian symphonists, or Mahler, his orchestral usage was conservative (no harp, no english horn). Two special features are his fanfares or similar declamatory figures (especially on the trumpet) and the *tremolando* strings which lend an expectancy to the opening of a first movement.

Several of Bruckner's symphonies exist in substantially differing versions because the composer, accepting criticism from others, made revisions – which, in turn, were later regarded as forced, leading to a posthumous publication of what are thought to represent the composer's unfettered intentions.

Symphony no.7 in E

Allegro moderato
Adagio: very solemn and slow
Scherzo: allegro – (Trio) Somewhat slower
Finale: with movement, but not fast
Duration: 64 minutes

The solemn *Adagio* movement, perhaps the most famous movement that Bruckner ever wrote, was said by the composer to be an elegy on the death of Wagner – though it had been sketched out before that event. An exciting cymbal clash at the climax of this movement was added at the persuasion of the conductor Artur Nikisch, who gave the first performance (30 December 1884 in Leipzig, at a concert to raise funds for a Wagner memorial). A later inscription on the score calling this addition 'invalid' may or may not come from the composer.

The connection with Wagner seems to be reinforced because in that slow movement, for the first time in the history of the symphony, Bruckner used a quarter of 'Wagner tubas' – instruments of a tone between that of horn and of trombone, made for Wagner's *Ring*, where they are associated with Valhalla and other solemn symbols. They are played by orchestral horn-players, eight of whom are therefore required for this symphony. To this Bruckner adds a lower-pitched model (contrabass tuba) of the normal orchestral instrument.

Against Bruckner's usual *tremolando* of violins, horns and cellos unfolds a long, assertive theme which sweeps up through an exceptional stretch of more than two octaves. It swells to a climax. Horns and trumpets then occupy the background while oboes and clarinets deliver a new theme. Both themes will later be recognized not only in straight recurrence but in upside-down shape. The underlying march-rhythm persistent, quickened at the end for a prolonged blaze of E major – 30 bars of the one chord!

The second movement, in C sharp minor, begins with two 'elegy' themes: the first with the Wagner tubas prominent, the second on the strings. The music fades out and a lighter, more flowing section begins (changing the pulse to triple time). This alternation of tempos, plainly indebted to the slow movement of Beethoven's Ninth Symphony, continues. At a huge change of harmony into C major, the cymbals and triangle make their sole (and disputed) entry. Quietly, C sharp major closes the movement.

The third movement (in A minor) is a Scherzo and Trio: its design and its feeling evoke Beethoven or Schubert. A fast, self-contained section in vigorous triple time is followed (after three bars of silence!) by a shorter section in more relaxed vein, and then by a literal repeat of the first section.

An urgent finale recalls the first movement in its march pulse and in the string *tremolando* of its opening. There is a wide-spanning opening theme, followed by a second and smoother theme on strings alone. The Wagner tubas, silent in the preceding movement, return. Eventually a mighty climax and a sudden quietness bring back the *tremolando* and lead through overlapping fanfares to a triumphant end.

Symphony no.9 in D minor

> Solemnly, misterioso
> Scherzo: with lively movement
> Adagio: very slowly, solemnly
> [Finale missing]
> Duration: 60 minutes

The composer was working on a final movement when he died, leaving three complete movements as one of the most imposing tokens of his genius. They were first heard – seven years after his death – on 11 February 1903 in Vienna, conducted by Ferdinand Loewe, who subjected the torso to various alterations. The authentic version was first publicly performed in Vienna under Clemens Krauss on 23 October 1932 and is now universally preferred. As in the Symphony no.8, the slow movement is placed third: as in the slow movements of the preceding two symphonies, additional weight comes from the Wagner tubas (to which 4 of the 8 horn-players change over). The other instruments required are 3 each of flutes, oboes, clarinets, bassoons, trumpets, trombones; 1 normal tuba, kettledrums and strings.

Beginning characteristically with a soft *tremolo* of the strings, the composer probes an extreme of harmonic tension. From a cushion of

D minor the horns suddenly leap to a remote region; and then the key seems to waver until the whole orchestra with a massive *fortissimo* asserts D minor again. After further uncertainty the strings embark on a long, 'songful' theme in A major. The music quickens, turns back to D minor and seems to fade out with a repeated horn-call, in F major. After this, the end of the exposition, Bruckner combines development and recapitulation in a span of music more than twice as long as what has gone before. The original *fortissimo* theme, in D minor, returns in the original key; then the reappearance of the songful theme suggests that a peaceful D major may end the movement. But the menacing D minor takes over again.

The second movement, though it uses the traditional overall form of the scherzo and the traditional lively 3/4 beat, is harmonically jolting. The *Scherzo* proper, divided into several sections, concludes in D minor with rough emphasis over a prolonged kettledrum roll. There is a sudden hush as the trio begins in F sharp major with a patter of strings. A violin melody rises above, and a flute joins in. Like the scherzo, the trio has several sections but the patter in F sharp major with the rising violin melody returns to conclude it. The scherzo is then literally repeated.

The slow third movement occupies a new region: E major. A climax with fanfares dies down to reveal a slow, descending theme on the solemn tones of the Wagner tubas. The strings begin a new, slowly moving theme in A flat. Eventually, a solo flute descends into silence. Here the exposition ends, and (as in the first movement) a combined development and recapitulation takes place. The opening theme eventually returns on the full orchestra, *fortissimo* and with the greatest harmonic tension. As the movement approaches its end, long-held chords are heard in the brass against which the horns intone a phrase from the *Adagio* of the Symphony no.7. (There have been previous allusions to other works by the composer.) With three chords of E major for *pizzicato* strings, the extant part of the symphony is finished. The absent finale would have restored the key of D minor.

CHABRIER

1841–94

Having first earned his living as a French government official, Emmanuel Chabrier became a composer of repute without venturing into symphony or concerto. He wrote operas, some songs of particular charm, and piano pieces – one of which, *Bourrée Fantasque*, also entered the orchestral repertory in an arrangement by the conductor Felix Mottl. To most lovers of orchestral music he is known only by the work discussed below, but his *Joyeuse Marche* is also occasionally heard and shares the same exuberance and melodic attractiveness.

Rhapsody, España

Duration: 6–7 minutes

Back from a journey to Spain in 1882, Chabrier is said to have played to the French conductor Charles Lamoureux a brilliant piano fantasia on Spanish themes which the conductor encouraged him to score for orchestra. Hence this *España*, which Lamoureux conducted in his Paris concert series of 6 November 1883. The orchestration is sumptuous and sparkling: two harps help to simulate the guitars of Spain and also add their sweeping sounds to the general glitter. The prominently used extra percussion includes a tambourine. The orchestra otherwise comprises piccolo, 2 flutes, 4 bassoons (very distinctively used), 4 horns, 2 cornets as well as 2 trumpets, 3 trombones, tuba, kettledrums and strings.

After an opening that sets the atmosphere, a solo muted trumpet in a low register delivers a pattering theme; a solo horn takes it over. Later all the horns peal out a joyous descending theme. After a climax, a change of mood brings a softer melody on violins and flutes. A movement which seems full of humour occurs when the trombones attempt to speak up for themselves and are met with a teasing jingle from the tambourine and others. Of such elements is this exhilarating piece made.

CHOPIN

1810–49

Poland's most famous composer was himself a virtuoso pianist: his recital tour in England and Scotland in 1848 was among the last of his engagements. He was to die in Paris, his adopted city, not much more than a year later. Frédéric Chopin (the French form of his name) left a rich store of works for piano solo, including the well-loved nocturnes, waltzes and ballades. Exploiting hitherto unknown resources of the keyboard and venturing into subtly advanced harmonic regions, these solo works influenced other composers (notably Liszt) and have retained the affection of both audiences and aspiring amateur performers.

Fewer, and less important, are his works for piano and orchestra (he wrote nothing for orchestra alone). His two piano concertos nevertheless maintain a place in the repertory, and we may remember that it was his variations (with orchestra) on an aria from Mozart's *Don Giovanni* that won for the young Chopin the famous salute from Schumann's pen: 'Hats off, gentlemen: a genius!'

Concerto no.2 in F minor for piano and orchestra, opus 21

> Maestoso
> Larghetto
> Allegro vivace
> Duration: 31 minutes

Of Chopin's two concertos this was the first to be written (when the composer was nineteen) but the second to be published – hence the numbering by which it is known. The temptation of the listener to identify its Romantic sentiment with an actual biographical experience may, for once, be justified. Chopin wrote to a friend of his worship of a woman to whom he had never spoken, 'of whom I dream each night and who was in my mind when I wrote the *Adagio* of my concerto' (meaning, of course, the slow movement, actually carrying a different designation, *Larghetto*).

The composer himself was, naturally, the soloist in the first performance, given in Warsaw on 17 March 1830. As often in those days, and not merely in such a secondary musical city as Warsaw, a 'serious' concerto was felt to be rather a burden on audiences, and a light *divertissement* for a horn separated the first movement from the others. Perhaps the audience thought it not so inappropriate, since a horn solo was to make a special point in the finale of the concerto. Chopin's orchestral requirement is modest: double woodwind, two horns, two trumpets but only a single trombone, kettledrums and strings.

The classical scaffolding of a concerto is used, with a full orchestral exposition to open the first movement – strings giving out the first subject and a solo oboe the second (in A flat). The soloist enters and deals characteristically with each. A central section develops the first-subject material with orchestral climaxes and the soloist ushers in a recapitulation: here the second subject again begins in A flat but modulates to the home key of F minor which provides the vigorous conclusion.

The second movement (in A flat) reveals itself after a few introductory bars as a piano solo, almost exclusively with the string accompaniment. Delicately meditative at first, later more passionate, the music eventually returns to the first strain with yet further delicacy or ornamentation.

The bold subject with which the piano opens the last movement has the flavour of a mazurka. There is extended comment on it; then, after the violins patter out a few bars *col legno* (with the wooden back of the bow), the piano gives out a contrasting subject in A flat and in *scherzando* mood, with prominent triplets. On these two themes the movement is based, the final section bursting into the key of F major with a flourish on the solo horn.

COPLAND

b. 1900

The emergence of American music into the international orchestral repertory dates from the period between the two World Wars, and Aaron Copland is one of its major figures. Like Virgil Thomson, four years his senior, he studied in Paris with that influential musician, Nadia Boulanger. Returning to his native New York he became known not only as a composer for the stage, film and concert-hall but also as pianist, lecturer, organizer, and spokesman for the dignity of his country's composers.

Three ballets, *Billy the Kid*, *Rodeo*, and *Appalachian Spring*, gave him the opportunity to tap the resources of American folk-music; a popular, jazzy style is also found in *El salón Mexico*. A different kind of Americanism in music made its appeal in two wartime works (1942), the *Lincoln Portrait* for narrator with orchestra and the *Fanfare for the Common Man* (later incorporated by the composer into his Symphony no. 3). In other works, particularly for piano solo and various chamber-music combinations, this ready melodious appeal is often sacrificed for more intellectual constructions.

Appalachian Spring

Duration: 27 minutes

The score carries the inscription 'Ballet for Martha'. *Appalachian Spring* was composed for Martha Graham's company, and with her choreography was given its first performance on 30 October 1944 in Washington, DC. Deliberate Americanism, equally characteristic both of Graham and Copland, achieved artistic success in this work. The original scoring was for only thirteen instruments; in 1945, Copland arranged the music for symphony orchestra. The scoring remains modest – 2 only of flutes, oboes, clarinets, bassoons, horns, trumpets and trombones, with kettledrums and harp – and also piano (a 'normal' orchestral instrument with Copland), and assorted percussion instruments including 'tabor', i.e. a rustic drum without snares.

The music is continuous but with frequent changes of tempo. A beginning in A major gives a typical Copland sound (suggesting stillness and openness). It will be recalled at the close of the work when the vigorous action is over. (But it is not a classical return of key: the work ends in C major.) In a programme note, the composer himself divided the music structurally as follows:

> Very slowly. Introduction of the characters, one by one, in a diffused light.

> Fast. A sudden burst of unison strings in A major *arpeggios* starts the action. A sentiment both exalted and religious gives the keynote to this scene.

> Moderate. Duo for the bride and her intended – scene of tenderness and passion.

> Quite fast. The revivalist and his flock. Folksy feelings – suggestions of square dances and country fiddlers.

> Still faster. Solo dance of the bride – presentiment of motherhood. Extremes of joy and fear and wonder.

> Very slowly (as at first). Transition scenes reminiscent of the introduction.

> Calm and flowing. Scenes of daily activity for the bride and her farmer–husband.

[This section presents five variations on a theme which is first given out by a solo clarinet – a tune called *Simple gifts*, which the composer borrowed from a collection of melodies from the rural American 'Shaker' community.]

> Moderate (coda). The bride takes her place among the neighbours . . . Finally the couple are left 'quiet and strong in their new house'.

El salón México

Duration: 11 minutes

A visit to Mexico City in 1932 stimulated Copland to write one of his best-known works. The title is that of a dance-hall. 'In that "hot spot"', Copland later wrote, 'one felt, in a very natural way, a close contact with the Mexican people. It wasn't the music that I heard, but the spirit that I felt there, which attracted me.' The first performance, appropriately in Mexico City itself, was given on 24 August 1937 under a conductor who was himself the leading composer of Mexico, Carlos Chavez.

A large orchestra is used including high clarinet in E flat and english horn – though the score marks these among the 'optional' instruments, with their parts cued in for others to play if necessary. As well as conventional forces (2 flutes and piccolo, 2 oboes, 2 clarinets, 2 bassoons and double-bassoon, 4 horns, 3 trumpets, 3 trombones, tuba, kettledrums and strings) Copland indulges his linking for a piano in the orchestra, and requires a large array of percussion including chinese blocks, wood block and 'gourd' – a scraper, as used in Latin-American dance bands.

The music gives a free treatment, not a literal quotation, of three Mexican folk-tunes. These tunes on which Copland exercised his skill (and which he does not say he heard in the dance-hall!) are found in printed collections of Mexican folk-music. At the outset the lively mood is set by a jumping, rising figure on violins and woodwind. After interchanges for a trumpet and a clarinet, a quieter tune is announced by the bassoon and is sentimentally embraced by the strings. These and similar figures are assembled into a brilliant mosaic – mainly strident but with contrasting, gentler passages, and with a final return to the 'jumping' figure of the opening.

CORELLI

1653–1713

Of the Italian violinist–composers whose style of pathos and
vivacity won a Europe-wide following in the seventeen and
early eighteenth centuries, none was more famous than Arcangelo
Corelli. Living in Rome, he attracted powerful patrons and
admirers, including the visiting Queen Christina of Sweden (to
whom he dedicated a set of trio-sonatas). More than anyone else
he established the *concerto* in its baroque sense of a piece for orchestral
strings in several movements, usually with one or more soloists
emerging in passages of brilliance and difficulty.

Handel, more than thirty years younger, met him in Rome and
turned Corelli's style to his own account. Confining his published
work to sonatas and concertos, Corelli seems to have been unique
among Italian composers of his time in essaying neither opera nor
church music.

Concerto grosso in G minor, opus 6, no.8 (Christmas Concerto)

> Vivace – Grave – Allegro
> Adagio – Allegro
> Adagio
> Vivace
> Allegro, *leading to*
> Pastorale: largo
> Duration: 14 minutes

Corelli's single published set of concertos (1714) comprises a dozen
works – a conventional number. Uniquely, no.8 has a movement
with a bagpipe-like drone bass and a gently swaying melody. It is
this movement (the last) which has won the concerto its nickname
through the traditional association of shepherds with the occasion of

the birth of Jesus. The 'Pastoral Symphony' in Handel's *Messiah* brings out this association by means of the same musical features.

The *pastorale* which ends this work and fulfils the composer's inscription for the whole ('Written for Christmas night') is, in fact, marked *ad lib* – meaning that it may be omitted or included at will. It is, however, linked to the previous movement. Moreover, apart from conveying the 'picture' of a shepherd's lullaby to the infant Jesus, it has a special effect in breaking out into G major for the first time in the work. The previous movements are all in G minor, apart from the *Adagio–allegro–adagio* (no.2) in E flat.

The concerto contrasts a group of three soloists (two violins and a cello) with a string orchestra in four parts – the cello line being reinforced an octave lower by the double basses. The participation of a keyboard continuo-player (harpsichord or organ) would also be assumed in Corelli's time. The three soloists plus the continuo-player would in fact suffice for this work; the composer makes it clear that all such concertos in his collection can be performed in this manner, with the orchestral parts added when players are available. The soloists continue to perform throughout, the orchestra's role being intermittent.

In terms of later concertos such as those by Vivaldi or Bach, all the movements are short (up to about eighty bars). The first movement is tripartite – the quick fast introduction and the following slow section both being forerunners of a third, longer section. Here the two violins in long notes are exhibited against the rapidly moving bass. This last section falls into two halves, each repeated.

The stringed instruments' capacity for gentle, expressive melody is shown in the *Adagio* which opens and closes the next movement. Between is a contrasting section of a faster, more emphatic character.

The *Vivace* that follows is a dance in lively 3/4 time: Bach would call such a movement a minuet. Here, too, the music is in two sections, each repeated.

The three solo instruments chase each other in snatches of counterpoint in the following *Allegro*, with contrasts of loud and soft to follow.

Linked to the previous movement, the *Pastorale* sets up a gently rocking rhythm and presents its melody with the sweetened effect of linked thirds. A central part makes a mild contrast, followed by a return of the opening and an extension to a very soft ending – a true lullaby.

DEBUSSY

1862–1918

'Impressionism' is the label that clings to the music of Claude Debussy, though it was not one he liked. It was a term first attached in the 1870s to the work of painters such as Monet, whose concern with the effects of light and colour made their images fleeting rather than firm. In outdoor paintings Monet would allow night and fog, for example, to obscure the outline of objects seen.

Thus Debussy's music often avoids regular, sharply outlined phrases; likewise its chords seem to pass meltingly from one to the next. Titles are often affixed to the music (in the case of the piano preludes, the title is printed at the *end* of each piece!) which may suggest some changing scene – or some remembered sight, sound or perfume. The piano, with sounds sustainable only for a limited time (then dying away) was one preferred medium; on the other hand the orchestra served Debussy not so much for force as for delicate variety of tone-colour and rich effects of motion and stillness.

From the late 1880s Debussy's highly individual style made its mark on musical life, first in Paris, then elsewhere. His music maintains itself firmly in the repertory of orchestras, pianists and singers, though some later compositions such as the ballet *Jeux* ('Games'), produced by Diaghilev in Paris in 1913, are rarely heard.

Three symphonic sketches, La Mer

> From dawn to midday on the sea
> Games of the waves
> Dialogue of the wind and the sea
> Duration: 24 minutes

'The sea has been very good to me – she has shown me all her moods'. Debussy's words (in a letter to his publisher) are fulfilled here. Such descriptive works are generally in one movement, but the clue to the presence of three is in the subtitle of 'symphonic sketches'. In Debussy's output this work stands in place of a symphony. The first movement particularly suggests a symphonic form; and like many a Romantic composer of symphonies, Debussy brings a theme from his first movement to prominence in the finale. He put the finishing touches to the score when he was staying in Eastbourne in the summer of 1905, and brought it to performance in Paris on 15 October of that year under the conductorship of Camille Chevillard.

The orchestration has what may be regarded as the French touch of two harps. The tinkle of a glockenspiel (with the celesta as an alternative) complements the booming excitement of the tam-tam. In the last movement, two cornets are added to the brilliance of the brass. Otherwise the requirement is: piccolo and 2 flutes; 2 oboes and english horn; 2 clarinets, 3 bassoons; 4 horns, 3 trumpets, 3 trombones and tuba; kettledrums, bass drum and cymbals; and strings – the cellos, unusually, being precisely specified as 16 in number.

The first movement ('Dawn') starts with low, muffled, slowly emerging sounds and is to end ('Midday') with blazing brass and cymbals. In form, it presents a slow introduction gradually increasing in pace up to the main tempo. Here the principal theme (in D flat) is a vividly coloured, 'wavy' figure high on flutes and clarinets which is followed by a smoother figure on muted horns. Later, after the music has sunk almost to nothing, a challenging new theme arises from the massed cellos in four-part harmony. Later, a slow section recaptures earlier material and briefly introduces a sustained, level theme on the horns against the background of a cymbal roll. A brilliant brassy chord of D flat ends the movement.

In the middle movement, the 'games' of the waves are suggested by flashing, restless musical figures. Soon a rising theme in the uncertainly anchored whole-tone scale is heard from the english horn. Later the same soloist delivers a more flowing theme – seized by a solo horn, then by strings. This rising whole-tone figure is soon heard distantly from oboe, flute and (a distinctly surprising tone-colour) muted trumpet. The double-basses' lowest note, E, is the keynote as the sound fades.

Surging sea and capricious wind are evoked in the finale, begun with rolls of kettledrum and bass-drum. A muted trumpet peals out a rising theme; a smoother theme is sounded by woodwind against choppy strings. A big climax dies on descending trombones, and the horns weightily deliver the theme briefly heard at the end of the first movement. But the earlier trumpet theme is the one which inspires the glittering conclusion – in D flat, paralleling the first movement.

Prélude à L'après-midi d'un faune

Duration: 10 minutes

With its delicate, suggestive orchestral colours, and with a time-span much briefer than that of most 'descriptive' orchestral works, this prelude was seen unmistakably as a revolutionary work. But, so far from having to battle with a puzzled public, it was an immediate success and won an encore at its first performance – in Paris, under the conductorship of Gustave Doret, on 22 December 1894.

The poet Stéphane Mallarmé, known personally to Debussy, published in 1876 his *L'après-midi d'un faune*: a faun (the mythical creature, half-man, half-goat), resting in a warm afternoon, speaks of his remembered love-ecstasies. In an early programme-note, written or at least approved by the composer, the piece is called 'a very free illustration of the poem'. In the final section the faun, 'tired of pursuing the timorous flight of the nymphs and naiads, succumbs to intoxicating sleep'. A flute, the traditional instrument associated with such scenes of rustic love-making, has a prominent solo part.

Three flutes are in fact used, the other instruments being 2 oboes, 1 english horn, 2 clarinets, 2 bassoons, 4 horns (no trumpets or trombones), the usual strings, 2 harps playing different parts (but one harp could accomplish all the notes) and 2 'ancient cymbals' or crotales, whose tiny delicate chime is used only towards the end. The air of haziness and languor is conveyed by the flute's opening tune, suggesting an ambiguity of key but eventually settling in E. A contrast of sound comes with smoother, rather heavier strain in D flat. The original languorous theme returns, again in E and again with flute tone, and the music fades into sleep.

DELIUS

1862–1934

The baptismal names Fritz Theodor Albert reveal Delius's German descent, but he was born in Bradford, called himself Frederick Delius, and won an intensely devoted British following – principally, though not solely, through the advocacy of the conductor Sir Thomas Beecham. He was in his mid-twenties before enrolling for study at the Leipzig conservatory; there he met Grieg, who was to influence him both in harmonic style and in a belief in folk-music as a composer's raw material.

Sliding harmonies, subtly mixed orchestral colours, and 'impressionistic' titles may suggest an English parallel to Debussy. Certainly there is a reticence and an avoidance of big, sweeping tunes which puts Delius beside Debussy rather than, say, Richard Strauss. But there is no closer kinship. English-German with Grieg's hand on his shoulder, Delius was always himself. His was a voice that sounded novel in English music, influencing many younger British composers but not going much beyond a localized fame.

He made his home in France but his appearance at a Delius Festival in London in 1929 (by which time he had become blind) was the moment of his most significant recognition.

English rhapsody, Brigg Fair

Duration: 16 minutes

Percy Grainger (1882–1961), the Australian composer who came to England and was one of the first to use the newly invented phonograph to record folksong from the lips of the singers, discovered in Lincolnshire a song which began as follows:

It was on the fift' of August,
The weather fine and fair,
Unto Brigg Fair I did repair.
For love I was inclined.

The tune is in an old scale (the Dorian mode) which preceded our conventional major and minor scales. Grainger showed his find to his friend Delius, who based on it this *English* rhapsody – the nationalistic title suggesting a parallel with Liszt's *Hungarian Rhapsodies*. The result was as much a tribute to native folk-song as a manifestation of his own genius. The work is dedicated to Grainger and was first performed at Liverpool on 19 January 1908, conducted by Granville Bantock.

A rich orchestral sound is made by very full orchestration, specifying 16 first and 16 second violins, 12 violas, 12 cellos, 12 double basses, 3 flutes, 2 oboes, english horn, 3 clarinets and bass clarinet, 3 bassoons and double-bassoon, 6 horns, 3 trumpets, 3 trombones and tuba, one harp (or more), 3 kettledrums, bass drum, triangle and 3 tubular bells.

Although made up of a series of variations, the work is divided into an introduction (in which the flute against a harp accompaniment provides a traditionally 'pastoral' feeling) and three sections which follow. In the first the theme is played four times with varying instrumentation and harmonies – (a) oboe solo, (b) flute solo, (c) strings, (d) flute and clarinet an octave apart. A freer variation with light semiquaver runs for violins, growing softer, is followed by two more straight harmonizations with rapid woodwind counterpoint – the first for two horns in unison, the second for trumpet.

A rhapsodic middle section starts with the flute solo from the prelude, after a time incorporating the folk-tune. A climax is reached and subsides. The final section now begins as the tune is solemnly declaimed by trumpet and trombone, and repeated by violins, horns, english horn and clarinets. The flute solo from the prelude reappears. The tune is further varied and finally comes back to the oboe – the instrument with which it began.

On hearing the first cuckoo in spring

Duration: 5–6 minutes

Several of Delius's works received their first performance in Germany, including this one (Leipzig, 2 October 1913, conducted by Artur Nikisch). It was later associated with his *Summer Night on the River* as 'two pieces for small orchestra'. *On hearing the first cuckoo in spring* requires only one flute and one oboe: 2 each of clarinets, bassoons and horns; and strings. Under the title of the work are the words 'introducing a Norwegian folk-song' – this being *In Ola Valley*, which had been previously harmonized by Grieg.

Nothing, even in the sweet-toned harmonies and the vocation of the far-off cuckoo, is more remarkable than the very opening chord, spaced out on the strings – a chord of C major but with a B natural on top. A flowing melody (Delius's own) begins on upper strings and passes into the (very similar) Norwegian tune. The cuckoo (clarinet) is repetitively heard – at two points in the short piece. Finally the first flowing tune reappears; and the music lingers and fades on strings alone.

DUKAS

1865–1935

A contemporary of Debussy's in Paris, Paul Dukas was a skilled, well respected, but far from prolific composer: shortly before his death he destroyed several manuscript compositions rather than allow them to submit to posterity's appraisal. He wrote a ballet, *La Péri* (the allusion is to the Persian fairy creature, the *peri* of Gilbert and Sullivan's *Iolanthe*), and an opera, *Ariane et Barbe-bleue* (*Ariadne and Bluebeard*), and the music to the former is occasionally given in concert form. But the work considered below is the only one on which his wider fame rests.

Scherzo, The Sorcerer's Apprentice

Duration: 11 minutes

The Sorcerer's Apprentice, as *L'Apprenti sorcier* is generally known in English, was first performed under the composer's baton in Paris on 18 May 1897, and is now the only work by which Paul Dukas is widely known. It achieved its greatest audience through Walt Disney's film *Fantasia* (1940), but the story which the music depicts is some 1600 years older. It comes from the Greek satirist Lucian (second century AD): Goethe made a ballad of it, and it is on this that the music is based.

Dukas's orchestration requires piccolo, 2 flutes, 2 oboes, 2 clarinets, bass clarinet, 3 bassoons, double-bassoon, 4 horns, 2 trumpets, 2 cornets, 3 trombones, kettledrums, harp, glockenspiel, bass drum, cymbals, triangle and strings.

The Apprentice, in the absence of his master, repeats a spell in order to make a broom go and fetch water (quick passage for woodwind). But he has forgotten the words to make the spell stop, and soon the room is flooded. He tries to chop the broom with a hatchet (orchestral climax); but, split in two, the broom does twice the work. It takes the return of the sorcerer (double-basses) to bring the mischief to an abrupt end.

DVOŘÁK

1841–1904

From the time of Beethoven to that of Mahler, the field of symphonic music was substantially occupied by composers of German mother tongue. But Antonin Dvořák took pride in Czech (or, as it would then have been said, Bohemian) inheritance. He did not think it unsuitable to bring Czech folk-dance rhythms even into the supposedly 'abstract' domain of chamber music. A strong and open national flavour is found also in Dvořák's orchestral *Slavonic Dances*, and in the choice of subjects for his operas.

But his symphonies do not reject the general plan of the German–Austrian symphonic tradition. They rarely seem to invoke national feeling: a dance-movement, a *furiant*, in Symphony no.6 is an exception. Principally, the music attracts by its energy and sheer melodic gift, strong structure, and occasional striking touch of orchestral colour. The same qualities are found in the *Symphonic Variations*, his Cello Concerto, and the overture *Carnival* – works which are dealt with below. A Violin Concerto (1883) is less often heard than the Cello Concerto and a Piano Concerto of the same year is generally considered a failure.

As a composer of choral as well as orchestral music Dvořák was warmly received in Britain. His arrival in New York in 1892 to head a conservatory of music led to his composing the famous *New World* symphony and other works. He assured Americans of his conviction that a coming development of American music must build on a 'folk' heritage as exemplified in Black and American Indian music.

The symphonies

As compared with the symphonies of his friend Brahms, Dvořák's are conspicuous for song-like, memorable tunes, infectious dance-rhythms and bright orchestration. They rely less on the close-worked development of themes The use of a motto theme to unite all the movements of the *New World* symphony creates a typical Romantic effect, such as Tchaikovsky loved but Brahms abstained from.

Only five of Dvořák's symphonies were published in his lifetime, but four more are dated from his earlier years. The well-known five are now numbered as 5–6–7–8–9 (corresponding to a former numbering 3–1–2–4–5): thus the *New World* Symphony is no.9. The numbering 1–4 is given to the youthful four, which although now published are still seldom heard.

Symphony no.8 in G major, opus 88

Allegro con brio
Adagio
Allegretto grazioso
Allegro ma non troppo
Duration: 38 minutes

Apart from its hint of birdsong, the relaxed and happy feeling of this symphony suggests the nickname of 'Dvořák's Pastoral'. It shows the composer's wish to bring freshness to symphonic form. Accepting an honorary doctorate of music from Cambridge University in 1892 he offered this work as his obligatory 'exercise' – though it was not new, Dvořák having conducted the first performance in Prague on 2 February 1890.

The orchestration is for 2 flutes (one doubling piccolo), 2 oboes (one doubling english horn), 2 each of clarinets and bassoons; the usual 4 horns, 2 trumpets, 3 trombones, and tuba; kettledrums and strings. Trombones and tuba are withdrawn from the two middle movements, making the outer movements more emphatic.

The opening is deceptive. A sustained tune in G *minor*, sung by the cellos, conceals the point that the movement is to be anchored in G major – which emerges on a solo flute in a high, chirruping tune. After a climax comes another pair of themes: a soft, inward-turning theme on the strings (E major) and a lively, march-like tune on the flutes (B minor) which is expanded on the full orchestra. A short, vigorous development quietens over a long, quiet kettledrum-roll and then the recapitulation begins – the first tune softly breathed by horns and cellos. After another climax, the voice of the english horn recalls the chirruping theme at a lower pitch; and the music sweeps off again, taking in the march theme on its way to a confident finish.

The slow movement has two contrasted moods. A section in C minor is pensive, even wistful (with lingering, repetitive phrases on the paired woodwind instruments); the second section is more vigorous in C major, and incorporates a high violin solo. Both are in turn brought back in varied guise.

In the form of a scherzo but without the usual suggestion of humour or abruptness, the third movement begins with a swinging song tune in G minor on the strings. No less attractive is the contrasting central section (trio) in G major with its tune on flute and oboe. After a literal repeat of the first part, a coda merrily turns the melody line of the trio from 3/4 into quick 2/4 time.

A trumpet fanfare begins the finale, ushering in a theme and variations. The theme (reminiscent of the chirruping theme of the first movement) is two short sections, each repeated. After the fourth variation the music diverts to a march with a mock-grumpy theme in C minor. The fanfare returns in varied form and four other variations follow – the last extended and quickened for a joyful finish.

Symphony no.9 in E minor, opus 95 (From the New World)

> Adagio – Allegro molto
> Largo
> Scherzo
> Allegro con fuoco
> Duration: 42 minutes

Carnegie Hall, New York, was the scene on 16 December 1893 of the first performance of the most famous work ever presented to America by a visiting composer. The title *From the New World* was Dvořák's own. But as to how much genuine American music went into it, and of what sort, his own reported words have left a somewhat confusing account. He seems to have been convinced that musical characteristics existed in common between American Indian music and Black (Negro) spirituals.

He claimed to have used the idioms of such music without borrowing actual melodies. In the symphony's first movement, the solo flute theme almost inevitably recalls the spiritual, 'Swing low, sweet chariot'. The tune of the slow movement (*Largo*) likewise suggests a folk origin, but here the composer claimed to have been prompted by the scene of Minnehaha's funeral in Longfellow's *Hiawatha*. He also linked the *Scherzo* to the Indian feasting and dancing in that poem – which he had read in translation long before he visited America's shores.

The basic orchestration is for 2 each of flutes, oboes, clarinets and bassoons, 4 horns, 2 trumpets, 3 trombones, tuba, kettledrums and strings. A triangle is added for the jollity of the *Scherzo*, the same player briefly taking up the cymbals in the finale. Most strikingly, an english horn enters solely for the famous melody in the *Largo*.

A fanfare-like motto-theme unifies the symphony. It is heard on the horns during the slow introduction to the first movement. With a change to *Allegro molto*, this vigorous horn-call (with an addition on clarinets and bassoons) becomes the movement's principal subject; in due course the flute quietly announces the 'Swing low' theme in G major. (From the next full-orchestral climax, there is an instruction, not always observed, to repeat from the opening of the *Allegro molto*.) The shaping of the final pages of the movement is highly individual: the 'Swing low' theme returns on the flute in an unexpected key (A flat) and is then loudly proclaimed by trumpets – but the horn-call and the original E minor have the end.

The second movement begins in hushed solemnity as the brass and lower woodwind take us to the new key of D flat. The english horn gives out its elegiac song; muted strings and muted horns follow. At the climax of a more animated middle section, while the trumpets give a new urgency to fragments of the 'elegy' tune, trombones bring back the horn-call motto from the first movement. The more peaceable mood returns, and with it the elegy. Finally, after an echo of the solemn opening, comes a unique farewell chord: four notes *pianissimo* on double-basses.

The designation *Scherzo* carries with it the traditional form of a light, vigorous outer section, a central contrast, then a return to the first section (A–B–A). In an attractive chain of moods, Dvořák compounds the construction: the outer section itself (A) has threefold form, two statements of a fast and merry tune in E minor being separated by slower, more easeful strains in E major with a new tune begun by flutes and oboes. A transition to C major leads to the new main section (B) in which a woodwind tune carries a prominent triangle accompaniment. There is then another transition and a literal repeat of section A. A distinctive coda follows, recalling not only themes of this movement but the motto-theme too.

The finale is a full-scale sonata-form movement based on a main theme asserted by horns and trumpets, a soft theme from a solo clarinet (with a charming afterthought from the cellos) and a strongly rhythmical full-orchestral theme. After their eventual recapitulation, the main theme of this movement unites majestically with the motto-theme of the symphony; then comes a recollection of the first themes of the *Largo* and the *Scherzo*. An accelerated ending has a final emotional surprise – a dying-away on the very last chord.

Concerto in B minor for cello and orchestra, op. 104

Allegro
Adagio ma non troppo
Allegro moderato
Duration: 41 minutes

Perhaps the most celebrated of all cello concertos, Dvořák's was composed at the end of his stay in America (the winter of 1894–5). Deeply affected by news of the illness of Jozefina Kaunitzová, who had been the object of his youthful love but had long been his sister-in-law, he incorporated into the slow movement an allusion to one of his songs of which she was especially fond. After he returned to Prague, she died, prompting him to extend and alter the final movement to give a further reminiscence of that song.

The work was dedicated to the composer's friend and compatriot, the cellist Hanuš Wihan, but circumstances led to the first performance being given by Leo Stern at a London concert which Dvořák conducted on 10 March 1896. The success of the work was striking and immediate, Dvořák having surmounted the difficulty of making the cello's voice heard against the strength of a large orchestra. Three (instead of the usual four horns are used, along with 2 each of flutes, oboes, clarinets, bassoons and trumpets, 3 trombones and tuba, kettledrums and strings. There are no cadenzas to be inserted by the soloist – indeed, no cadenzas, the music flowing without halt.

A long orchestral section opens the first movement, presenting a theme immediately (clarinets, joined by bassoons, in B minor) and a second theme in D major in which a solo horn seems to express romantic longing. The cellist enters in decisive mood, expanding on the first of these themes, then sinks to a hushed tone in the 'longing' theme. The solo instrument leads the music passionately forward, yielding to the full orchestra at a point which carries one of Dvořák's favourite markings, *grandioso*. Typical of the formidable technique demanded of the soloist is the scale in octaves which is followed by a restatement of the longing theme, now strongly proclaimed by the orchestra in B major. The return of the other main theme is not long delayed, and the *grandioso* mood is again invoked at the end.

The slow second movement in G major conveys a gentle, pastoral feeling: a solo clarinet begins the melody, then two clarinets link their voices as the cello comments. *Pianissimo* trombones (a subtle, unusual touch) add their sustaining chords. A central contrasting section which begins in G minor is more agitated: within it, the cello delivers its song-theme (Jozefina's) in high, impassioned tones. The return of the opening strain sends the soloist on a rhapsodic, meditative path, the cello's sound fading at the end to dreamy high notes in ethereal harmonics.

A march-tune on the horns, reverting to the concerto's key of B minor, initiates the finale. The cello soon takes it over. Melodies succeed one another with a considerable flexibility of mood and tempo. Eventually the key of B major (destined to end the concerto) arrives, not with a bang but in a delicate tapestry of string sound: a solo violin rises above the cello's trills. At length cello and orchestra summon a reminder of the opening theme of the concerto, now strongly confident in the major key. The slow movement is also recalled in Jozefina's song. Like a gesture of individual passion, the soloist's part dies away with just one final surge of tone before the orchestra rounds off the work.

Overture, Carnival, *op. 92*

Duration: 9–10 minutes

Three concert-overtures by Dvořák (that is, not overtures to theatrical performances of operas or plays) arise from an impulse to show different aspects of human experience, and all three share a motto-theme. But of these, only the present is frequently played, the others (*Amid Nature* and *Othello*) rarely occurring in concert programmes. Joyous acceptance of life is represented in *Carnival*. (The form sometimes encountered, *Carneval*, is simply the older German spelling – modern German *Karneval* – and, not being the Czech original, has no value in English-speaking use). The first performance of all three overtures was conducted by the composer in Prague on 28 April 1892.

A brilliant, joyous-sounding orchestration is a feature of this work: three extra percussionists are needed for the cymbals (without their usual heavy companion, the bass drum), triangle and tambourine. The composer requires piccolo as well as 2 flutes, english horn as well as 2 oboes, 2 clarinets, 2 bassoons, 4 horns, 2 trumpets, 3 trombones and tuba, kettledrums, harp and strings.

The form is very clear but unusual. A fast movement in sonata-form is not *preceded* by a slow section but has the slow section inserted in the middle. The initial joyous section is in A major, moving to E major. (Note the continuing beats of tambourine and triangle even when a quieter, softer mood takes over.) The harp enters and the music reaches a moment of stillness. The slow section now starts with a dreamy melody on the english horn accompanied by muted violins and violas. The faster tempo is then resumed for a development of the opening material, in the main lightly scored – the full, joyous orchestral sound (without the english horn and the harp) being reserved for the moment when the opening is recapitulated. The brass takes a prominent share in the excitement of the ending.

ELGAR

1857–1934

Without formal conservatory training, Edward Elgar rose from modest provincial origins to become his country's leading composer, and the first native-born Englishman to establish a firm place in the international repertory of symphony, overture and concerto. Hans Richter, who had been Wagner's chosen conductor at the Bayreuth Festival, championed Elgar in conducting his first orchestral masterpiece, the *Enigma Variations* of 1899; three years later Richard Strauss acclaimed him after a German performance of *The Dream of Gerontius*, destined to be Elgar's most enduring choral work.

Two long, amply scored symphonies (1908, 1911), each in four movements, display an outgoing, positive feeling, but a succeeding generation which treasures the extremities and ironies of Mahler's music will look in vain for those qualities. The two concertos, however, have been prized from the first by the great solo interpreters. Besides these and the other works discussed below, Elgar's orchestral music includes the radiantly coloured (but perhaps too long) concert overture, *In the South* (1904) and the Shakespearean *Falstaff* (1913) which he called a 'symphonic study'.

Standing as the supreme example of his popular touch, four *Pomp and Circumstance* marches date from before 1914, a fifth from 1930. A. C. Benson's words 'Land of hope and glory' were fitted afterwards to a tune taken from the first march. Their aggressive imperialism was modified when Elgar incorporated the tune in the *Coronation Ode* which greeted Edward VII in 1901. That Elgar should range from this to the Wagnerian chromaticism of the prelude to *The Dream of Gerontius* is a measure of his range as a composer. His mastery as an orchestrator, comparable to that of Richard Strauss, is evident throughout.

Concerto in B minor for violin and orchestra, opus 61

Allegro
Andante
Allegro molto
Duration: 48 minutes

Fritz Kreisler, the Austrian violinist (and composer) was the dedicatee of Elgar's Violin Concerto, and gave its first performance on 10 November 1910 in London, under the baton of the composer. The score bears an inscription in Spanish, *Aquí esta encerrada el alma de.* ⌒ . . (Here is enshrined the soul of . . . .). The identity of the person indicated has never been definitely established, nor the reason for the Spanish language.

Elgar, who had himself been a professional violinist in his younger years, knew how to exploit the full brilliance and emotional power of the solo instrument. He also invented a new sound-effect for the orchestral strings. To accompany the cadenza in the last movement (the other movements have no cadenzas) he prescribed what he called *pizzicato–tremolando*: 'the strings of the instrument should be "thrummed" with the soft part of three or four fingers across the strings' (a guitar-like effect).

The concerto displays the composer's full virtuosity as an orchestrator. The double-bassoon part is marked 'ad lib', i.e. optional, but that is only a reflection of the fact that not all symphony orchestras before the First World War could be sure to have a player available! The scoring is for 2 each of flutes, oboes, clarinets and bassoons, plus double-bassoon: 4 horns, 2 trumpets, 3 trombones and (similarly marked ad lib) tuba; kettledrums and strings. Though the movements do not flow into one another, there is a strong interconnection between them. The upward-moving pair of slow notes which begins the first movement (F sharp, G) is paralleled by the upward G–A of a theme in the slow movement and the A–B of a theme in the finale; moreover, those themes of the first two movements are *literally* recalled in the finale, just after the cadenza.

An upward pair of notes and then a downward turn – like a sigh – constitutes the opening theme. A more forceful descending figure follows. When the violin enters it is with the 'sigh' (subtly altered). After elaborating the previous orchestral material, the soloist arrives at its own distinctive new, restful theme in G major – marked *semplice* (simply) and accompanied by orchestral strings alone. A forceful climax leaves the orchestra in charge with a restatement of the forceful descending theme in the new key of F sharp minor; but the development is short and the opening theme re-enters, with the violin soon adding its eloquence. The violin's special theme in G major returns too, and more majestically. The music takes on new impetus to end the movement in B minor.

A big shift of key can be felt as the strings (with woodwind backing) softly deliver the opening theme of the slow movement. It is in B flat major. After a further thematic figure from the strings, beginning with a slow upward pair of notes, there is another surprising shift; the violin chooses E major to suggest a second theme of its own, then settles it into D flat major. The soloist's line becomes ever more passionate and rapid until the opening theme returns in its original key: eventually the soloist's own theme comes home to that key, and fades with a long-sustained low note.

If the second movement was an elegy (for 'the soul of . . .') the third is buoyant. What happens first, in B minor, is an athletic running rather than a theme: the very definite second theme follows – decisive, rising orchestral strokes which the violin is quick to take up. Quieter and smoother, a theme on the solo violin begins in E major. The interplay of mood and theme is vigorous until, under a high trill from the soloist, the orchestra intimates a reminder of the opening of the concerto. Soon, against the hushed strings with their thrummed sounds (see above), the soloist begins the cadenza – starting with another reminder of the opening movement. The mood of wistful reminiscence is suddenly banished – the athletic run returns, the music passes joyously from B minor to B major. In that key, the third movement's own second theme of decisive strokes is delivered in double time (twice as slowly) in triple stops by the solo violin, the trombones and tuba stepping in to clinch the harmony. A quick, brilliant flourish and the concerto is over.

Concerto in E minor for cello and orchestra, opus 85

       Adagio – Moderato, *leading to*
       Allegro molto
       Adagio
       Allegro ma non troppo
       Duration: 28 minutes

Elgar's 'autumnal' period after the First World War is marked by this
concerto, which was given its first performance under the composer's baton on 27 October 1919 with Felix Salmond as soloist. It is
unusual in being in four movements rather than three, and in its
nominally 'heavy' (but lightly used) brass component – 4 horns, 2
trumpets, 3 trombones and optional tuba – besides double woodwind, kettledrums and strings. A further unusual touch is the slow
introduction declaimed by the soloist before the orchestral violas
present the flowing main theme of the first movement, which the
soloist soon takes over. A contrasting theme with a distinctive lilt is
heard from clarinets and bassoons. The music takes on a new
warmth in moving from E minor to E major, but dies away in the
minor key. Orchestral cellos and double basses hold a single low
note as a link into . . .

    . . . the second movement. After an echo of the slow introduction
to the first movement the soloist launches into a kind of scherzo,
basically in G major. Rapid articulations of repeated notes for the
solo instrument contrast with a particular rhetorical phrase which
has a gap like an intake of breath. The impetus is continuous to the
end.

The third movement in B flat is short and, in its brevity and
eloquence, perhaps the most remarkable of all. The orchestral
accompaniment is reduced to clarinet, bassoons and two horns. It
starts with an introductory, questioning phrase in the orchestra. The
answer is supplied by a sweeping, elegiac melody for the solo
instrument passing to remote keys and then returning to B flat. The
original questioning phrase needing an answer returns, but the
movement ends there, unsatisfied.

Can the finale provide the 'answer'? The orchestra begins softly
but almost gruffly. After a few bars the cello intervenes with the
original introductory music from the first movement and passes to
an eloquent cadenza. Now, in a more resolute vein than anything
previously in the concerto, the main part of the finale begins. It is
built on a rhythmic transformation of that introductory material to
the first movement. The soloist's skills both of expression and of
agility are tested and at length a new intensity envelops the music.
There is a change to the triple time of the slow movement and a
passionate recall of it by the soloist, followed by a recall of the
opening bars of the concerto in their original key. The time for
tender recollection is now over; a brisk coda in E minor ends the
concerto.

Overture, 'Cockaigne', opus 40

Duration: 26 minutes

The composer's subtitle for the work is 'In London Town', and its main title is a pun – *cockaigne* as a literary term for a land of make-believe, and cockney as the nickname for a Londoner. It celebrates the pomp and high spirits of London life, and was born at a time when patriotism found satisfaction in the successful military campaign which was bringing the South African War to an end. The first performance, in London on 20 June 1901, was conducted by the composer.

Celebration is conveyed not only by the themes but also by the exuberant orchestral writing, culminating in the addition of an organ. In a section imitating a marching band, the printed score suggests the reinforcement of the three standard trombones by another two. A combination of small bells and triangle presumably represents the jingles of a horse's harness. The orchestration is for 2 each of flutes, oboes and clarinets, 2 bassoons and double-bassoon; 4 horns, 2 cornets as well as 2 trumpets, 3 (optionally 5) trombones and tuba, kettledrums, bass drum, cymbals, snare-drum, tambourine, triangle and bells; and strings.

Although a pattern of sonata-form (exposition – development – recapitulation) can be traced in the work, it hits the listener as a continuous development, with reappearances of principal themes and an enormous climax at the end. Given the 'scenic' character of the whole, the commonly accepted labelling of principal themes makes sense. The animated opening section produces a broad 'citizens' theme' in C for full orchestra; a quieter section yields a smooth and gentle 'lovers' theme' in E flat for strings; later there is a military-band march and the hint of a Salvation Army presence in the beat of tambourine and bass drum. The citizens' and lovers' themes and the marching-band themes, with subsidiary material, all recur. Finally, as the organ enters, the citizens' theme gets its apotheosis *not* in the home key of C but in E flat, shifting quickly home to C major for the final few bars, clinched by the kettledrums.

Variations on an original theme (Enigma Variations), *opus 36*

CAE
HDS-P
RBT
WMB
RPA
Ysobel
Troyte
WN
Nimrod
Dorabella ('Intermezzo')
GRS
BGN
*** ('Romanza')
EDU
Duration: 31 minutes

Elgar's title was simply *Variations on an original theme*, with the dedication 'to my friends pictured within'. Over the theme itself he placed the word 'Enigma', about which he wrote elsewhere as follows:

> The enigma I will not explain – its 'dark saying' must be left unguessed, and I warn you that the apparent connection between the variations and the theme is often of the slightest texture; further through and over the whole set another and larger theme 'goes', but is not played.

A few degrees short of certainty is the conjecture that this hidden tune is *Auld Lang Syne*. But the work is, needless to say, self-sufficient. To follow it, the chief necessity is to grasp the three-part form of the theme itself – G minor, G major, G minor again – and to note which of the variations come to a full stop and which flow into the next.

But the listener may also feel that the work has its larger dimensions or 'movements' in the symphonic sense. An opening 'movement' in forthright vein spans the first four variations and pivots on the keynote G (minor and major). A new movement now begins (Variations V–VII) in C minor and major – two 'serious' variations sealed by a jocular one. A third movement has two variations in G

(VIII, X) enclosing the centre-piece of *Nimrod* in E flat. A finale begins with Variation XI, which asserts a G minor opening (last used in Variation IV). This finale culminates in XII (representing the composer himself) which, with its midway plunge into E flat (the key of *Nimrod*), is like a distillation of all preceding.

Theme Begins in the minor key; after a few bars there is a new tune (clarinet solo) in the major key; then (strings) back to the first tune. Strings and clarinets hold a chord which leads without a break into . . .

Variation I ('CAE' – Elgar's wife, Caroline Alice). Begins softly; leads to a climax in the middle in which trombones, tuba, and kettledrums join; quiet end.

Variation II ('HDS-P' – Hew David Steuart-Powell, an amateur pianist). Fast and light. Begins on violins alone and ends with a single note on cellos and double-basses *pizzicato*.

Variation III ('RBT' – Richard Baxter Townshend). Rather light and waltz-like; a prominent bassoon solo and a quiet end.

Variation IV ('WMB' – William Meath Baker, apparently an emphatic man!) Loud, heavily accented, and bringing in all departments of the orchestra at the end.

Variation V ('RPA' – Richard Penrose Arnold, a son of Matthew Arnold, the poet). A serious mood is struck in the violins' lower register; in contrast is a sunny outbreak on the woodwind. The first strain returns, then the second, then again the first. A long, subdued kettledrum roll leads without a break from the minor key into . . .

Variation VI ('Ysobel' – Isabel Fitton, a viola-player). The major key takes over for this graceful and thoughtful melody, the violas having the main tune.

Variation VII ('Troyte' – Arthur Troyte Griffith, a very close friend). Rather fierce. Kettledrum solo at the start and most of the way through.

Variation VIII ('WN' – Winifred Norbury). Clarinets begin the tune: the mood is fresh and delicate. At the end the violins hold a single note which leads into . . .

Variation IX ('Nimrod' – August Johannes Jaeger: the Bible refers to 'Nimrod, the mighty hunter', and Jaeger, whose name is German for hunter, was a close friend who worked for Novello's, Elgar's publishers.) Slow and majestic. Full orchestral climax, dying away right at the end.

Variation X ('Dorabella' – Dora Penny). Muted strings start a playful dialogue with woodwind. Brass silent throughout.

Variation XI ('GRS' – George Robertson Sinclair, with an energetic bulldog!) Fast and boisterous.

Variation XII ('BGN' – Basil Nevinson, a cellist). A solo cello begins this expressive variation – and ends it, passing straight into . . .

Variation XIII ('***' – Lady Mary Lygon, a friend who had been on a sea voyage; this attribution has been queried but not toppled). Shortly, over a slow, wavy accompaniment, a clarinet plays a falling scrap of melody from Mendelssohn's overture *A Calm Sea and Prosperous Voyage*. This comes back at the end.

Finale ('EDU' – Edoo being a pet-name of his wife's for Elgar himself). Beginning quietly, like a far-off march coming nearer, it builds gradually into the mightiest climax of the work.

FALLA

1876–1946

Spanish national idiom was imitated by French, Russian and other composers of the nineteenth century (a good example being provided by Chabrier's *España*: see p.125), but not until about 1900 did Spain itself establish a lively presence in the international concert-hall with the music of Albéniz, Granados and Falla.

Manuel de Falla trained in Madrid and then, in his thirties, found encouragement and stimulus in Paris from Debussy, Ravel and others. He is best known for vigorous, richly scored orchestral music (some of it taken from ballets) which makes use of national Spanish dance-rhythms and occasionally evokes the strong strokes of the Spanish guitar. A harpsichord concerto (1926) pursues a leaner style: with an accompaniment of only five instruments, its melodic patterns pay homage to Bach and Domenico Scarlatti. After enduring the tensions of the Spanish Civil War Falla spent the later (and unproductive) years of his life, from 1939, in Argentina.

Dances from The Three-Cornered Hat

> The Neighbours' Dance (Seguidilla)
> The Miller's Dance (Farruca)
> Final Dance (Jota)
> Duration: 12 minutes

London, surprisingly enough, saw the first performance of the ballet *The Three-Cornered Hat* (known in French as *Le tricorne*, in Spanish as *El sombrero de tres picos*) on 22 June 1919. It was one of the many commissions of the Diaghilev company. The score remains, in the concert-hall, one of the most vivid evocations of the Spanish idiom. The instrumentation naturally adds castanets to the other percussion (kettledrums, snare drum, bass drum, cymbals, triangle, tam-tam, xylophone). The orchestra otherwise comprises 2 flutes and piccolo,

2 oboes and english horn, 2 clarinets, 2 bassoons, 4 horns, 3 trumpets, 3 trombones and tuba, piano, celesta, harp and strings.

The complete ballet opens with a mezzo-soprano solo on stage as part of the action, but there is no vocal part in the three well-known concert extracts. The action, in two scenes, concerns the attempts of an amorous Corregidor, or Governor, to seduce a miller's wife, who fools and tricks him. In one episode he falls into a stream and the end sees him tossed in a blanket by the derisive populace who have gathered at the mill to feast on St John's Eve (midsummer).

The three dances excerpted all come from the second scene, as described in the score: 'The neighbours come to celebrate. Men and women drink and dance. It is a fine Andalusian night, perfumed, starlit and mysterious.' The neighbours' dance is in the triple time of the *Seguidilla*, alternating between 3/4 and 3/8, and starting softly with a characteristic rhythmic phrase on the violins which haunts the movement.

More energetic, preluded by a spirited solo horn-call, is the *Farruca* danced by the miller. A stamping figure (strings and snare drum prominent) is succeeded by a tune on the oboe which ends in a flurry of scales. Energy and excitement are sustained to the end.

Although called Final Dance, the third number in fact covers the Corregidor's continued amorous pursuit and the attempt of his henchmen to arrest the miller, as well as the final turning of the tables on the would-be seducer. After a few bars' introduction, the main tune is heard (*Jota*), in vigorous combination of 6/8 and 3/4 time. After the interposition of other lively material the main tune returns with renewed exuberance, and half a dozen upward rushes (xylophone, piano, harp) indicate the tossing of the hapless Corregidor.

Symphonic Impressions, Nights in the Gardens of Spain *for piano and orchestra*

> In the gardens of the Generalife
> Dance in the distance, *leading to*
> In the gardens of the Sierra de Córdoba
> Duration: 22 minutes

According to the composer, this work is 'not descriptive but expressive'. It calls on the idiom and some characteristic effects of Andalusian folk-music but without direct quotation of tunes. In its title (and in its label of 'symphonic impressions') it shows its affiliation to the impressionism of Debussy and to such works as *La Mer*. The three movements, respectively centred on C sharp, A and D, do not make the traditional tonal unity.

Enrique Fernandez Arbos (himself a noted composer) was the conductor of the first performance, given in Madrid on 9 April 1916, with José Cubiles as pianist. The piano, sometimes with romantic opulence and sometimes imitating the thrumming of a guitar, joins with a glittering texture provided by a full orchestra: 2 flutes and piccolo, 2 oboes and english horn, 2 clarinets, 2 bassoons, 4 horns, 2 trumpets, 3 trombones and tuba, harp, celesta, kettledrums, triangle and cymbals.

The Generalife refers to one of the buildings of the famous Alhambra of Granada. The opening movement begins softly and somewhat mysteriously with a minor-key theme on the violas which dwells within a deliberately narrow range of notes. The piano takes it up and is then heard in animated dialogue with the orchestra. The texture thins as the piano presents a new theme. The narrow-range theme swells to a passionate climax, then subsides, a solo horn recalling the opening phrases of the movement, but with a sweetened major-key ending.

The second movement sets a slightly faster pace for a tune in 3/4 dance-rhythm, with flutes prominent, then the piano. Eventually the dance music hangs in the air (a long, soft cymbal-roll forms a background) and fades. The piano moves in with animation, leading upward to . . .

. . . the finale. On a hillside above Cordoba, we glimpse a party entertained by gypsy musicians. The orchestra delivers the first, dance-like theme, taken up by the piano; the piano, itself in octaves, enunciates the second, with its obsessive near-repetitions – surely those of a gypsy singer. This second theme later returns in varied form, but its energy is eventually spent and the work ends in stillness.

FAURÉ

1845–1924

A small but distinguished output in the fields of song, piano music and chamber music was left by Gabriel Fauré. He also wrote a *Requiem* which remains a favourite of choral societies. A *Ballade* for piano and orchestra, now not often heard, is among his few orchestral works. The *Elegy* for cello and piano exists also in the composer's own version for cello and orchestra.

Pavane

Duration: 7 minutes

This short orchestral piece is a curiosity. It has a setting of words for chorus, in which male and female lovers of some bygone elegant festivity tease one another – but the choral part is marked 'optional' and the orchestral part stands self-contained, which is how it is usually given. The first performance took place in Paris on 28 April 1888, conducted by Charles Lamoureux.

The scoring is light – for two each of flutes, oboes, clarinets, bassoons and horns, plus strings, whose harp-like sounds accompany the opening main theme, at first in the low register of a solo flute. The strain is plaintive and in a minor key; a louder, contrasting central part (in D major, after F sharp minor) is heard before the original, languorous mood returns in music which is nearly but not quite the same and which fades in farewell.

FRANCK

1822–90

In an obvious way they were opposites: the extravagant Berlioz, whom no institution could have tied down, and the sober Franck, professor at the Paris Conservatoire and for more than thirty years organist at the Paris church of Ste Clotilde. But both composers triumphed in the symphony, a form mastered by few others in nineteenth-century France, and chose to let one theme reappear in transformed guise through several movements. Belgian by birth, César Franck trained in Paris and made his career there. His achievement in orchestral, organ and chamber works is credited with shifting the weight of French composition away from opera and ballet towards 'absolute' music.

His use of sliding, chromatic harmony is characteristic. Other orchestral works of Franck include the sparkling *Symphonic Variations* (1885) for piano and orchestra, and several symphonic poems (among them *The Accursed Huntsman*, 1883): he was the first major French composer to essay this Lisztian story-telling form.

Symphony in D minor

Lento: Allegro non troppo
Allegretto
Allegro non troppo
Duration: 27 minutes

This symphony and Dvořák's *New World* (No.9) have slow movements which enshrine the most famous symphonic uses of the english horn. Franck apparently encountered criticism (magnified in the history books) for daring to use it *in a symphony*, a form restrictive in its instrumental tradition. The precedent of Berlioz (page 81) must have been ignored or forgotten!

Unusual too, was the participation of a bass clarinet in the score. French practice is followed in the use of two trumpets *and* two cornets – the former for strength, the latter for agility. The complete orchestration is for 2 each of flutes, oboes (plus english horn), clarinets (plus bass clarinet), and bassoons; 4 horns, 2 trumpets (plus 2 cornets), 3 trombones and tuba; kettledrums; harp and strings. The symphony was first performed on 17 February 1889 in Paris, Jules Garcin being the conductor.

The themes of Franck's only symphony present strong outlines, vivid orchestral colour and exultant climaxes. It has a highly individual construction – the finale quotes from other movements, and the middle movement combines the concepts of lyrical slow movement and more animated intermezzo. Moreover, the tempo-scheme of the first movement is strikingly unusual. Instead of a slow introduction and faster main section, as so often occurs in earlier symphonies, the two tempos alternate.

After the main theme, in D minor, has been presented slowly at the outset, the same theme comes more urgently at the tempo of an allegro. The slow tempo returns, but this time switches the theme to F minor, and a resumed allegro likewise adopts that key, then changing to F major for a smooth, song-like tune on the strings, leading to an ardently proclaimed theme – the so-called 'motive of faith', on the full orchestra, with trumpets conspicuous. After the expected development, the end of the movement again brings back the opening theme in slow, then in fast tempo, though with a different key-sequence. The motive of faith, even more ardent, rings out in D *major*. But there is more to come, the conclusion being given to the original opening theme and a glowing, final D major chord.

The second movement displays the english horn as soloist in a gentle, evenly measured tune in B flat minor; a sequel in the major key is heard on the violins. Then, though the beat remains the same, the music appears to move faster: a winding triplet motion is set up by the violins, and soon a new tune issues from the clarinets. Returning, the english horn theme is combined with the other material.

The third and final movement has a sweeping onward drive. Its march-like song in D major may remind us of the song of joy in the finale of Beethoven's Ninth Symphony. Later, the english horn's solo from the middle movement returns, and after a development it returns yet again. There is also a reappearance of the motive of faith from the first movement and a version of the first theme from that movement. Nevertheless, it is the march–like song which, led by trumpets, ends the symphony.

GERSHWIN

1898–1937

Probably the most famous name among American composers, George Gershwin won early success as a song-writer: *Swanee*, selling over a million copies, was composed when he was only 19. That a song-writer in the jazz idiom should establish himself in musical comedy (or, as it was later termed, 'the musical') was normal: but what Gershwin exceptionally did, and what Jerome Kern, Cole Porter and others did not do, was to make the successful crossing into the concert-hall. Although the *Rhapsody in Blue* was tailored to the special instrumentation of a jazz orchestra, such later works as the Piano Concerto (1925) and *An American in Paris* (1928) were written for symphony orchestra and maintain their place in the orchestral repertory.

In rhythms and the occasional sliding figure or suggestion of a 'blue' note (see note on the work that follows), Gershwin brings a flavour of jazz into nominally classical forms. It is, in fact, that characteristic flavour and the bounce that goes with it which give these works their principal appeal.

Rhapsody in Blue

Duration: 17 minutes

The work which the dance-band leader Paul Whiteman commissioned for his New York concert on 12 February 1924 was destined to be perhaps the most famous non-vocal work America has ever produced. The orchestration for the band's use by Grofé, (though with an unusual part for piano), is now commonly used in concerts. It asks for a banjo and (optionally) 3 saxophones, as well as 2 flutes, 2 oboes, 2 clarinets and bass clarinet, 2 bassoons, 4 horns, 3 trumpets, 3 trombones and tuba; kettledrums, snare drum, bass drum, cymbals, triangle, gong; and strings.

The imitations of vocalized 'blue' notes, the use of added-note harmonies favoured by dance-bands of the time, and a profusion of appealing melodies gained an immediate following for this piece. The term *rhapsody* seems to allude to Liszt's *Hungarian Rhapsodies* and Gershwin emulates their succulent tunes with (this time) an American flavour. The design has no complications. A low trill on the clarinet and a skyward ascent lead to the first theme in B flat; a later more sentimental theme in E flat becomes the main and most memorable theme of the piece. The clarinet's theme is assumed by the full orchestra towards the end.

GLINKA

1804–57

The 'father of Russian music' was not the first composer to arise in his country: among earlier figures, Dmitri Bortnyansky (1751–1825) is remembered for his contributions to the choral repertory of the Russian orthodox church. But Glinka, by the vigour and richness of his style and especially his treatment of Russian words and his use of Russian folk-music, was the figure venerated by such later, more widely celebrated composers as Rimsky-Korsakov and Tchaikovsky.

Glinka grafted this Russian nationalism on to an idea of opera mainly received from his studies and experiences in Italy (where he met Donizetti and Bellini). Symphonic music was barely established in the Russia to which he returned, and his chief energies went into his pair of celebrated operas, *A Life for the Tsar* (1836) and *Ruslan and Ludmila* (1842). As an orchestral composer he is best known for his overture to the latter, but some of his independent short pieces are occasionally heard. Among these are *Kamarinskaya*, a treatment of a Russian folksong, and *Jota Aragonesa* (originally called *Capriccio brilliante*) on the Spanish dance, the *jota*.

Overture to Ruslan and Ludmila

Duration: 6 minutes

Produced in St Petersburg on 9 March 1842, *Ruslan and Ludmila* is an opera where fantasy creatures interact with an episode of ancient Russian history. Tunes from the opera are taken to make a brilliant, colourfully scored overture. The orchestration is for double wood-wind plus double-bassoon, standard brass (4 horns, 2 trumpets, 3 trombones), kettledrums and strings.

The slow opening so often found in operatic overtures is absent: fast, vigorous themes take charge at once. In contrast with the dashing tune of the opening, a more sustained theme first heard on violas and cellos is taken from a song in which the warrior-hero, Ruslan, recalls his beloved, absent Ludmila. Towards the end of the overture a heavy, strange descending scale on the trombones portrays the threat of the wizard Chernomor. It is, in fact, a presentation of the whole-tone scale, which would be systematically used more than half a century later by Debussy.

GRIEG

1843–1907

More than 75 years after his death, Edvard Grieg still stands with unique distinction as the representative of Norwegian music. Like Sullivan (one year his senior), he attended the Leipzig Conservatory; but the skills he acquired in the German orchestral tradition were put to the production of music with a distinct flavour of Norwegian dance and song at a time when national sentiment was rising. Norway remained under Swedish royal rule (though possessing its own parliament) until 1905. The cultural backwardness of the country drove Norway's greatest literary figure, Ibsen, to live mainly abroad, but Grieg's music did not raise social controversies and the composer's eminence was recognized by a substantial state pension.

Grieg discarded an early symphony and the works that brought him greatest fame are those treated below. The incidental music to a play, *Sigurd the Crusader* (not by Ibsen but by another distinguished Norwegian writer, Bjørnson) includes a famous *Homage March*.

Concerto for piano and orchestra in A minor, opus 16

>   Allegro molto moderato
>   Adagio, *leading to*
>   Allegro moderato molto e marcato
>   Duration: 29 minutes

Grieg was only twenty-five, and newly married, when he composed his piano concerto. He was himself the soloist at the first performance, given in Copenhagen on 3 April 1869. Three years later it won the approval of Liszt, not only Europe's most famous pianist but the champion of whatever music possessed a strong individual and national colouring. The concerto gained speedy popularity but the composer continued to make revisions to it until his last years.

It follows Schumann's Piano Concerto (see p. 297) not only in its key but in its swift play of mood. There is no long-sustained tension, no menace, but a predominance of tender, lyrical feeling. But Grieg's concerto shows the later nineteenth-century preference for a heavier orchestra: it has four horns instead of Schumann's two, and the trio of trombones which Schumann omitted. Other instruments are 2 flutes (one doubling piccolo), 2 each of oboes, clarinets and bassoons; two trumpets, kettledrums and strings.

A piano flourish opens the work, and then – instead of an orchestral exposition followed later by a solo entry – the orchestra and pianist share the exposition between them. The pace is slowed down for the arrival of the second subject in C major on the cellos. After an animated development the opening material returns – the second subject being again heard on the cellos, but in A major and more warmly accompanied. A long, exciting cadenza (fully written out by the composer) is followed by a quick coda.

The key shifts to the remote D flat for the soft-breathed melody on muted strings which opens the second movement. The tune is finally glorified by the piano at its full emotional strength. The sound dies away, but there is no pause . . .

The finale follows immediately: a rhythmic utterance of clarinets and bassoons and a flourish on the piano lead to the main theme – given out by the soloist in a Norwegian folk-dance rhythm. In the next main theme the piano also takes the lead with three strong, detached chords. Later, in stronger contrast, the strenuous pace is dropped as a solo flute meditates in stillness. After more presentation of previous material, a cadenza leaves us with an expectancy which is resolved by a transformation of the opening theme into a light, triple rhythm. The concerto ends with a majestically transformed version of the flute tune.

Incidental music to Peer Gynt

Ibsen's play *Peer Gynt* has been described as a disillusioned *Pilgrim's Progress*: a sort of morality play, though its lessons are elusive. The great Norwegian dramatist commissioned music from Grieg for a revival of the play in Oslo (then called Christiania) on 24 February 1876. The composer revised the music later, and selected two concert suites which won more universal acquaintance than the play itself.

The first suite is the more popular of the two: in both, the orchestration is highly skilful without being showy. The scoring is for 2 flutes (one doubling piccolo), 2 each of oboes, clarinets and bassoons; 4 horns, 2 trumpets, 3 trombones and tuba; kettledrums; and strings. The items in the suites do not follow the order of their appearance in the play.

Suite no.1

Duration: 16 minutes

Morning: A tone-painting of a dawn in which (as Grieg said) the sun breaks through the cloud.

The Death of Ase: the death of his mother serves in the play to show Peer's callousness. He sits on her bed recounting some of his adventures and does not realize the moment of her death.

Anitra's Dance: despite the indication of *Tempo di mazurka*, this represents not a Polish but a Moroccan scene – hence the exotic touch of melody and percussion. By the end of the scene, Peer and Anitra have become lovers.

In the Hall of the Mountain King: the music points to the strangeness of the underground domain of the king with his three grotesque-looking daughters. Peer has seduced one of them and at the excited part towards the end they shout 'Kill him!'

Suite no.2

Duration: 17 minutes

The Abduction of the Bride begins with a brief, furious theme which represents the violent Peer who dragged Ingrid away when she was about to be married to someone else; the slower, sadder tune represents *Ingrid's lament*.

The **Arabian Dance** is sung in the play as well as danced by young women. The quieter episode (strings and triangle only) is sung by Anitra alone.

Peer Gynt's Homecoming bears the subtitle 'stormy evening off the coast': the ship bearing Peer is wrecked. A long wail is heard from the woodwind; the music moves on to . . .

. . . **Solveig's song**, belonging to the woman who has waited lovingly for Peer. Heard in various contexts in the play, finally represents consolation to the tormented, worthless 'hero'.

HANDEL

1685–1759

One of the great masters of his time, George Frideric Handel (to give him the spelling he used when exchanging Hanoverian for British nationality) was among other things a master of the orchestra. He used the strings with the vivacity and idiomatic style which he had learnt from Corelli and others in Italy; he called on oboes and bassoons mainly but not entirely to reinforce the strings; he gave lively, characteristic music to horns and trumpets. He sometimes employed the flute in the orchestra, sometimes the recorder. Characteristically, a keyboard instrument (harpsichord or organ) fills in the harmony. Its player would often have served as director of the performance.

Overtures (and some other orchestral numbers) from Handel's operas and oratorios serve admirably as concert pieces. Expressly designed as such were his 'concertos': he used the term broadly, as in a famous set of six (opus 3) and another of twelve (opus 6). Handel's *Water Music* and *Music for the Royal Fireworks* were re-ordered and re-scored by Sir Hamilton Harty (1879–1941) for the large, twentieth-century symphony orchestra. But more and more performances in recent decades have shown a preference (in these and other works) for a nearer approximation to Handel's own scoring, whether or not with the special colouring lent by 'early' instruments such as the one-keyed wooden flute.

Concerto in Alexander's Feast (Concerto for strings in C)

Allegro
Largo
Allegro
Andante, non presto
Duration: 18 minutes

The odd-seeming title arises from the custom by which Handel (and other composers) interspersed an instrumental piece in the middle of performances of an oratorio or similar work. *Alexander's Feast*, a setting of a festive ode by Dryden, was first given in London, under Handel's direction, on 19 February 1736. This concerto for strings, originally performed on that occasion, is an outstanding example of Handel's skill in the management of the *concerto grosso* – in this case with a solo group of two violins and cello contrasting with the orchestra.

In four movements (not the three usually cultivated by Vivaldi and by Bach), it starts with a fast movement in which soloists and orchestra mainly alternate with each other, rather than inter-acting. The second movement relegates the orchestra almost to an accompaniment of the expressive music given to the soloists.

In the third movement Handel begins by displaying his fugue style – often favoured by him as a beginning – which then merges into less rigid contrapuntal music. The soloists gradually show their vivacity. A finale which is in fact a gavotte has the 'Scotch snaps' (accented short note followed by an unaccented long one) which were in vogue at that time, and conveys the elegance of Handel's most polished music.

Music for the Royal Fireworks

> Overture
> Bourrée
> La Paix
> La Rejouissance
> Minuets 1 and 2
> Duration: 25 minutes

A firework display disappointed, but a musical performance triumphed, at a public concert in London on 27 April 1749 in celebration of the newly concluded Peace of Aix-la-Chapelle. 'A hundred musicians' are said to have played, but therein lies a historical puzzle. Handel wanted to include strings as well as wind instruments and drums, but was refused permission by the organizers. However a calculation of the total of wind-players and drummers known to have been present would hardly make more than 60, so perhaps Handel had 40 string-players after all. Whether he had or not, he certainly wanted strings and those modern concert-givers who put on a supposed 'original' performance with wind only do him no favour. The complete string parts survive.

Until recently, twentieth-century audiences have usually heard the work in an arrangement for conventional symphony orchestra made by Sir Hamilton Harty (see below for his more extensive editorial work on the *Water Music*). But now the preference is to follow Handel's own choice of instruments as far as possible – even if indoor performances do not need his twenty-four oboes! The other wind instruments comprise bassoons, double-bassoon, horns and trumpets.

The overture has the pompous dotted notes of the formal French overture (see p. 14), and its key of D major facilitates the participation of the (originally valveless) trumpets. Two dances follow, a *bourrée* and *siciliana*, the latter given the French name corresponding to 'peace'. The next movement, whose French title means 'rejoicing', is a cheerful fast piece to be played three times – by trumpets, wood-wind and strings; by horns and woodwind; and by everyone. Two minuets follow, one in D minor and the second in D major which brings the full orchestra into play for a joyful end.

Water Music

Suite no. 1 in F for 2 oboes, bassoon, 2 horns and strings

> Overture: Largo – Allegro
> Adagio e staccato
> Allegro – Andante – Allegro
> Presto
> Air
> Minuet
> Bourrée
> Hornpipe
> [Allegro]
> [Andante]
> Hornpipe
> Duration: 35 minutes

Suite no.2 in D for 2 oboes, bassoon, 2 horns, 2 trumpets and strings

Allegro
[Allegro]
Minuet
Lentement
Air
Duration: 10 minutes

Suite no.3 in G for 2 recorders, flute, 2 oboes, bassoon and strings

[Andante]
Presto
Minuet
[Andante]
Country Dance
Duration: 6 minutes

(For the arrangement by Hamilton Harty, see below)

Its fame began early. Even in Handel's own time it was published as 'the celebrated Water Musick'. But what was its origin? The old story that it was the means of reconciling Handel with George I in 1719 is now discredited for lack of evidence. The music appears to have been compiled for the King's river trip from Whitehall towards Chelsea on 17 July 1717, about fifty musicians being stationed on an accompanying barge. Some of the pieces may have been composed earlier. The Prussian Resident (diplomat) in London, in a letter, noted the instruments as flutes, recorders, oboes, bassoons, horns, trumpets and strings. In normal non-water-borne performance the addition of kettledrums (playing with the trumpets) and harpsichord could have been expected.

The music won its twentieth-century popularity in a skilful arrangement of six numbers made by Sir Hamilton Harty (1879–1941), published in 1922 and freely combining different numbers of the original. Though Harty's suite is not quite superseded, a more recent preference is to give the work in the composer's own scoring and in a recognition that Handel designed the work as three separate suites, each suite with its own scoring. The first suite, in F, gives

prominence to two horns – perhaps the first time that this characteristic orchestral sound had been heard in Britain. Much shorter are the
second suite in D with prominence for the trumpets and the third in
G with prominence for flute and a pair of descant recorders.

Handel's manuscript is lost, but a contemporary manuscript copy
plus early printed editions have been collated in Roger Fiske's
authoritative 1973 edition and yield the sequence above. The headings are not consistent, some being indicative of tempo, some of
dance rhythms, some missing altogether, leaving it to the performers to recognize the tempo required. For his opening movement
Handel used the French title 'Ouverture', i.e. the French overture,
with a slow stately section followed by a faster. The final item of the
first suite is actually headed 'Alla hornpipe', the Italian first word
(like the French *à la*) indicating 'in the style of'. The hornpipe in this
context (as in Purcell's earlier use) is a dance in triple time, not the
more familiar (nineteenth-century) 'sailor's hornpipe'. In some
movements he gives instructions for repetitions of the whole in
different ways ('All the violins', 'all the oboes', 'all together').

The music of the individual movements hardly needs comment,
except to point the contrast between the dance movements with their
parallel 'blocks' of equal numbers of bars, and those of freer form
where melodies are inventively extended. Strings and wind may be
placed in vivid opposition, as in the *Allegro* which stands in the first
suite as the last number but two. Note two other characteristic
features in this number: a fast movement with a slow finish, and a
movement in D minor, as a change from the prevailing major key.

HAYDN

1732–1809

Acclaimed as the leading composer of Europe, Joseph Haydn paid
two visits to London, in 1791–2 and 1794–5, and presented there his
last twelve symphonies. They marked the ripeness of an orchestral
style which had developed over the long years when Haydn had
served, in a humble social capacity, as musical director to the
Austro-Hungarian family of Esterházy. From Austria his fame had
spread as a composer both of symphonies and of string quartets: in
both forms, he stands (if not as the originator) as the earliest
composer substantially represented in the standard repertory.

Modest orchestral forces were available to him at his princely
employer's establishment; larger sonorities (an orchestra of about
sixty) as well as larger audiences were at hand in London. But the
type of orchestra remains the same – the 'classical orchestra', as it is
now known and as described on p. 19. Strings, two oboes and two
horns are its basis, which suffice in the two cello concertos (early
works) discussed below. In later works Haydn adds one or two flutes
and a pair of bassoons to the woodwind, and a pair of trumpets plus a
pair of kettledrums (one player). In some of the symphonies of his
second London visit he called in also a pair of clarinets (an instrument
of relatively new invention). Departures from this, for instance the
extra percussion in Haydn's *Military* Symphony (no. 100, see below),
are rare and special.

To this instrumental list, however, the harpsichord or piano
should be added as a means of directing orchestral performances in
those days (see p. 19). In the case of at least one symphony, no. 98,
evidence has come down to us of a special little solo which Haydn
contributed at the keyboard to brighten up the last few bars of the
finale.

The grouping of Haydn, Mozart and Beethoven as musicians of
the 'classical' or 'Viennese classical' era implies more than their use of

a typical orchestra. It implies also their use of 'classical' forms: those of the symphony and concerto are discussed below. From these forms, with their balance between movements and within movements, the seasoned listener has expectations which the composer fulfils or teasingly turns aside. Beneath a smooth surface, Haydn's works show mastery of the ingenious choices which the classical style permits.

Haydn's works are now numbered as Hob. (for Antony van Hoboken, their modern American cataloguer) followed by a roman figure for the series (symphonies, concertos, quartets, etc.) and an arabic figure denoting the work itself. These numberings are used for the concertos below. But for the symphonies the older numbering still serves, since Hoboken follows it too – the Symphony no. 100 becoming Hob I:100, etc.

The symphonies

The prodigious span of Haydn's symphonies is hardly to be paralleled: it stretches from around 1760 (he was not yet 30) to the period of his London acclaim three and half decades later. Inevitably the later works are more often heard, but not to the exclusion of the others, and all are recorded. The mature Haydn symphony has the classical four-movement form (see p. 12) with two special features in the first movement: Haydn usually (but Mozart rarely) precedes the main, fast section by a slow introduction, and the fast section itself often follows a construction which analysts tend misleadingly to call 'monothematic'. It does not mean that only one theme or tune is used. It means that in the exposition, when the music has turned to a new key and we might immediately expect a new tune, we get the *first* theme again, but in the new key. (A new theme may indeed occur later.)

Haydn's slow second movements more often suggest grandeur than pathos: trumpets and drums here have their own stately effect. The third movements of the symphonies retain their dance-like appeal as minuets: they are not slow, but have not acquired the faster, one-beat-to-a-bar pulse that was to characterize a Beethoven scherzo. The final movement is fast – sometimes very fast, as indicated by presto. (Exceptionally, for the sake of a special occasion explained below, the *Farewell* Symphony ends in slower tempo.) The fast finale most commonly takes the form of a rondo (see glossary), offering the listener the gratification of an immediately catchy tune and the further gratification of recognizing its return several times, always in the same key.

Symphony no.45 in F sharp minor (Farewell)

Allegro assai
Adagio
Minuetto: Allegretto
Presto – Adagio
Duration: 26 minutes

The presumed origin of this symphony has made it famous. It is said that, in order to remind his princely employer that his orchestral players were hard worked and needed a holiday, Haydn contrived a symphony in which the players gradually leave the stage. The exact date of its first performance, some time in 1772, is not known. A small orchestra only is required: 2 oboes, a single bassoon, 2 horns and strings.

If the circumstances of its production are unique, then another fact about it is at least rare: it is one of the few minor-key classical symphonies. There is no slow introduction and the opening fast movement has a particular urgency which is later reinforced by off-beat accents and harmonic clashes.

The first three movements are engagingly individual but with no clue to the later surprise. The opening movement, with the pathos of its minor key, follows a variant of sonata-form (with a new, warm tune in the development section). In the slow second movement, the muted violins impart a new tone-colour: beginning in A, the music moves to E and then (with a new strand of argument from the lower strings) back to A again, each half being marked to be repeated.

The customary minuet movement follows: unlike the first movement it is in F sharp *major*. Its central trio brings a prominent and characteristic contribution from the horns.

The finale is remarkable musically, even apart from providing for the players' exits. As it proceeds, it appears to be a regularly built sonata-form movement in fast time (*Presto*) and in F sharp minor. But as we are supposedly brought towards the conclusion, the music stops and restarts as a slow movement in A major. Here at last the single bassoon, which so far has simply doubled the cello line, takes on a part of its own. The music turns to F sharp minor, then major. During this slow section the different players' music ends in turn, allowing them to leave the platform while the others continue; finally, deserted by all the others, only a pair of violinists are needed to sustain the final bars.

Symphony no.88 in G major

> Adagio – Allegro
> Largo
> Minuetto: Allegretto
> Allegro con spirito
> Duration: 22 minutes

Outside the *London* symphonies and (because of its novelty) the *Farewell*, none of Haydn's symphonies is better known than this. It combines his greatest warmth and animation with prodigious contrapuntal skill (especially in the last movement). The score was one of two symphonies taken to Paris by a former player of Haydn's Esterházy orchestra, Johann Tost, when he decided to try his professional fortune in the vigorous Parisian musical environment. The symphony was duly published in Paris in 1789 (and presumably first performed there, though no exact date is known). Delay in receiving payment made Haydn suspicious of Tost's business methods, but they later re-established an amicable relationship.

Within a conventional list of instruments (1 flute; 2 each of oboes, bassoons, horns, trumpets; kettledrums and strings), two unusual features of orchestration are concealed. The trumpets and drums are silent in the opening movement but enter spectacularly in the second; and in this movement also a solo cello detaches itself from the others to carry the opening melody.

The first movement has a 3/4 slow introduction to precede a 4/4 main section in which the horns prominently join. Sonata-form is followed, with the exposition repeated, the strings then initiating the development. When the main theme reappears on the violins for the recapitulation, a happy ingenuity is the addition of a counter-melody high on the flute.

The second movement, with its spacious tune on a solo cello, is in D. Trumpets and drums make a fierce interruption and will do so again and again. Meanwhile the smooth melodic flow progresses: when the cello's tune finally returns, now on the violins, a richer orchestral web supports it.

The third movement (in G) follows the normal minuet-and-trio form. But the trio is apt to take the listener pleasantly by surprise with its 'rustic' melody supported by a bagpipe-like drone on bassoons and violas.

The finale is a rondo, its main theme being one of Haydn's most gaily irresistible. In due course the theme takes off in several directions: the most artful is the canon in which violas, cellos and double-basses unitedly begin a version of the theme pursued by the identical melody half a bar behind on the violins. There is an amusing suggestion of 'Will he, won't he?' before a later return of the theme in its original form.

Symphony no.94 in G major (Surprise)

> Adagio – Vivace assai
> Andante
> Minuet: Allegro molto
> Allegro di molto
> Duration: 23 minutes

The symphonies of Haydn's first London visit (nos.93–98) begin his final and richest period of symphonic writing. Their standard orchestra is 2 each of flutes, oboes, bassoons, horns and trumpets, with kettledrums and strings. They were not performed in the order of that (later) numbering. Nos.95 and 96 had already been given when the concert of 23 March 1792 introduced no.94. The 'surprise' (which, as we know from surviving manuscripts, was an after-thought of the composer's) consists of the suddenly loud chord, with drum-stroke, in the seemingly placid tune of the second movement.

The opening movement has a slow introduction contrasting the tone of woodwind-plus-horns with that of the strings. Not merely a call to attention, its rising-then-falling melody dovetails into that of the following main faster section. For once, Haydn delivers a 'real' second subject with a character of its own: after a syncopated 'wait-for-it' figure, the tune is a sudden quick scurry on the first violins, to which the flutes are added. After the expected recapitulation, another special feature occurs: a long coda begun when the main theme re-enters on lower instruments, including bassoons.

The slow-movement tune with its unmistakable surprise is itself as regular as a nursery-rhyme melody and not dissimilar to one. But in three varied restatements, the second one being in a minor key, Haydn raises it to considerable grandeur, followed by a graceful withdrawal at the end.

The marking of a fast tempo for the minuet prevents its tune from being rather heavy, while the contrasting central trio with its reduced orchestra offers the piquant sound of violins and solo bassoon sharing a melody an octave apart.

Finally, a rondo of immense good humour and the most ingenious manipulation of themes: towards the end, a long drum-roll, suddenly louder, leads to a switch to an unexpected key (from the basic G to the remote E flat) and then home again.

Symphony no.96 in D major (The Miracle)

> Adagio – Allegro
> Andante
> Minuetto: Allegretto
> Vivace assai
> Duration: 25 minutes

The nickname serves as a convenient identification but has for some years been known to rest on a historical mistake. At one of Haydn's London concerts a chandelier fell down, killing nobody; but this was at a later concert when the Symphony no.102 was given, not on 11 March 1792 when Haydn first presented the present work, no.96.

The slow introduction, ending with a conspicuous little cadenza for solo oboe, leads to the main faster section which is in Haydn's favourite, so-called 'monothematic' pattern (see above, p.178). As it unfolds there is one special, 'teasing' feature: the development reaches a climax of sound, then two bars of complete silence, and plainly something important is about to happen. We hear the main opening theme again – but it is a 'false' recapitulation, in the wrong key (G instead of the home key, D): not until later, after a little downward scale on the first violins, is the true recapitulation begun, working up to an assertive end. Both 'halves' of this faster section of the movement are marked to be repeated.

A superb specimen of Haydn's typically grand, spacious kind of slow movement follows, with decorated melodies, trills, and occasional, striking rhythmic reinforcement from horns, trumpets and drums. Towards the end two solo violins have their own say, then a long trill is built up by oboes, flutes and bassoon which yields to a final resting point.

The standard minuet movement follows, with a solo oboe winning prominence in the enclosed central trio.

A merry rondo forms the finale, with a catchy main tune relished at each appearance. The scoring is light at first, finally made exciting with bold kettledrum rhythms and (a rarity at this period) a trumpet joining in the actual theme in the very last bars.

Symphony no.100 in G major (Military)

Adagio – Allegro
Allegretto
Minuet: Moderato
Presto
Duration: 28 minutes

The five remaining symphonies selected here are works which Haydn presented on his second visit to London. This symphony's complement of normal instruments includes a pair of clarinets, but only in the second movement. A more special addition to this work is a set of extra percussion, namely the 'military' triangle, cymbals, and bass drum. Their unfamiliar colour, decisive rhythms and extra weight bring a touch of the parade-ground slow march into the second movement. Silent in the first and third movements, they are summoned back to join the jollity of the finale.

The opening introduction is substantial, even suggesting a development of its own. Contrasting with its heavy-sounding final cadence, the high, light sound of one flute and two oboes begins the main faster section. When the music reaches its new key, this theme returns, again with flute and oboe tone only. But what follows is new: a cheery strain on the violins like a whistled street-tune, this impression reinforced when a solo flute joins in. It is this theme which begins the development; and later the flute and oboes (again) can hardly decide whether it is this theme or their 'own' one which will make the bridge to the full orchestra's recapitulation.

The march-like strain of the slow movement begins on the normal orchestra instruments only: Haydn reserves the effect of the added military instruments (plus the orchestra's own kettledrums) until the music moves to the minor key. Towards the end of this movement in C, a trumpet fanfare and kettledrum roll yield to the grandly surprising chord of A flat, but with the home key of C soon to be regained.

The minuet is announced with full sound and weighty rhythm, to which the central Trio at first offers the contrast of a lighter air – but it, too, undergoes a sudden full-orchestral reinforcement.

In 6/8 time, the cheery and ingenious rondo-theme of the fourth movement will later take off on its own developments. The basic rhythm of the movement (*rum-ti-ti, rum-ti-ti*) naturally lends itself to the kettledrums, even to a bar of solo. The entrance of the additional military instruments is again postponed for heightened effect.

Symphony no. 101 in D major (The Clock)

Adagio – Presto
Andante
Minuet: Allegretto
Vivace
Duration: 28 minutes

First given in London on 3 March 1794, the symphony soon acquired its nickname from the 'tick-tock' which is persistently suggested by the slow movement. All movements feature Haydn's standard orchestra (p. 177) with the addition of clarinets.

In the first movement, the slow introduction unusually suggests, by its climbing scale in triple time, the similarly ascending theme which is to initiate the main faster section – marked, for once, *presto* (faster than the usual *allegro*). This *Presto* offers a clear example of Haydn's so-called monothematic plan (see p. 179), in which the eventual arrival of a new key is established not by a new theme but by a varied statement of the old. The exposition ends with a downward scale which vanishes off the bottom of the cellos and double-basses: only in a performance which includes a repeat of this exposition (that is, which goes back to the beginning of the *Presto*) does one get the witty juxtaposition of this descent followed by the climbing figure. The whole of the *Presto* preserves the impetus of jollity.

The attractiveness of the second movement is not just in the allusiveness to a clock. It is in the tune which the 'clock' accompanies, and in the varied way that the ticking itself is presented – now low, now high, now in one instrumentation and now in another. A witty point occurs in a bar of silence when the clock fails to tick, followed by a tentative resumption of music in the 'wrong' key (E flat instead of G), shortly overtaken by a loud, full-orchestral resumption in the right key.

The Minuet encloses, as usual, a contrasting trio, which this time gives a smiling pretence of simplicity, with repeated chords in the strings above which a solo flute climbs in isolation. Later, solo flute and solo bassoon exchange remarks.

The final movement is a rondo of great vivacity. The main key of D major switches for one energetic episode to D minor, after which the main theme returns in the major, but *pianissimo* and in the unexpected texture of a fugue, each of four string sections (without double-basses) delivering the subject in turn. The 'counter-subject' (the fragment of tune delivered simultaneously with the main theme) is heartily embraced when the whole orchestra enters to give the theme a final assertive statement, concluding the symphony with prominent horns, trumpets and drums.

Symphony no.102 in B flat

> Largo – Allegro vivace
> Adagio
> Minuet: Allegro
> Presto
> Duration: 26 minutes

The common naming of Haydn's last twelve symphonies as his 'Salomon set' is incorrect; the last three (nos.102–4) were commissioned not for the concerts promoted by J. P. Salomon but for the 'Opera Concerts' of G. B. Viotti, himself a noted composer. Under those auspices the London public first heard this symphony on 2 February 1794.

The orchestral forces are as above (p.177), but without clarinets. Not that this turns out an impoverishment: a rich, inventive sound is notable in this symphony. Quite exceptional for its time is the use of muted trumpets (in the second movement) and, accompanying them, 'muted' kettledrums, that is, covered with a cloth to deaden the sound.

The slow introduction to this first movement ends with a fanciful little ascent for solo flute. The first violins, announcing the main theme of the faster section, are vigorously reinforced by other instruments on the accented beats. The arrival of a new key brings a disturbance – a loud unison, a bar of silence, a soft string response, then more in similar vein. After a long drum-roll, this exposition ends on strings alone. The development continues with the same energy, then sinks to a pause: a solo flute now softly tries a 'false' recapitulation in the 'wrong' key (C), but the orchestra vehemently squashes the attempt. In due course the recapitulation arrives in its true form with drums to usher it in.

The slow second movement, in F major, presents a complicated tracery of melody on woodwind and strings. Not till the repetition of the principal tune is a new richness of sound added by horns, muted trumpets and covered kettledrums. A continuous thread of thought takes the music to new keys and to a return.

The third movement takes the minuet frame for broad melody with subtle harmonic and rhythmic displacements. The lighter, more open feeling of the central trio is no less subtle: hear the tiny two-note phrases added by the high solo flute.

A vivacious rondo forms the last movement, its playful main theme beckoning the listener through many a turn – this way or that way? After the last occurrence of the playful twists, an unusually full sonority gives a glow to the final page: cellos, double-basses and bassoons, normally sharing the same bass-line, are here given different roles to play.

Symphony no.103 in E flat (The Drum-roll)

Adagio – Allegro con spirito
Andante più tosto allegretto
Minuet [Allegro]
Allegro con spirito
Duration: 27 minutes

Viotti's 'Opera Concerts' in London launched this symphony on 2 March 1795. The nickname *The Drum-roll* appears to have originated a few years later, but as the special opening feature of the symphony it is unmistakable. Moreover, and unusually, Haydn re-quotes the material of the opening *Adagio* section (including the drum-roll) near the end of the movement. Perhaps because of that double helping of slow tempo, the conventionally 'slow' second movement is not so slow as usual, being marked 'or rather *allegretto*'. Clarinets are absent from this movement, present in the others (with otherwise the usual forces – p.177).

The drum-roll (conductors must decide how long, how loud it is to be) leads to a slow-moving bass theme in even notes, a theme destined to reappear within the main, faster section. This section, couched in a tripping 6/8, has a happy second subject on a solo oboe. After an exposition which closes on full orchestra, the development begins softly – but has gone only a little way when the bass theme of the introduction (now speeded up, but still mainly in the bass) makes its contribution. Soon another full orchestral sonority, with drums, builds an expectancy answered by the soft recapitulation of the opening theme. The former oboe subject is now delightfully exchanged between violins and oboe. Dramatically, the opening drum-roll and the bass theme in original slow tempo interrupt before the lively end.

The second, slow (or rather, slowish) movement cloaks its passion in stately gravity. A tune in two parts, in C minor, is the subject of variations. The first statement of the tune (each half repeated) is for strings alone; further statements follow, its various emotional shades interpreted in various scoring. Some statements switch to C major, including one with prominent solo violin and another where the oboes sustain the tune with flute decorations above and a 'popping' bassoon beneath. The insistent rhythm throughout suggests a march, an impression which the ending with its long drum-roll does not dispel.

The third movement follows conventional minuet shape. A main section with sweeping, sonorous melody finds charming contrast in a central trio in which two clarinets exchange graceful phrases while other woodwind (except for a single bassoon) is silent.

The finale announces a sturdy horn-call: loudly by itself, then softly with a lively counter-statement from the violins. Both recur, and the latter theme with its four-note repetition is most ingeniously handled (a commentator has counted more than 150 appearances!) in a genial, spirited flow.

Symphony no.104 in D major (London)

>Adagio – Allegro
>Andante
>Minuet: Allegro
>Spiritoso
>Duration: 29 minutes

The nickname *London* makes no sense, since it could apply to any of Haydn's last twelve symphonies. No.104 was first launched at Viotti's concerts in the spring of 1795, perhaps on 13 April, and was certainly given at a benefit concert for the composer on 4 May. Haydn's full orchestral forces (with clarinets) are used in a work of particular robustness and jollity: it is not just because it is his last symphony that it is one of Haydn's most popular.

There is the usual slow introduction, made especially weighty by

the pauses in the opening couple of bars. The opening theme is due to
recur when a new key is reached (the 'monothematic' construction)
but the fragment that Haydn plucks from it for later development is a
figure of four repeated notes followed by two more notes. This
development reaches a climax of sound and a pause of silence before
the recapitulation starts.

The second movement too is marked by pauses of halted expectation as the tune moves from a fairly simple major-key statement to a
weightier minor-key transformation and then back again. A solo
flute then raises its own questions (with its own pauses!) before the
theme undergoes yet another variant.

Off-beat accents give a special rhythmic quality to the third
(*Minuet*) movement, with an unusual shift of key for the trio: a B-flat
enclosure amid the surrounding D.

In the eighteenth century the low-sustained keynote (a drone bass)
with a simple tune above was an evocation of the bagpipe, not as
Scottish but as a rustic instrument of various peoples. In Haydn's
idiom it goes with uncomplicated merriment, and here provides the
accompaniment and main theme of the fourth movement: the theme
itself being confined to a restricted scale in another 'rustic' gesture.
This is not a rondo but a full sonata-movement with contrasting
second subject, repeated exposition, and then development and
regular recapitulation. A coda follows in which Haydn revels in his
fullest orchestral sound: the drone bass is not only sustained by lower
strings and wind but rhythmically rat-tatted on the kettledrums.

The concertos

Unlike Mozart, Haydn is not as highly rated for his concertos as for
his symphonies. Not himself a solo concert-performer as Mozart
was at the keyboard, he seems not to have developed that dramatic
relationship between solo instrument and orchestra which make
Mozart's concertos so fascinating to follow. Most of Haydn's concertos are early works, among which a violin concerto in C (Hob
VII:1) is occasionally heard. So is one of the later concertos for
harpsichord or piano, in D (Hob XVIII:11).

But it is his two surviving concertos for cello (another is apparently lost) and his single concerto for trumpet which have been most
keenly embraced. Virtuosos of those instruments need to scour the
field for a repertory! Haydn also left a work of the hybrid type for
which he used a French form of title, *Symphonie concertante*, em-

ploying violin, cello, oboe and bassoon. Seemingly written in haste, it does not rank with those last symphonies which he was writing at the time (1792).

Concerto for cello and orchestra in C major (Hob VIIb:1)

Moderato
Adagio
Allegro molto
Duration: 24 minutes

Haydn himself listed a cello concerto in C among his works, but it had disappeared until a set of parts (an early copy, not the composer's original manuscript) was found in Prague in 1961 and given its first modern performance on 19 May 1962 by Milos Sadlo (with Charles Mackerras conducting) at the Prague Spring Festival. Scholars consider the work to date from 1765 or a few years earlier. For much of it, the cello is accompanied by strings only, the two oboes and two horns entering only to signal the ritornello sections which are the structural pillars of the first and third movements: in the second movement they are silent. In the conventional place, towards the end of the first and second movements, occurs a cadenza, fully written out in the cello part discovered. The last movement has no cadenza.

Unusually, the first movement is *not* marked allegro but something slightly less fast. The soloist, who in eighteenth-century performance would join with the orchestral cellos in the opening ritornello section, today probably reserves his or her entry until the grand solo proclamation of the main theme. The soloist proceeds to a new key (G) and new material, presenting the conventional (this time very brief) trill just before the full orchestra re-enters to emphasize the new key. The eventual re-presentation of the thematic material leads to the cadenza.

The soloist takes the lead for most of the peaceful slow movement (in F) which follows a readily appreciable shape of *statement–detour–return*.

The third movement, unusually in a classical concerto, is the longest (in number of bars) and seemingly the weightiest: not a light rondo but laid out in the same, full-tensioned form as the first movement. The cellist's command is exerted in rapid passages, unusually high notes, double-stopping and finally a climax of scales and trills.

Concerto for cello and orchestra in D major (Hob VIIb:2)

> Allegro moderato
> Adagio
> Allegro
> Duration: 28 minutes

Previously conjectured to be the composition of Haydn's cellist of Esterházy, Anton Kraft (who was also Haydn's pupil in composition), this concerto is now confidently ascribed to Haydn himself, with the date 1781. It is an unassuming, charming piece in which the cello seems to chat with the small orchestra (2 oboes, 2 horns, strings) rather than engage in bold confrontation.

In the opening movement, the solo cello at first simply doubles the line that the orchestral violas are playing (it gets the soloist warmed up and in tune with the orchestra!), then is heard in an accompanying figure, but soon takes what has been established as the main tune. After announcing the second subject in A, the soloist with the conventional trill heralds the full orchestra's emphasis of the new key. The music is shaped by the use of three levels of sound – full orchestra, soloist plus strings, and soloist alone: a cadenza (we have no surviving original) is envisaged at the usual point near the end.

The slow movement is dominated by the opening, self-contained eight-bar tune on cello and strings, repeated with fuller scoring. The final return makes room for a cadenza.

The 6/8 rhythm of the finale displays a recurring tune which reminded the great analyst Donald Francis Tovey of 'Here we come gathering nuts in May'. The music is strengthened by a turn to D minor and an emergence from it. The cellist displays energetic command with octave passages, but it is left to the orchestra to bring the lively movement to a close.

Concerto for trumpet and orchestra in E flat major (Hob VIIc:1)

> Allegro
> Andante
> Allegro
> Duration: 14 minutes

A recording made by the British trumpeter George Eskdale in the

1930s awoke the public to this sprightly and charming concerto, which had previously been little known. It now ranks as easily the most familiar work for trumpet and orchestra. Though modern soloists frequently play it as their normal instrument in B flat or C, it was designed for a higher-pitched and more brilliant trumpet in E flat. The concerto was composed for Anton Weidinger, a Viennese trumpeter, who had developed an instrument with finger-operated keys – not as efficient as the valve system which was to be later invented, but at least permitting chromatic passages impossible on the unmodified tube of the earlier trumpet.

This happens to be Haydn's last purely orchestral work (that is, not counting those for voices and orchestra). Weidinger is known to have given the first public performance on 28 March 1800 in Vienna. The orchestration rather surprisingly includes 2 further trumpets (Haydn might have dispensed with them in order to emphasize the soloist's tone still more) as well as 2 each of flutes, oboes (no clarinets), bassoons and horns, together with kettledrums and strings. The first movement requires the insertion of a cadenza: no cadenzas by Haydn or by the original soloist survive.

After a condensed orchestral presentation of the main themes, the trumpet gives a full exposition which demonstrates its 'singing' capacity as well as its authority. After its second theme – in B flat, with sustained long notes – the trumpet hands over briefly to the orchestra before joining in a lively development. The recapitulation brings sprightly descending triplets to the solo part. After a cadenza, the orchestra alone provides a brisk conclusion.

The orchestral opening to the second movement, in A flat, is as smoothly lyrical as that in any of Haydn's symphonies. The solo role is like that of a singer – with a main tune, middle section, return of the main tune, and tenderly lingering coda.

The finale is a cheerful rondo, the opening tune given quietly by the strings, loudly by full orchestra (with a new tune added, in B flat), and then by the soloist. In due course the 'added' tune finds its way to the home key of E flat (solo trumpet and first violins). There is some entertaining dialogue between orchestral horns and the solo instrument before the work ends with the trumpet's traditional fanfare figures.

HINDEMITH

1895–1963

Troubled political times affected the life and musical career of Paul Hindemith. Having become famous for an 'advanced' musical style, freely discordant and cutting, he could not pursue his art freely in his native Germany once the Nazi regime (from 1933) had begun to enforce its cultural dictatorship. So Hindemith (though not a Jew, and therefore not forced into exile like Schoenberg) voluntarily emigrated to the United States in 1939, eventually taking American citizenship. But he returned to Europe after the Second World War and died in Germany.

His music (like Bartók's in this respect, though not otherwise) generally avoids emotional or descriptive titles. *Concert music* (in German, *Konzertmusik*) is the heading for three different works, of which the last, for strings and brass, celebrated the 50th anniversary of the Boston Symphony Orchestra in 1951. Though some of his vocal music written in the United States has English texts, the two orchestral compositions by which he is best known both place him firmly in a German tradition: the three-movement symphony based on his opera *Mathis the Painter* (*Mathis der Maler*), 1934, and the work discussed below.

Symphonic Metamorphoses of themes by Carl Maria von Weber

> Allegro
> 'Turandot' Scherzo
> Andantino
> March
> Duration: 19 minutes

The unique title *Symphonic Metamorphoses* indicates that Hindemith has given a free treatment to themes originally derived from music by Weber (who is separately dealt with in this book: see p. 362). The result is a rather playful work which has proved one of the most approachable of Hindemith's. The New York Philharmonic Orchestra, under Artur Rodzinski, gave the first performance on 24 January 1944.

The designation of the second movement makes its source easy to trace – Weber's overture to Schiller's play *Turandot*, itself derived from the same Italian play which was to lead to Puccini's opera more than a century later. The title-role is that of a Chinese princess, and the atmosphere is evoked by Weber's (and Hindemith's) use of a supposedly authentic Chinese melody. For the other movements Hindemith gives no clue in his score, but they have been traced to various pieces by Weber for piano duet.

The orchestration includes an unusually large variety of percussion, shared between three players in addition to the kettle-drummer.

The music has a forthright, square-built feeling (several sections are literally repeated, which makes for easy recognition). The first movement, in A minor, is dominated by the theme delivered immediately by the first violins. Rather teasingly, the final statement of that theme is in D minor, not in the home key, but the composer immediately asserts a bright, A major ending.

The second movement, in F, opens with a prominence of solo flute and bells – lending 'oriental' colour to the 'Chinese' theme which, however, carries a twentieth-century Western twist of its own. The theme is subjected to continuous variations displaying various sections of the orchestra. After a climax, trombones begin a brass fugue. Finally, and quite unexpectedly, the kettledrummer delivers the theme while the other percussionists provide accompaniment.

A wistful third movement, in B flat minor, sets up a tune in gently swaying rhythm (the *siciliana* rhythm of the Bach period). Later the smoothness of that theme is counterpointed by a high, flowery, very rapidly articulated outpouring from a solo flute.

The fourth movement is also in B flat (minor and major). The brisk march, with a definite military-band flavour, presents two main themes – one heard almost immediately with the tune in the woodwind against a snare drum beat; another, later, from the horns against rapid triplets in the woodwind.

HOLST

1874–1934

Experience as a professional trombonist enhanced Holst's skill as an orchestral composer, just as his celebrated work as teacher (at St Paul's Girls' School and Morley College in London) guided him in writing so inventively for choirs and amateurs. English-born but of Swedish descent, Gustav Holst (originally 'von Holst') shared many ideas with his close friend Ralph Vaughan Williams – among them a willingness to find inspiration in English folk-music. Both enriched the repertory of the military band and brass band as well as the orchestra: his *Hammersmith* (prelude and scherzo), sometimes heard orchestrally, is a military band original.

As well as *The Planets*, Holst's orchestral works include the much-liked *St Paul's Suite* for strings (written for his school, and incorporating the folk-tune *Greensleeves* in the finale) and *Beni Mora*, an 'oriental suite' with some deliberate evocation of Arab music. The ballet music from his opera *The Perfect Fool* is also heard at concerts, as is the *Fugal Overture* which was used for that opera.

Suite The Planets

    Mars, the bringer of war
    Venus, the bringer of peace
    Mercury, the winged messenger
    Jupiter, the bringer of jollity
    Saturn, the bringer of old age
    Uranus, the magician
    Neptune, the mystic
    Duration: 52 minutes

The new, enlarged orchestras with which Richard Strauss and Stravinsky had transported their listeners to new excitement were not readily available to British composers under the concert conditions which were then current. In staking his conception of *The Planets* on just such a large orchestra, Holst was venturesome, particularly because this was the time of the First World War with its increased economic difficulties. By the private generosity of a wealthy fellow-composer, H. Balfour Gardiner, Holst was lucky enough to have a private performance of this work in London, conducted by Adrian (not yet Sir Adrian) Boult, on 29 September 1918. Presented to the public, under the baton of Albert Coates in London on 15 November 1920, it became his most successful work.

The significances which Holst attached to the seven planets are mostly unusual but serve to characterize the movements sharply – all of them ending in normal, self-contained fashion except the last, where the sound vanishes in the wordless voices of a female choir, which takes part only in this final movement. The orchestra, apart from sheer size, is notable for including a tenor tuba (euphonium) and the rare *bass oboe* or *heckelphone* (Delius also used it). An organ is also required. The full listing of instruments is: 4 flutes (2 doubling piccolo, 1 doubling alto flute), 3 oboes (1 doubling bass oboe), english horn, 3 clarinets and bass clarinet, 3 bassoons and double-bassoon; 6 horns, 4 trumpets, 3 trombones, tenor tuba and bass tuba; kettledrums (2 players), triangle, snare drum, bass drum, cymbals, tambourine, gong, tubular bells, glockenspiel, xylophone (4 players), celesta, 2 harps, organ and strings.

Mars menaces in an unrelenting 5/4 time. The originality of scoring is immediate – the kettledrums struck with wooden-headed sticks, the strings played *col legno* (with the back of the bow), the gong keeping up a continuous rumble, the two harps reinforcing the rhythm with low sonorities. Chords clash unresolved as the full brass brings a climax. Later, a tenor tuba solo delivers a new threat, backed by trumpet fanfares.

Where the sound of Mars was dense, that of **Venus** is airy – a slow tune rising on a solo horn, with flutes and oboes answering. A change of mood brings a violin solo; the celesta enters, its faint tracery of sound tapering off in the final bars.

Mercury brings flying sound, with woodwind dominating at first. A theme in stronger rhythm carries authority. A solo violin intervenes. Finally the woodwind fly upwards (from bassoons and double-bassoons to 2 flutes and 2 piccolos) and the messenger has gone.

The best-known of the movements is **Jupiter** (raided by other hands to produce the hymn tune, 'I vow to thee, my country'). Six horns begin a jovial tune in irregular rhythm. Later a trumpet interjects characteristically and the horns are again thrust forward for a theme like a bell chime. A large section of the movement passes before the 'hymn tune' arrives on the strings. It will later return in unexpected form, penetrating through a swirl of musical clouds. Both cloud and hymn tune are blown away by a final, brief presto.

Saturn symbolizes old age in an endlessly repetitive, dragging theme, given to low-sounding chords on 3 flutes plus alto flute. An upward theme slowly rises from the trombones. The flute theme flows in new urgency, summoning the full orchestra including the jangle of tubular bells. The end is soft but uneasy, the pedals of the organ contributing single low notes.

Uranus opens disturbingly on long, loud notes delivered by the brass and kettledrums. Bassoons follow, leading the combined woodwind into a chopping theme which almost suggests that this magician is the one of *The Sorcerer's Apprentice* (see p. 140). A new, slightly smoother theme also chooses to enter on a solo bassoon, transferring to solo clarinet. Eventually comes a huge climax requiring a glissando (slide) up the keys of the full organ – and suddenly cut off, leaving only a faint sound of seven string-players. But the magician has another tricky reappearance to make.

In **Neptune, the Mystic** the orchestra is instructed to play with 'dead tone', very softly throughout. Sequences of chords ascend or oscillate; an eerie theme arises high on muted violins; a misty effect is set up by harps, celesta and the organ's low pedal sounds. Imperceptibly, wordless female voices enter. They arrive at an alternation of strange chords which they repeat (the instruments falling silent) 'until the sound is lost in the distance'.

IVES

1874–1954

Now recognized as one of the most adventurous and prophetic of twentieth-century composers, Charles Ives attracted scant recognition even in his native America until the last two decades of his long life. Nor did he seek it. Composing at his own pace (he earned his living in his own insurance business), he lived as a virtual recluse, never went to concerts, did not own a radio or record-player, and showed little concern for the generally acknowledged masters of modern music. But his music went into regions of atonality ('keylessness') and clashes of one sound-stream against another, long before these became commonplaces of the European avant-garde.

With such modernisms went a deep attachment to traditional hymns, band music, and other musical manifestations of American community life. Of his four symphonies, the third was completed by 1904 but received its first performance only in 1946, thereafter being widely heard; the Fourth Symphony dates from 1910–16 but reached its first complete performance only posthumously, in 1965. Not numbered among these is *A Symphony: Holidays*, in four separable parts of which *Decoration Day* is most often heard.

The Unanswered Question

Duration: 8 minutes

Completed by 1908, but long remaining unpublished and unperformed, this work is scored for four flutes, a solo trumpet, and a 'distant choir' of strings. Some optional replacements for the solo trumpet and two of the flutes are specified in the score.

A hushed, long-sustained chord of G on muted strings begins and ends the piece. The solo trumpet enters with a melody which completely cuts across that chord as though not inhabiting the same world. A clue may be sought in the composer's own words (quoted in David Wooldridge's biography):

The strings play *ppp* throughout, with no change of tempo. They are to represent 'The Silences of the Druids' who speak, see and hear nothing. The trumpet intones 'The Perennial Question of Existence' and states it in the same tone of voice each time. But the hunt for the 'Invisible Answer' undertaken by the flutes and other human beings becomes gradually more active, faster and louder through an *animando* to a *con fuoco*. The 'Fighting Answerers', as time goes on, seem to realize a futility, and begin to mock 'The Question' – the strife is over for the moment. After they disappear, 'The Question' is asked again for the last time, and the 'Silences' are heard beyond in undisturbed solitude . . .

The first datable performance of this work (and of a companion-piece, *Central Park in the Dark*) took place in New York on 11 May 1946. The conductor was the distinguished composer Elliott Carter, who afterwards recalled: 'I wrote to Mrs Ives to ask if these were in fact first performances and for other programme information. She wrote back a very charming letter quoting her ill husband, that they would not want to say those works were having their premieres – Mr Ives wanted to be fair to those 'old fellers' who had played them between the acts of a theatrical performance in 1907 or 1908.'

JANÁČEK

1854–1928

Now considered the most distinguished of Czech composers to arise since Dvořák's day, Leoš Janáček never knew in his lifetime the international success which his operas have come to enjoy in the theatre and on records. He made his home in Brno, where he had been a boy chorister, and led an active life as conductor and as teacher and conservatory director. He was a diligent collector of his country's folk-songs, making many choral arrangements of them; his music in general shows their influence as well as that of the melodic and rhythmic characteristics of Czech speech (and his own local Moravian variant).

The preludes to *Jenufa* (staged 1904) and to some other operas can be (questionably) detached for orchestral performance. Janáček's designated orchestral works are few: they include some folk-dance suites and, notably, *Taras Bulba*, a descriptive work founded on the novella of Ukrainian heroism by the Russian writer Gogol.

Sinfonietta

Allegretto
Andante
Moderato
Allegretto
Andante con moto
Duration: 25 minutes

At 72, Janáček delivered a work which carries a national feeling as well as showing his own striking individuality in form and instrumentation. Despite the title's suggestion of a 'little symphony', it rejects traditional symphonic moulds and is rather a suite in five movements. It was first performed in Prague, under the conductorship of Václav Talich, on 29 June 1926.

The unique orchestration gives the *Sinfonietta* a special impact, but also restricts the opportunity for performance. In addition to 'normal' constituents, the orchestra must be augmented by an extra brass contingent of 9 extra trumpets, 2 bass trumpets and 2 tenor tubas (in British terms, euphoniums). The work originated in a commission to write fanfares for a public exercise of the Czech gymnastic movement, Sokol, in Prague. Hence comes the first movement of the work, which uses only the additional brass instruments plus kettledrums.

The other movements originally bore the titles *Castle–Convent–Street–Town Hall*, representing the city of Brno, where the composer lived. But they may have set up misleading expectations – there is no conventional church sound in the second movement, for example – and do not appear on the published score. These movements employ the main orchestral: 4 flutes (1 doubling piccolo), 2 oboes (1 doubling english horn), 2 clarinets (1 doubling high clarinet in E flat), bass clarinet, 4 horns, 3 trumpets, 3 trombones, tuba, kettledrums, cymbals, glockenspiel, harp and strings. The finale brings back the additional brass.

All the movements have internal changes of tempo (only the opening tempo indications are given above). Throughout, the construction in fixed sections or blocks, often immediately repeated, clarifies the impact. The initial Fanfare, the shortest movement, is based on a single theme – mostly in rhythms conventionally suited to a fanfare but with a brief central section in a sort of waltz-time.

Another type of fanfare will peal from the trumpets to crown the second movement which begins with a few introductory bars followed by the suggestion of a rather grotesque dance.

A slower, smoother theme on muted strings opens the third movement, with a later, more static theme on brass chords. Both these recur, the opening theme eventually dying away.

The fourth movement is built from a single, polka-like theme which, at the start, is lightly pattered out by the three trumpets in unison. The end is a brief, highly accented *prestissimo*.

A slow theme on three flutes which opens the fifth movement is extended and, after contrasting material, will later return. Then occurs the grand climax of the whole work. The opening movement returns literally, in its special brass scoring – but this time it is surrounded by trills from woodwind and strings. Seven additional bars give a blazing conclusion.

KHACHATURIAN

1903–78

From the late 1930s Aram Khachaturian became famous as a representative of the 'cultural nationalism' encouraged by the Soviet rulers. The culture in this case is that of Armenia, on whose folk-music the composer drew. Concertos for piano, for violin and for cello are among his works as well as three symphonies. But his chief fame is probably in numbers from the two ballets *Gayaneh* (see below) and *Spartacus* (1954).

Three dances from Gayaneh

Dance of the young maidens
Lullaby
Sabre Dance
Duration: 15 minutes

Produced on 9 December 1942 by the ballet company of the Kirov Theatre, Leningrad, when it was in war-time evacuation in the city of Molotov, *Gayaneh* has a patriotic plot. A villainous husband, a traitor to the Soviet Union, joins a group of smugglers and attempts to murder his wife, Gayaneh. Animated by Armenian folk-dance elements, the score is optimistic in tone and the story has a happy ending. Several suites have been extracted for concert performance. The most popular numbers have proved to be these three, the 'Sabre Dance' achieving an extraordinary success in various arrangements. In its original form the colourful scoring includes an alto saxophone and a full percussion section, as well as 2 flutes and piccolo, 2 oboes and english horn, 2 clarinets and bass clarinet, 2 bassoons, 4 horns, a cornet as well as 3 trumpets, 3 trombones and tuba, harp and strings.

The 'Dance of the Young Maidens', marked *allegro*, has a graceful opening tune which later acquires a counter-melody on the solo cornet, unusually backed by a tubaphone (a percussion instrument like a glockenspiel, but with an array of small tubes instead of metal bars).

The 'Lullaby', in the slow, rocking 6/8 rhythm often used for such pieces, presents its chief melody on the flute, then on muted violins. With piquant interjections from other woodwind, the music rises to a climax, then subsides.

The 'Sabre Dance' is marked *presto* and is characterized by the percussive, athletic rhythms set forth at the opening. Over it a quick theme, starting with the same note 15 times over, is hurled out, the xylophone's tone being prominent. The 4/4 beat changes to 3/4, with a more sustained tune from saxophone and cellos; then the former headlong drive is resumed.

KODÁLY

1882–1967

Zoltán Kodály has a double fame: as the international representative of Hungarian music (along with Bartók and Dohnányi) in his time, and as the deviser of an internationally renowned educational method based on singing and group activity. But the two are in fact related, as parts of Kodály's evident belief in a 'people's' music. Many of his orchestral and other works have Hungarian national associations, apart from those which are actual arrangements of traditional material, like the two orchestral sets, *Dances of Marosszek* and *Dances of Galánta* (1930, 1933).

Kodály's orchestral works, though not numerous, span his life. Before he was twenty-five he had written *Summer Evening* for orchestra, later subjected to a revised orchestration; in his late seventies (1957–61) he wrote a symphony. Better known, though not as well known as the work treated below, are the *Variations on a Hungarian Folksong* (also called *Peacock Variations*), first heard in 1939, and the Concerto for Orchestra written for the Chicago Symphony and first heard in 1939.

Suite, Háry János

> The Tale Begins
> The Viennese Musical Clock
> Song
> The Battle and Defeat of Napoleon
> Intermezzo
> The Emperor and his Court
> Duration: 23 minutes

Háry János is a light-hearted opera (sometimes called 'a musical play') on a Hungarian national theme which was produced in Budapest on 16 October 1926. Its comically boasting hero is named in Hungarian fashion, surname first. Though the opera has travelled little, the orchestral suite drawn from it has become the composer's most popular work. It opens with an orchestral 'sneeze' which is supposed to guarantee the truthfulness of the events narrated by János about his feats of fighting and diplomacy in the war between Austrian and Napoleonic France. The order of items in the suite does not correspond to their operatic sequence but form a lively contrast.

The novel participant in the large orchestra is a *cimbalom*, the traditional Hungarian dulcimer (like a small harp laid on its side and struck with hammers) – an instrument sometimes imitated in earlier concert music of Hungarian flavour, but here brought into the orchestra. The other requirements are 2 flutes and piccolo, 3 clarinets, alto saxophone, 2 bassoons, 4 horns, 3 trumpets *and* 3 cornets, 3 trombones and tuba, kettledrums, snare drum, bass drum, triangle, celesta, piano and strings.

After the truth-telling 'sneeze', the first movement presents a questioning theme. Swelling to a climax and dying away to a reminiscence of the opening, the music presumably evokes the power of the narrator's imagination.

In the second movement, the chiming and movements of the Viennese musical clock are amusingly depicted on woodwind, piano, tubular bells and other percussion – with strings and brass (except for horns) silent throughout.

The 'Song' of the third movement, a genuine folk melody, represents the love of János and his betrothed. It is introduced by a solo viola. The clang of the cimbalom is then heard, persisting when the melody is begun on an oboe and then passing to other instruments.

The 'Battle and Defeat of Napoleon' has an obviously parodied air as the trombones' tune is heard over a beat of bass drum and cymbals. After a musical 'battle' a big thud and a perceptible pause indicate the defeat: a funeral march follows with a lamenting alto saxophone. In this movement also the strings take no part.

The ensuing 'Intermezzo' again features the cimbalom, this time in a fiery dance. Kodaly borrowed the tune from an early nineteenth-century source: it is an example of traditional Hungarian *verbunkos* (recruiting dance). Its strenuous D minor has a gentler interlude in D major.

A toy-like fantasy seems to show in the processional music entitled 'Entrance of the Emperor and his Court' (the Austrian emperor is meant). Trumpets and cornets unite in a cheeky, mock-pompous theme and the good humour continues to the end.

LALO

1823–92

A piano concerto, a violin concerto, and a cello concerto are among the works of Edouard Lalo. None of these is often heard, but the success of the violin concerto when launched in Paris in 1874 led to the creation of the composer's most celebrated work, the *Symphonie espagnole*. In both of these the soloist was Pablo Sarasate, the Spanish virtuoso who enjoyed an unsurpassed fame at the time.

Lalo, though born in the French city of Lille and trained at the Paris Conservatoire, was himself of Spanish descent. Professionally active as violinist and viola-player, he was slow to win fame as a composer and passed his 65th birthday before achieving success in opera with *Le Roi d'Ys*.

Symphonie espagnole *for violin and orchestra,* opus 21

> Allegro non troppo
> Scherzando: allegro molto
> Intermezzo
> Andante
> Rondo
> Duration: 31 minutes

The curious title of 'Spanish Symphony' seemingly points to the avoidance of the three-movement pattern which is standard for works called 'concerto'. Nevertheless, the soloist behaves very much as in a concerto, with a particular emphasis on dazzling display. Sarasate, to whom the work was dedicated, gave its first performance in Paris on 7 February 1875, Edouard Colonne being the conductor.

Triangle and harp are the picturesque and (for a concerto) somewhat unusual additions to an orchestra of piccolo, 2 flutes, 2 oboes, 2

clarinets, 2 bassoons, 4 horns, 2 trumpets, 3 trombones, kettledrums, bass drum and strings.

Orchestra and soloist begin the first movement by offering a hint
of the main thematic idea, and then – after the violin's two sweeping
upward scales – present the main statement of the idea, in D minor.
After a climax and a moment when the violin is heard alone, a change
to B flat major brings the gentler second subject on bassoon and
lower strings, then on the solo instrument. The rest of the movement follows sonata form. There is a development, followed (after a
recurrence of the soloists' sweeping upward scales) by a recapitulation in which the second subject duly falls into D major. A coda
brings the end into D minor again.

All the brighter, for the previous movement's ending, is the
sudden G major with which the strings now give out their guitar-like
pizzicato. Over the orchestra's syncopated phrases floats the violin,
with an airy tune and further cross-rhythms. Later comes something
more languorous, in a minor key, but suggestions of the opening
section constantly interrupt. Eventually this opening section itself
returns, but the end is (rather surprisingly) quiet, and in G minor.

The third movement borrows the dance-rhythm of the *habanera*.
The orchestra begins and the violin follows with a swaying, persuasive, but rather sad tune in A minor. A contrasting middle section in
6/8 time later leads back to a varied repeat of the first section.

The almost sombre, chorale-like opening of the fourth movement
is the perfect counterpoise to the rest of the work. The theme begins
in D minor, and even when it later touches the placid region of D
major the cellos keep up an undertone of restless repeated notes.

The *Rondo* which constitutes the fifth and final movement begins
with an orchestral introduction. The soloist then presents the main
theme, in D major. A contrasting section is rather martial at first, the
violin later becoming more passionate (*habanera* rhythm again). The
main tune comes back in F sharp, B flat and finally D once more – full
orchestra, with tambourine and triangle, after which the soloist leads
the dance-like progress to the closing bars.

LIGETI

b.1923

The cultivation of the more radical kinds of modern music was as severely restricted in the Communist regimes immediately after the Second World War as it had been in Nazi Germany. Composers wishing to join that radical stream had little recourse but to emigrate – if possible. In the wake of the Hungarian political upheavals of 1956, György Ligeti left for the West and has since lived mainly in Vienna. From 1960 he was recognized as a leading innovator, particularly in composing with whole blocks of shaded sound at the sacrifice of clearly defined melody and rhythm.

Orchestral works which best show his method include *Atmospheres* (below) and *Lontano* (1967). Earlier he had composed a 'symphonic poem' not for orchestra but for 100 metronomes controlled to run at different speeds – a type of creation characteristic of one side of Ligeti. A liking for the jokey and satiric is also evident in his opera, *The Great Macabre* (1978).

Atmospheres

Duration: 9 minutes

The novel and complex scoring of this work is its most striking feature. Each instrument, including those of the string section, has its independent part, these instruments comprising: 4 piccolos, 4 flutes, 4 clarinets, 4 high clarinets in E flat, 3 bassoons, double-bassoon, 6 horns, 4 trumpets, 4 trombones, a piano (with two players who use brushes and cloths to sweep across the strings) 14 first and 14 second violins, 10 violas, 10 cellos and 8 double-basses. There are no percussion instruments. With the web of sound so constituted, the composer aimed to establish a new kind of continuous musical texture, having 'no contours or forms but, instead, an uninhabited, imaginary musical space'. Dedicated to the memory of the composer's fellow Hungarian Mátyás Seiber (1905–60), who spent most of his creative life in Britain as composer and conductor, *Atmospheres* was first performed at Donaueschingen (Germany) under Hans Rosbaud on 22 October 1961 and achieved fame through its incorporation in Stanley Kubrick's film, *2001*, alongside such unlikely companions as Johann Strauss's *Blue Danube* waltz.

Written in 22 sections, each of which is precisely timed in seconds, the music presents a kind of blurred sound which yields to gradual, sometimes microscopic changes. Once the listener has absorbed the shock of the 'blur', the music reveals an appreciable flow between extremities of dense and spaced-out sounds, highs and lows, louds and softs. One effect, nearly five minutes from the start, is particularly striking: a very dense, very loud sound of strings suddenly ceases, and then there is a concentration of sound in the extremely narrow region comprising middle C plus the two notes either side of it (B and C sharp). Shortly afterwards the various instruments are again spaced out over a huge spectrum in long-sustained chords reminiscent of the beginning. The final audible sound consists only of the faintest brushing of the piano strings.

But it is not the end of the piece. The last of the composer's measured sections comprises 19 seconds of silence for players and audience – after which, presumably, the conductor may put down the baton!

LISZT

1811–86

Apart from his celebrity as the greatest, most sought-after pianist of his time, and also as a conductor (he gave the premiere of Wagner's *Lohengrin*), Liszt was a composer of the greatest historical importance. His harmonic language bridges the gap between Chopin and Wagner and some of the chord-formations associated particularly with Wagner can be found in previous works by Liszt. Sharing in the general tendency of Romantic composers to associate music with description or narration, Liszt pioneered (and is sometimes said to have invented) the extended, one-movement, multi-tempo orchestral form called the symphonic poem, bearing the title of a non-musical event or topic.

His two piano concertos, like his equally famous Piano Sonata in B minor, appeal by marrying his pianistic dazzle to his pioneering of a unified form. But modern taste has moved against his orchestral works in general. Even in such a superior example of the symphonic poem as *Mazeppa* (1854, after Victor Hugo's poem of unconquerable heroism), the depiction of successive moods tends to seem too blatant, lacking the lyric pathos that Tchaikovsky was later to bring to musical narrative. Nevertheless, *Les Préludes* (below) manages to survive as an example of this type. Two descriptive symphonies, the *Faust* Symphony (after Goethe) of 1857 and the *Dante* Symphony of ten years later, have considerable intrinsic interest but remain rarities today.

The piano concertos

Apart from some smaller compositions and arrangements for piano and orchestra, including a celebrated version of Schubert's *Wanderer Fantasia* (originally for piano alone), Liszt left two full-scale piano concertos. Conforming to the Romantic ideal, they break free of the traditional form of three separate movements. The brilliant writing of the solo parts is supported by a large orchestra; trombones had been freely used in symphonies beginning with Beethoven's, but their presence in a concerto was novel.

Concerto for piano and orchestra No.1 in E flat major

> Allegro maestoso, tempo giusto, *leading to*
> Quasi adagio – Allegretto vivace – Allegro animato, *leading to*
> Allegro marziale animato
> Duration: 19 minutes

Attached to the grand-ducal court of Weimar as musical director from 1842, Liszt was the soloist there in the first performance of this work on 17 February 1855, with the visiting Berlioz as conductor. The printed score sets out the work in three movements, as above, but concert programmes occasionally give four, splitting the central movement into its slow and scherzo parts; and since the scherzo is followed by yet another section, a further division could be made. In performance, however, the whole concerto is given without pause. The listener encounters music which seamlessly unfolds, with an obvious relation between the end and the beginning. Liszt's idea of unifying a long musical work is firmly achieved.

The unusual constituent of the orchestra is a triangle – the use of which in a concerto was something that Liszt felt he had to defend. Cymbals are also used. Otherwise the orchestra is standard for a mid-nineteenth-century concerto: 2 flutes and 1 piccolo, 2 each of oboes, clarinets, bassoons, horns, trumpets; three trombones, kettledrums and strings. To the strings in octaves is given the proclamation of the opening theme, which serves as a kind of motto for the work. It is said that Liszt's private vocalization of it took the German form, 'Das versteht Ihr alle nicht', which might be translated in the same rhythm as 'None of you can understand!'

The first movement is quite short – hardly more than an exposition, which is to find its recapitulation, later in the concerto. It opens with the main theme (the 'motto') on the strings, punctuated by exclamations from the wind instruments. The piano storms in with a cadenza. Then the main body of the first movement begins in exchanges between orchestra and soloist, who pursues an individual train of thought, joined shortly by a solo clarinet, then by other instruments. The emotion swells and dies down; as the theme is quietly restated on the strings at its original pitch, the piano's *arpeggio* prepares for a transition without pause to . . .

. . . the second movement. Cellos and double-basses, muted, offer in subdued tones a theme which will come into flower on the piano in B major. After a climax, a trill on the piano accompanies a new theme on a solo flute, continued by a solo clarinet. There is no development, the music passing immediately to the scherzo – for so this light, capricious movement may be called. The tinkling triangle, the skittering octaves of the piano and the trills of a solo flute all contribute. Vigorous dialogue continues until the piano breaks loose for a cadenza in which the 'motto' is restated. The piano leads the way to a recapitulation (*Allegro animato*) of material from the first movement. The rhythm of the 'motto' is firmly recalled on a kettledrum and the second theme (originally on a solo flute) is now transferred to an oboe. Excited octaves for the piano make a transition towards . . .

. . . the finale. The 'martial' air indicated in the movement's heading is fulfilled in the firm rhythm and in the beat of cymbals (silent till now!) and triangle. Trombones reinforced by bassoons and double-basses deliver a heavy theme which is derived from the piano's theme in the second movement. Similarly the theme at which the piano arrives (after some preliminary flourishes) is based on the flute and clarinet theme from that earlier movement. The scherzo element also reappears (with triangle) and the motto-theme is summoned for the grandiose ending of the work. On the way, the piano's full technical range is displayed – not only the soloist's mastery of rapidly articulated passages of all kinds, but the instrument's ability to dominate the orchestra in heroic posture.

Concerto for piano and orchestra No.2 in A major

> Adagio sostenuto assai, *leading to*
> Allegro agitato assai, *leading to*
> Allegro moderato, *leading to*
> Allegro deciso, *leading to*
> Marziale: un poco meno allegro, *leading to*
> Allegro animato
> Duration: 20 minutes

As musical director at the grand-ducal court of Weimar, Liszt directed the first performance of this concerto on 7 January 1857 with his pupil, Hans von Bronsart, as the soloist. Like his previous concerto it is in one continuous movement, freely constructed so as to appear as a unity despite the variations of tempo. As well as strings, the orchestration consists of 3 flutes (one interchangeable with piccolo), 2 oboes, 2 clarinets, 2 bassoons, 2 horns, 2 trumpets, 3 trombones and tuba, kettledrums and (a novelty for a piano concerto, especially of that period) cymbals.

The first theme, announced by a clarinet, is transformed by the piano. A new tune (marked 'dreamy') is announced by a solo horn as the piano line expands in florid arabesques. The piano breaks off to announce a stronger, almost martial theme in D minor, which is reinforced by the kettledrums. With a cascade of descending notes from the piano, the music turns to its second section (*Allegro agitato assai*) which corresponds to a scherzo, with heavy accents in 6/8 time.

After a climax for the orchestra alone, the soloist joins in, passing to a tiny cadenza and to a new section which is a sort of miniature slow movement (though marked *Allegro moderato*). Here, in D flat, against a rippling accompaniment, a cello reminds us of the opening theme. Later, a new, impassioned theme is added by the soloist and taken up by an oboe and then by a flute. A long cadenza leads to the *Allegro deciso*, a forceful fantasy in which piano and orchestra confront one another with grandiose gestures.

Now comes the *Marziale* section – the real point of arrival after all that has gone before, when the initial key of A major is regained and the opening theme is declaimed by soloist and orchestra over a martial rhythm, emphasized by the trombones. Cymbals, heard for the first time, add their clashing excitement. The piano, with all the technical resources and fiery expression at the soloist's command, now takes the lead right up to the end of the work.

Les Préludes

Duration: 16 minutes

The 'symphonic poem', or descriptive piece of orchestral music (p. 14), is said to be Liszt's invention; but whereas most such works have a narrative thread, a minority do not – such as this one. It was first given under the composer's own direction at Weimar on 28 February 1854. The orchestration calls for 3 flutes, 2 oboes, 2 clarinets, 2 bassoons, 4 horns, 2 trumpets, three trombones, tuba and strings, with the kettledrums supplemented by bass drum, snare drum, and cymbals. A harp plays a characteristic role.

By no means constituting a *prelude* to something else in the musical sense, the work takes its title from a now forgotten poem by the contemporary French writer, Lamartine. From it Liszt derived the inscription on the score: 'What is life but a series of preludes to that unknown song, the first solemn note of which is sounded by death? The enchanted dawn of life is love, but what is the destiny where the first delights of happiness are not interrupted by storm, whose fatal breath dissipates its beautiful illusions? . . .' It is known, however, that Liszt composed the music before annexing the poem.

Two quiet Cs from the *pizzicato* strings herald the quick opening theme in C major around which most of the work is built. It swells to vigorous assertion on the brass in a new tempo. A second main theme, corresponding to 'Love' in the verbal programme, undulates on the horns in a gentle E major. (The sentiment makes this an appropriate entry point for the harp.) After long-held notes on high woodwind, the 'storm' of life sweeps in. Repose arrives in a 'pastoral' section, with a theme on the horn which passes to the oboe. A further change brings martial confidence, with emphasis from the 'military' percussion, and the opening theme in its brass version concludes the work.

LUTOSŁAWSKI

b.1913

Together with Penderecki, Witold Lutosławski represents the emergence of modern Polish music into the forefront of the European musical scene. Like all composers working in Poland immediately after the Second World War, he was at first under the restriction of conforming to the conservative, nationalist style ordained from the Soviet Union. A Concerto for Orchestra (composed 1950–54) is among works of this period which won him notice.

Greater freedom led him at different times in different directions – in the use of quarter-tones (in a Prelude and Fugue for 13 strings), of the 12-note row, of 'indeterminate' passages of music with choice for the performers. But, unlike so many modern composers, he has not abandoned the traditional way of 'thinking with themes', and his output accordingly includes two symphonies as well as a cello concerto (1970) – which, like Britten's Cello Symphony, was composed for the eminent Russian virtuoso, Rostropovich. A number of his vocal works have French texts.

Symphony no.3

Duration: 30 minutes

Sir Georg Solti and the Chicago Symphony Orchestra, to whom it is dedicated, gave the first performance of this work on 29 September 1983. Only part of it, however, is conducted. Interspersed are *ad lib* sections in which (says the composer) the note-values are approximate only, so that music written in the score for the different instruments will not necessarily be heard exactly together.

A piano played by two performers as a duet (as in Saint-Saëns's Symphony no.3, p.281) is an unusual constituent of the orchestra, and there is an exceptionally strong component of percussion: kettledrums, snare drum, tenor drum, bass drum; 5 tomtoms, 2 bongos, 3 cymbals (of different pitches), tambourine, gong, tam-tam, xylophone, vibraphone, marimba, glockenspiel. Other requirements are 3 flutes (2 doubling piccolo), 3 oboes (one doubling english horn), 3 clarinets (one doubling high clarinet in E flat, one doubling bass clarinet), 3 bassoons (1 also playing double-bassoon), 4 horns, 4 trumpets, 4 trombones, tuba, 2 harps, celesta and strings.

The music is performed as a single uninterrupted span. It both begins and ends with a kind of exclamation, a quick hammering of the note E, four times repeated. But the work falls into two parts, corresponding (says the composer) to the introduction and main part of the opening movement of a Haydn symphony. The first part, in this case, presents the main musical material but in a way that is meant to leave the listener unsatisfied, awaiting the fulfilment of the second movement.

After an introduction both opened and closed by the 'exclamation', this first movement has three contrasting statements, each full sounding and active but rounded off by a sparse refrain of long-sustained notes. In the first two occurrences the refrain is given to the clarinets and followed by the 'exclamation'; the third is given to oboe and flute, then extended before the 'exclamation' arrives.

The main movement begins by making more of the 'exclamation': the repeated, hammered E is heard 12 times, then 16 times. The main material of the movement begins with urgent activity on strings and clarinets, followed by another extended 'exclamation' and a contrasted section of increasing complexity. Swift interchanges of phrase and rhythms give prominence to various instrumental colours in turn, including a tuba solo. At length ensues a series of frenzied climaxes from which a sustained string tune can be heard trying to emerge.

There is yet more battling, but after a sudden snare drum-roll the string tune grows firmer and more continuous, over a low E which now establishes itself as keynote. Horns join in, then the other instruments: stability and solidity have been reached. The tempo quickens for a coda with conspicuous jangling percussion, leading for the last time to the 'exclamation'. It forms the very last bar, the note E now not only rhythmically emphatic but also a satisfying harmonic centre.

MAHLER

1860–1911

Though Gustav Mahler had established his particular kind of symphony by 1900, and by then had also become director of the Vienna Opera, it was in the last years of his life and the first years of the twentieth century that he consolidated a career which was to be so influential. Doubly influential: firstly on the music of Schoenberg and other composers who directly trod his footsteps in Vienna, secondly (and at a distance) on international taste. After the Second World War the public in Britain, America and elsewhere responded strongly to the intensity and hugeness of his music. At this time too, such composers as Shostakovich and Britten (outside his Austro–German culture) acknowledged their debt to him.

Mahler wrote for the instruments of the orchestra sometimes in a traditional way (for instance in horn-calls and trumpet-calls), sometimes extraordinarily – incorporating sleigh-bells into the Symphony no.4, a mandolin into nos.7 and 8. Mahler's harmony sometimes (in late works) screws the tension to the bursting point of the tonal system; but it can be deliberately simple as part of an evocation of the simple and child like. A master of the colossal in orchestration, Mahler can surprise (like Berlioz) by the occasional delicacy of his effects – as in the song-cycle with orchestral accompaniment, *Songs of a Wayfaring Lad* (Lieder eines fahrenden Gesellen), a work which also shows the connections Mahler made between song and symphony.

Remarkably, the Second Symphony begins in one key (C minor) and ends in another, closely related one (E flat) – Mahler being the only composer at this time except for Carl Nielsen (see p.257) to essay in a symphony what was later to be called 'progressive tonality'.

The symphonies

Mahler completed nine numbered symphonies and enough of a tenth for a completion to be attempted by others (notably by Deryck

Cooke, whose version was first performed in 1960). Additionally, he stretched a point in referring to one of his other works as a symphony – the orchestrally accompanied song-cycle *The Song of the Earth* (Das Lied von der Erde) on German translations of Chinese poems.

In the purely orchestral symphonies (nos. 1, 5, 6, 7 and 9) and in no.4 (which adds a soprano voice in the last movement only) his symphonic form displays a clear descent from the historical Austro-German types, with scherzos and 'song-like' phrases which may recall Bruckner. In the remainder the text must influence the musical form – as in the finale of Beethoven's *Choral Symphony* (p.60) which was surely to some extent the inspiration of such works. Within twentieth-century music there is no series of symphonies, except those of Shostakovich, to parallel the variety and scope of Mahler's.

Symphony No.1 in D major

> Slow, dragging
> Strongly moving, but not too fast
> Solemn and steady, without dragging, *leading to* . . .
> Stormy
> Duration: 52 minutes

At its first performance, under Mahler himself at Budapest on 20 November 1889, the work appeared as a 'symphonic poem' (that is, a descriptive or pictorial work) in five movements, with titles. Later distrust of such titles, too easily taken in literal detail, led him to present the final, revised version of the work as a four-movement symphony, without titles. (The omitted movement, *Blumine* or *Flora*, is occasionally restored by well-meaning conductors.) But he admitted that his stimulus for the present third movement had been a picture for children of a 'hunter's funeral' at which the burial procession is escorted by weeping animals.

No external props are in fact needed for this powerful first symphony. Nor does Mahler buttress it with words. His means of pushing expression to his personal extreme was the use of an outsize orchestra: in particular, the proclamations of the brass require 7 horns and 4 trumpets as well as the usual 3 trombones and tuba. The remaining requirement is for 4 flutes (two doubling piccolo), 3 oboes (one doubling english horn), 4 clarinets (2 doubling on high clarinet in E flat or bass clarinet), 3 bassoons, kettledrums, bass drum, cymbals, triangle, and tam-tam, plus harp and strings.

A still, suspended note ('like a sound of nature', wrote the composer) opens the introduction, which soon gives the sound of a distant fanfare and of a falling figure in the woodwind imitative of a cuckoo. The pace quickens, the main faster section of the movement begins, and the 'cuckoo' phrase is re-identified as the beginning of a long, song-like melody. It *is* a song: one which Mahler had included in his set, *Songs of a Wayfaring Lad* (see above, p.216). The exposition, based on this extended melody, is repeated. A short development, with a new theme for horns, reaches a point of increased tension at which the fanfare of the introduction is recalled. The music is led back to a recapitulation and a happy mood prevails.

Nostalgia pervades the second movement. A *Ländler* or German waltz (in A major) has a lilt that recalls Schubert or Bruckner, and equally redolent of tradition is the central contrasting section or trio in C major and in more relaxed vein. A condensed version of the opening section rounds off the movement.

The round known by its French words, 'Frère Jacques' is grotesquely shifted into the minor key to form the funeral march of the third movement. Muffled kettledrums tap the rhythm; a solo double-bass, muted, begins the tune in D minor and other instruments join in. There is an interruption as if from vulgar street music, including bass drum and cymbals; the round resumes; a quite different interruption comes from a delicate melody (also, originally, one of Mahler's songs). Again the 'round' is heard but (subtly disturbed) it is now in E flat. It comes to an uneasy end – and the music now moves, without pause, to . . .

. . . the finale. What seem to be shrieks of despair are heard, banished by an upward-striving theme. It is in F minor, with a gentler theme in D flat major following. The 'home' key of D major will not emerge until after the argumentative middle section, when it manifests itself in an exultation of brass. But there is more to come. Already the movement has in several ways recalled the opening movement, and now a quieter section brings back the cuckoo-calls as in a remembered pastoral vision. But the heroic note returns on the brass and a prolonged blaze of D major ends the symphony.

Symphony No.2 in C minor (Resurrection)

   Allegro maestoso. With serious and solemn expression
      throughout
   Andante moderato. Very leisurely

With quietly flowing movement
'Primal Light'. Very solemn, but simple
In the tempo of the scherzo (i.e. of the third movement),
    wildly breaking out . . . Slow
Duration: 85 minutes

This is the first of Mahler's symphonies to summon the help of
words. In the fourth of the five movements, a contralto solo sings
verses from a famous German collection (supposedly of 'folk' origin)
called *The Youth's Magic Horn* ('Des Knaben Wunderhorn'); in the
finale a chorus as well as soprano and contralto soloists sing a text
partly by the eighteenth-century poet Klopstock, partly by Mahler
himself, affirming resurrection to immortal life. Hence the nickname of the symphony.

To one of Mahler's mentality the preaching of such a momentous
text went inescapably with the creation of massive musical sound.
The orchestra is one of the largest ever used at that date, and demands
to be listed as in the printed score:

    4 flutes (all interchangeable with piccolo)
    4 oboes (two interchangeable with english horn)
    3 clarinets (one interchangeable with bass clarinet)
    2 high clarinets in E flat
    4 bassoons (one interchangeable with double-bassoon)
    10 horns (4 sometimes placed remotely from the main
        orchestra)
    8 trumpets (4 similarly sometimes remotely placed)
    4 trombones
    1 tuba
    2 harps
      organ
    6 kettledrums (2 players)
      other percussion (5 players) including glockenspiel, high
        and low tam-tams, and 3 deep bells of indeterminate pitch
      strings

The presence of such a huge number of performers in a vocal work,
plus the use of sounds off-stage, lend a certain theatrical dimension to
performances (anticipated in earlier works such as the *Requiems* of
Berlioz and Verdi). On 29 June 1894, in Berlin, the first three
movements were heard under Richard Strauss's direction; the complete work was first performed, under Mahler himself, in Berlin on
13 December 1895. Within each movement, the composer creates an

emotional tension through the use of an extreme range of keys. The length of the symphony led the composer to stipulate a pause of 'at least five minutes' after the first movement. Conductors generally allow much less.

The first movement seems to suggest the human agony which only the divine message of the finale can heal. It opens with disturbances and fanfares in C minor, and suggestions of a tragic march in that key. But when the violins unfold a soaring phrase seeming to promise peace, they shift to a remote E major. There is a fade out on low notes in the harps and a development begins. Through the jagged march a serene hymn tune rises from trumpets and trombones. After a massive climax and a prolonged bass drum roll a shortened recapitulation begins. In a coda (with the two kettledrummers softly but urgently active) a surprising conclusion with a chord of C *major* is hinted at – and immediately rejected. The tragic C minor will not be moved.

The next two movements, according to the composer, are in the nature of interludes, fleeting fancies after funereal grief. The second movement, in A flat, presents a tune in Viennese dance-rhythm (a *Ländler*) at first on the strings alone. A single note on a solo horn moves the music to a more animated section. A variant of the first section ensues, then a variant of the second, then of the first again. The orchestration has a light touch throughout, and at the end only strings and the two harps are sounding.

A scherzo (though not so entitled) forms the third movement, in 3/4 time and in the traditional form. Mahler borrows from his own song, *St Anthony's Sermon to the Fishes* in order to suggest the humorous contemplation of wasted effort. It opens in C minor, gruff and grotesque on kettledrums and bassoons, soon joined by other low woodwind and percussion. (The swish of a brush on wood makes a notable sound.) The violins strike up an angular, wandering tune, to which an oboe and a bassoon later add a counter-theme. A contrasting section, faster, brings boisterous horn-calls in D major and E major. In vain: the opening strain returns. The next movement follows without a break (but not actually linked).

From the one note C which ends the previous movement, the unaccompanied contralto soloist moves up one single semitone to D flat to begin her solemn song in D flat major: 'O rosebud red!' (a mysterious reference, the 'rosebud' being unidentified). A solemn hymn-like strain is then heard from horns and trumpets standing apart from the main body of the orchestra. The voice continues:

> Mankind lies in greatest need!
> Mankind lies in greatest woe!
> I would fain to Heaven go.

Later, softer sounds including those of a harp and solo violin seem to portray a heavenly vision:

> . . . I am from God and wish to return to God.
> The dear Lord will lend me a little light . . .

Without a break the music passes to the last and longest movement. An orchestral cry of horror acts as a memory of things past. Now the message of redemption begins. A prayer-like theme in C major for horns and others has a symbolic upward movement which will later take vocal form. There is a gap of silence, a summons to attention, a march, a huge orchestral climax, and yet another summons: this time, the horn-call is unexpectedly followed by flute and piccolo in bird-calls which the composer must have seen as a nature symbol. The bird-calls end on the note C sharp. That note (in its other guise, D flat) is the key of the hushed choral section that now follows. The setting of Klopstock's Ode begins with the word 'arise' ('aufersteh'n').

> Arise, yes, arise you shall, after a short rest!
> Immortal life he shall give you who summoned you,
> To grow again shall you be sown.
> The lord of harvests goes
> To gather sheaves of us who died . . .

Elements of the previous orchestral music join with the vocal utterance. The contralto solo enters:

> O believe, my soul, believe,
> Nothing is lost to you . . .

Later, soprano and contralto sing in turn:

> O pain! thou ever-present,
> From thee I have escaped . . .

With the next choral entry the final key of the symphony, E flat, is reached and the symbolic upward phrase first heard much earlier takes new meaning from the addition of words. Moreover, from this point the words are the composer's own:

> With wings I have won for myself I shall soar . . .

Soon, *fortissimo*, over a kettledrum roll with brass support comes a further choral affirmation ('Sterben werd' ich, um zu leben'):

> Die I shall – in order to live!

A reprise is heard of the first words ('Arise . . .') – now raised to E flat and proclaimed with the utmost power, the organ entering for the first time as the symphony draws to its fervent close.

Symphony No.4 in G major

> Deliberately
> In easy motion, unhurried
> Peacefully, *leading to*
> Very leisurely
> Duration: 52 minutes

The vocal symphony takes many forms with Mahler. Here three purely instrumental movements are followed by a vocal – not, this time, a heaven-storming chorus but a soprano solo singing of a naïve, child-like vision of heaven. The sleigh-bells of the opening likewise suggest the idea of simplicity as a gateway to poetic truth.

Mahler himself conducted the first performance on 25 November 1901 in Munich. Afterwards he revised the work several times – finally in 1911, conducting that version in New York a few months before his death. That final version requires the following unusual orchestra, with no trombones but an expanded woodwind section: 4 flutes (two doubling piccolo), 3 oboes (one doubling english horn), 3 clarinets (one each doubling high clarinet in E flat, and bass clarinet), 3 bassoons (one also playing double-bassoon). 4 horns, 3 trumpets, harp, kettledrums, other percussion (triangle, cymbals, bass drum, tam-tam, glockenspiel, and sleigh-bells) and strings.

The symphony begins in G, and the last movement naturally also begins in that key – but ends in E major, by a kind of side-slip as though the heavenly vision cannot be brought down to earth. This is a particularly graphic use of the procedure which Mahler also used in the Symphony no.2 (see above), and which was later to be called 'progressive tonality'.

The first movement is introduced not merely with sleigh-bells but with bird-like flute calls. This opening strain recurs as happy agitation within a kind of freely varied sonata-form movement of which the first theme proper is a sunny, song-like melody on the first violins. After the last appearance of the sleigh-bells' theme the music seems about to fade but is strikingly reanimated.

A scherzo, though not a hurried or bumpy one, is placed as the second movement, in C minor. Its special sound comes from a solo violin (played by the leader of the orchestra) which derives an unusual tone from being tuned a whole tone higher than normal and is directed to be played 'like a fiddle', i.e. in a sort of country style. Mahler let it be known that this was a dance led by the figure of Death. A more cheerful trio stands in contrast. The first part and the trio both return in varied form.

Serenity falls on the orchestra with the strings' unfolding of a theme in G which becomes the subject of free variations with various changes of tempo and rhythm. After some anguished interruptions the opening serenity is never quite re-established. Loud kettledrums introduce a call from horns and trumpets which prefigures the main theme of the following movement and, what is more, is in E major which is to be that movement's eventual goal. Strings and harp pull back the present movement to the key of G. It ends on the note D, poised to lead into . . .

. . . the finale. Smoothly and simply, a clarinet gives out in G the theme just prefigured. The soprano voice now enters to deliver a song in nine stanzas, three times interrupted by 'bird-song' music recalled from the opening of the first movement. The first two stanzas conclude with an archaic, church-like harmony at the reference to St Peter ('Sankt Peter in Himmel sieht zu!')

> All heavenly joys are ours,
> Pleasures of earth we disdain.
> No worldly strife
> Mars our heavenly life.
> We live here in sweetest peace.
>
> We lead an angelic life,
> Yet are merry as can be.
> We dance and spring,
> We jump and sing
> While St Peter in Heaven looks on.

In similar vein the singer continues to describe the heavenly music. Again the archaic harmony is heard with the line 'Sankt Martha die Köchin muss sein' – 'St Martha must be the cook'. But then the orchestral music shifts key to E major and the voice describes the distinguishing feature of Mahler's heaven:

No music exists on earth
That can be compared to ours. . . . .

In that vein and that key, with a harp prominent, the symphony
attains its peaceful end.

Symphony No.8 in E flat major (Symphony of a Thousand)

Part I: Hymn, 'Veni, creator spiritus'
Part II: Closing scene from Goethe's *Faust*
Duration: 86 minutes

The so-called *Symphony of a Thousand* was introduced, under
Mahler's own baton, on 12 September 1910 in Munich. On that
occasion the nickname was literally justified with a total of 1003
performers – 146 orchestral players, two mixed choruses of 250
voices each, a children's choir of 350, and the required seven vocal
soloists.

The orchestral scoring, which marked an extreme of gigantic
conception which has hardly been exceeded, is for 2 piccolos (more if
possible), 4 flutes, 4 oboes, english horn, 2 high clarinets in E flat
(more if possible), 3 clarinets, bass clarinet, 4 bassoons, double-
bassoon, 8 horns, 4 trumpets, 4 trombones, tuba, kettledrums, bass
drum, cymbals, tam-tam, triangle, bells, glockenspiel, celesta,
piano, harmonium, organ, two harps (more if possible), mandolin
and strings. Mahler recommends further doubling of the principal
woodwind parts when large choral and string forces are available. A
separately disposed group of four trumpets and three trombones is
also required. The vocal forces comprise three sopranos, two con-
traltos, tenor, baritone and bass soloists, a boys' choir and two
mixed choirs from whom a semi-chorus is drawn.

Part One

Though fulfilling something like the form of a vast sonata-allegro,
with exposition, development and recapitulation, the material im-
poses itself chiefly as a musical response to the text. It is a Whitsun
hymn in Latin, an invocation to the Holy Spirit. In the key of E flat, it
begins (with the marking 'impetuously') with a loud choral cry. The
downward pair of notes on 'Veni' remains an important motive
throughout the symphony.

> Veni, Creator Spiritus,
> Mentes tuorum visita.

> Come, O Spirit of Creation,
> Enter into the minds you made:

The seven solo voices enter, led by the first soprano:

> Imple superna gratia
> Quae tu creasti pectora.

> Fill with highest grace
> The hearts you created.

An orchestral transition leads to the remote key of D minor and a new thought:

> Infirma nostri corporis
> Firmans virtute perpeti . . .

> To the frailty of our bodies
> Give perpetual strength

leading to an ecstatic shout from all:

> Accende, accende lumen sensibus

> Kindle, kindle the light of our understanding.

After musical development, a recapitulatory section begins. The initial words and musical theme are heard, and a further prayer:

> Da gratiarum munera,
> Da gaudiorum praemia.
> Dissolve litis vincula,
> Adstringe pacis foedera.

> Grant us the gift of thy graces,
> Grant us the reward of joys,
> Break the chains of strife,
> Bind us in the bonds of peace.

Acclamations of glory to God follow (on the original 'Veni, creator' theme). As the pace gathers urgency towards the end, a group of trumpets and trombones placed apart from the main orchestra sounds a fanfare based on the previous 'accende lumen'.

Part Two

The second part of the Symphony, much the longer, sets (like an opera in concert form) the scene which concludes Goethe's two-part drama, *Faust* – and at the same time takes up and fulfils many of the musical ideas of the first part of the symphony. Its long, slow, purely orchestral introduction is in E flat minor. A recurrence of its opening strain (flutes above, *pizzicato* cellos and double-basses far below) leads to the choral entry – complete with an imaginary stage direction in the score – mountain gorges, rocks and desert, with stations for the heavenly beings and clefts which furnish the dwelling for holy hermits.

The chorus is divided into two, at first with an echo effect:

> Waldung, sie schwankt heran . . .
>> Forests are swaying round our sacred refuge . . .

As the music turns to E flat major, saints voice their rapture:

> *Pater Ecstaticus* (baritone):
> Ewiger Wonnebrand, glühendes Liebesband . . .
>> Endless fire of God's love in my breast . . .

> *Pater Profundus* (bass):
> Wie Felsenabgrund mir zu Füssen . . .
>> Vast as the caverns at my feet is almighty love . . .

A trumpet motive, based on the 'accende lumen' of Part 1, grows ever more urgent and is a signal of the redemption of the sinner:

> *Chorus of Angels (bearing the immortal part of Faust):*
>
> Gerettet ist das edle Glied . . .
>> Rescued is this noble being . . .

> *Choir of Blessed Boys (together with the Chorus of Angels):*
> Hände verschlinget . . .
>> Hands joined in a circle, you shall see God . . .

A lighter (scherzando) element is interposed:

> *Chorus of Younger Angels:*
> Jene Rosen, aus den Händen . . .
>> Roses fashioned by penitent women aided the fight . . .

Further development leads to the entry of Doctor Marianus (tenor), hailing Mary, queen of heaven. Harps play their traditional 'celestial' role (reinforced here by piano and celesta) in signifying her appearance. Three women pray to her in turn for the repose of Faust's soul: the Magna Peccatrix ('the great sinner', Mary Magdalen), the Samaritan Woman and Mary of Egypt. A change of orchestral colour, with the entry of a mandolin (its first entry into the symphony) brings the soprano voice of 'a penitent, formerly named Gretchen' – pleading on behalf of her former seducer, Faust. Finally amid hushed tones the acceptance of Faust into heaven is signalled by Mary:

> Komm! Hebe dich zu höhern Sphären!
> Come, rise to higher spheres!

Doctor Marianus, with chorus, now continues in praise of Mary; then comes a stillness and expectation. So arrives the final *Chorus Mysticus*, beginning with the famous words, *Alles Vergängliche ist nur ein Gleichnis* (All earthly things are but a parable). This chorus, in E flat major, is an apotheosis of the musical phrase that was first sung, on his entry, by the Pater Ecstaticus. The massed voices begin in a whisper (the very low notes of the basses are notable). A soprano soloist, then another soprano soloist, delivers what is to be the concluding, much-repeated line:

> Das Ewig-Weibliche zieht uns hinan
> The Ever-Womanly leads us on

– from which the choral voices will pick out the 'Ewig' (ever). The full orchestral sound – including piano, harmonium and organ – wells up as the chorus now repeats the above line at a brighter, higher pitch. As the voices end, the group of off-stage trumpets and trombones contribute (as at the end of Part 1) their solemn proclamation. Cymbals and tam-tam do likewise, leading to a purely orchestral end to a choral symphony.

MENDELSSOHN

1809–47

Musical history provides no more remarkable example of a musical prodigy: to compose the overture to *A Midsummer Night's Dream* at the age of seventeen represents a maturity of artistic genius such as even Mozart's work hardly shows at that age. Felix Mendelssohn Bartholdy (the 'Bartholdy' was his father's addition to the family name) was favoured by the wealthy circumstances of his upbringing in a Hamburg banking family – Jewish by origin, Protestant by choice. The composer proceeded to win the highest acclamation in many cities, first visiting London in 1829 and unveiling his famous oratorio, *Elijah* in Birmingham in 1846. His *Songs Without Words* were a staple of the domestic and concert repertory for the piano in the Victorian age.

That popularity has waned. The formerly well-known Piano Concerto no. 2 in D minor is now rarely heard, and the quotation from Mendelssohn's overture *Calm Sea and Prosperous Voyage* in Elgar's *Enigma Variations* now makes no point until it is explained. But what gives continuing life to Mendelssohn's best works is vigour, conciseness and an inventive freshness of melody. He is also recognized as a master of light, pointed orchestration with each instrumental entry deftly characterized.

Symphony No. 4 in A major (Italian), *opus 90*

> Allegro vivace
> Andante con moto
> Con moto moderato
> Saltarello, Presto
> Duration: 25 minutes

The fruit of the young composer's journey to Italy in 1830–1, this symphony was first conducted by him in London on 13 May 1833.

Along with the *Hebrides* overture (see below) and another work, it fulfilled the commission which Mendelssohn had received from the Philharmonic Society of London. Twice revised later, it had a vivacity and charm which have made it the most performed of Mendelssohn's five symphonies.

The overall form is classical, though the third movement has a gently lyrical flow rather than the strong energy of a minuet or scherzo. In the instrumentation, too, Mendelssohn restricts himself (though with such skill that it seems no restriction) to the basic classical orchestra (see p.19): double woodwind, two horns, two trumpets, kettledrums and strings.

The first movement is in a dashing 6/8 rhythm. An opening theme is heard on the strings and a contrasting theme rises from clarinets and bassoons in thirds. After this exposition (which is repeated), we might expect only a development of the material, but Mendelssohn incorporates into that development the surprise of another tune, distinctively in the minor key. The recapitulation of the two first themes comes unmistakably, and finally the minor-key theme itself is happily transformed to the major.

The second movement, in D minor, is based on an Italian pilgrims' march – the final effect being of a dying away in the distance.

The third movement is in A major once more. Though not minuet-like in feeling, it summons the simplicity of the minuet form (almost!). A graceful opening section is followed by a contrasting section, begun with a kind of call to attention from horns and bassoons. The first section then returns. But (an individual touch) the call to attention makes a soft re-entrance towards the end.

The fourth movement, unusually for a symphony begun in the major key, is in A minor – a brisk Italian dance (*saltarello*). Midway, a smoother theme steals up from the violins. The dance theme, deceptively quiet on the flutes, swells over a drum roll to give the symphony an emphatic end.

Concerto for violin and orchestra in E minor, opus 64

Allegro molto appassionato, *leading to*
Andante, *leading to*
Allegretto non troppo – Allegro molto vivace
Duration: 28 minutes

One of the most popular of all violin concertos, Mendelssohn's is an example of how an intense, 'romantic' feeling can be combined with 'classical' clarity of form and restriction of resources. The orchestra is the same as for the symphony described above. For technical advice on the solo part, Mendelssohn sought the advice of his friend Ferdinand David – the violinist–leader of the Leipzig orchestra under Mendelssohn's conductorship. David gave the first performance in Leipzig on 13 March 1845, conducted, in the absence of the composer, by his Danish disciple Niels W. Gade. The solo part, though not of the difficulty which was to be demanded by Brahms or Tchaikovsky, is sufficient to challenge a virtuoso's skill and interpretative feeling.

Two features of the first movement which were innovations at the time were the *immediate* entry of the soloist with the main theme (without a preliminary exposition by the orchestra) and the placing of the cadenza just before the return of the principal subject in its own key (instead of nearer the end of the movement, before a coda). Likewise a new device was the expressive linking of the first movement to the second; the third also follows its predecessor without pause, though not with a melodic link.

In E minor, the violin enters with the passionate principal theme of the opening movement. A *tutti* section follows in which the soloist joins. As the violin sinks to a long-held low G, clarinets and flutes deliver a quiet, contrasting theme in G major. In that key, too, the soloist briefly recalls the principal theme. A development leads, quite suddenly, to the cadenza – fully written out (not left to the performer's choice). It forms the bridge to the re-entry of the principal theme in E minor, on the orchestra beneath the spread of the soloist's *arpeggio* figures. The original clarinet-and-flute tune calmly reappears in E major. But an accelerated tempo ends the movement in the original minor key and with renewed passion.

From the final chord of that movement, the single note B is sustained by a bassoon. It rises . . . is joined by others . . . and takes us to the C major in which the violin serenely gives out the main theme of the second movement. A more agitated section follows, then a modified return of the opening.

The second movement ended (as it began) in C. Now the violin, instead of launching the expected fast finale, first dreamily meditates in A minor . . . but soon the happy finale arrives in E major with unmistakable emphasis from trumpets and drums. A scampering theme for the soloist and a slightly more stately one (trumpets and drums again joining) provide the main material with both vigour and delicacy required from the soloist in rapid, exhilarating music.

Incidental music to A Midsummer Night's Dream

Overture
Scherzo
Nocturne
Wedding March
Duration: 34 minutes

In 1826, when he was barely seventeen, Mendelssohn and his sister Fanny read German translations of Shakespeare's plays. A direct result was his overture, *A Midsummer Night's Dream*. It was written first as a piano duet, then orchestrated, receiving its first public performance in that form at Stettin on 29 April 1827, when Carl Loewe conducted it from manuscript. In 1843 a commission from King Frederick William IV of Prussia to write music for his theatre led Mendelssohn to compose the further numbers of *A Midsummer Night's Dream*. The production, complete with this music, was given in the theatre of the New Palace at Potsdam on 14 October 1843. The first concert performance took place under Mendelssohn's own direction in London, on 27 May 1844.

Of the 13 numbers which comprise the music to *A Midsummer Night's Dream*, the four described here are the best known. The basic orchestral force is of double woodwind, 2 trumpets, kettledrums and strings. An ophicleide (an obsolete bass instrument, now replaced by the tuba) is added in the Overture; ophicleide, 3 trombones and cymbals reinforce the Wedding March.

Overture. The four long chords for woodwind rise up like a summons to the imagination. They have that peculiar shading (being in E major, but the third chord in A *minor*) which lends enchantment to this overture. The scampering theme – fairy music, clearly! – is in E *minor*. Later, the music contrives to suggest the comic braying of Bottom when turned into an ass (long notes on the tuba) and the stamping dance (a hefty melody on the violins) which will conclude the rustic entertainment provided by Bottom and his friends for the court. Development and recapitulation lead to a reappearance of the soft 'magic' chords of the opening.

Scherzo. Between Acts 1 and 2 of the play, this fleet-footed piece in

G sharp minor begins on two flutes and later introduces a sturdier, good-humoured major-key theme on the strings. Fairy music again? A solo flute dances away at the end.

Nocturne. The sustained melody of the solo horn depicts the stillness of the wood at night in which the four lovers lie asleep – of which Puck, with his magic eye-drops, takes advantage. The music has a more urgent middle section, then a return to the peaceful opening.

Wedding March. So familiar that one scarcely notices its ingenuities and felicities in detail, this forms the entr'acte before the last (fifth) act of the play, in which the royal marriage and that of the two young couples are celebrated. The key is C major, the trumpets proclaiming that with their opening fanfare, but with the following festive full-orchestral chords *not* in that key! Contrasting episodes separate the recurrences of the principal section and maintain the joyful tone.

Overture, The Hebrides, opus 26

Duration: 9 minutes

'In order to make you understand how inordinately the Hebrides have affected me, I have written down the following, which came into my mind . . .' Twenty bars of music follow. So Mendelssohn wrote home to his family on 7 August 1829, after a Scottish steamer trip from Fort William to Oban and from Oban to Tobermory. He did not see the famous Fingal's Cave (on the Isle of Staffa) till the next day. So those famous bars which open the present overture cannot be directly linked with the cave.

Nevertheless, *Fingal's Cave* was the title which Mendelssohn's publishers were to attach to the first full published score of the work (1835) (the composer's own preference was for *The Hebrides* – in German, *Die Hebriden*). The work was first performed, under the twenty-three-year-old composer's baton, in London on 14 May 1832. Mendelssohn made a few further alterations in the following month. A letter to his sister Fanny, criticizing his own work in the course of working on it, shows his wish that the music should convey not just scenic beauty but the realities of the journey: 'The so-called development smacks more of counterpoint than of oil and seagulls and dead fish – and it should be just the opposite!'

The concert-goer may not find the dead fish, but the Romantic effects of seascape and storm are irresistible. The agitation and climaxes are the more remarkable because Mendelssohn did not extend the orchestra beyond its 'classical' size with double wood-wind, horns and trumpets, but no trombones. So-called 'hairpin' dynamics – a swelling from soft to loud and back again – are prominent.

The scene-painting is accomplished within a traditional overture form. The wave-like opening theme (B minor) rises to a climax before cellos and bassoons offer a more assuring theme in D major. In a further climax an insistent, fanfare-like figure rings out from horns and trumpets; this in turn dies down but a new section starts (the development proper) which soon brings a fresh, challenging theme on the woodwind. The biggest climax is still to come – after which the first 'wavy' theme returns in its original peaceful form, and the contrasting theme follows in B major on a solo clarinet. At last, all seems at peace – but no, an extension of the music (formally the coda) brings yet more disturbance. The sea is deceptive! The end is not in sunny B major but in the sombre B minor with which the overture began.

MESSIAEN

born 1908

Distinguished for orchestral music, organ music (he was himself an organist), songs and chamber music, Olivier Messiaen became the outstanding French composer of his generation. An exhaustive and scientific interest in birdsong as a spur to composition gave rise to such works as *The Blackbird* (Le merle noir) for flute and piano (1951) and *The Awakening of the Birds* for orchestra (1953). Much of his work has Catholic associations but he also drew on oriental imagery as in the work discussed below. A more recent orchestral work (1974) took the grandiose title *From the Canyons to the Stars*.

A distinguished teacher whose students included both Pierre Boulez and Karlheinz Stockhausen (who were to rank among the leading modernists of their own generation), Messiaen was himself in the forefront of technical advances in methods of composition. His music is the essential bridge between Stravinsky and Boulez. Marriage to the pianist Yvonne Loriod stimulated his composition of many works for her. He also gave exposure to one of the first (1928) practical electronic instruments, the *martenot* (see below).

Turangalîla Symphony

Introduction
Love–song no. 1
Turangalîla no. 1
Love–song no. 2
Joy in the blood of the stars
Garden of the sleep of love
Turangalîla no. 2
Development of love
Turangalîla no. 3
Finale
Duration: 90 minutes

One of the longest works in the orchestral repertory, and like no other in its inspiration, structure and scoring, the *Turangalîla-Symphony* had its first performance in Boston on 2 December 1949 under Leonard Bernstein's direction. The composer has described the work as 'a song of love, a hymn to joy', noting that the word *turangalîla* (in Sanskrit, the ancient Indian tongue) derives from two stems: *turanga*, galloping time, and *lîla*, play, divine action, love.

On the title-page it is described as being for 'solo piano and full orchestra'. In a programme-note, the composer wrote that the piano part is so important and so difficult as to make the work almost a piano concerto, with long and brilliant cadenzas 'binding together the elements of development and forming part of the structure'. At least as striking, however, is the use of the piano in company with two other keyboard instruments, the celesta and the keyed glockenspiel, to suggest the percussive melody of Far Eastern music.

A large role also falls to an electronic instrument, the Martenot (in full, 'ondes Martenot' or Martenot waves, named after its inventor). 'Everyone will notice it,' commented the composer, 'at those moments of paroxysm when it dominates the *fortissimo* with its expressive, very high voice. But it is also used in the lower register for effects of gentleness'. The Martenot can hold a pitch for an infinite period, or flutter round a pitch, or swoop up and down without seeming to dwell on any intermediate note – but it cannot sound chords, only one note at a time.

The other instruments include no kettledrums but a large variety of other percussion requiring five players: triangle, temple blocks, wood-block, various cymbals, tam-tam, tambourine, maracas, snare drum, tenor drum, bass drum, tubular bells. The orchestra otherwise consists of 2 flutes and piccolo, 2 oboes and english horn, 2 clarinets and bass clarinet, 3 bassoons; 4 horns, 3 trumpets, 1 high trumpet in D, 1 cornet, 3 trombones and tuba; glockenspiel, celesta, vibraphone; and strings precisely numbered – 16 first and 16 second violins, 14 violas, 12 cellos and 10 double-basses.

Three musical themes recur conspicuously during the ten movements, each having a characteristic instrumental colour: a heavy, brutal theme (called by the composer the *statue theme*) on trombones and tuba; a fragile theme (the composer's *flower-theme*) on two clarinets; and a smooth, singing *love-theme* on the Martenot and strings. Despite the richness of sound and complexity of notes, the work comes over clearly in short, often repetitive sections, differentiated by heavy accents and special combinations of percussion.

This might be a kind of latter-day *Rite of Spring* (see p. 326) save that, unlike the earlier work, it emphatically centres on, and concludes in, a definite key.

The opening movement, after a few bars in fast time, arrives at a section marked 'heavy, fairly slow': under high trills, the statue theme (see above) is delivered *fortissimo* by trombones and tuba. A big climax quietens to expose, on their own, the two clarinets in the flower-theme. Later comes the first of the piano cadenzas and the statue-theme concludes the movement.

The 'Love-song' that follows, opening with heavy clanging of bells, cymbals and piano, is plainly not a conventional fulfilment of its title. With a prominent piano part it oscillates between energetic and reposeful sections – the latter exposing the love-theme of the work, as the *glissando* (sliding) tones of the Martenot soar above.

Next comes the first of three movements headed *Turangalîla*: the beginning, marked 'dreamily', has a coaxing utterance on the clarinet echoed by Martenot. The oriental-percussive effect is later prominent.

A second 'Love-Song', beginning with an angular melody played by piccolo and bassoon four octaves apart, moves through a dance-like urgency to a passionate, almost sentimental statement of the 'love-theme' – sung out on all the high instruments of the orchestra, including the Martenot. Later the piano interpolates bird-calls. The 'angular' tune, now enmeshed with counterpoint, returns before another long piano cadenza. Statue-theme, flower-theme and love-theme all return briefly for the orchestral coda.

Now occur two central movements (nos. 5 and 6) of a new individuality: they resemble the scherzo and slow movement of a traditional symphony. The scherzo, entitled 'Joy in the blood of the stars', is a, fast, joyful song in exhilarating rhythm. It is in the key of D flat. There follows, in F sharp, the movement entitled 'Garden of the sleep of love': here the only instruments heard are muted strings and Martenot, playing a long, uninterrupted version of the love-theme, against which a constant counterpoint of bird-song issues from the piano.

The second *Turangalîla* begins with a further cadenza (and more bird-song), leading soon to a remarkable few bars for percussion alone. Later, the statue-theme returns prominently. A piano flourish and a loud solo bass drum stroke end the movement.

The next movement's title, 'Development of love', apparently embraces the idea of musical 'development' also. Beginning and ending with chimes, it has three points of climax at which the surge of passion seems to reach its height.

The third *Turangalîla*, like the first, begins with the seductive clarinet but proceeds to involve the whole orchestra in a dance-like pulse, the Martenot soaring above.

The Finale in its joyful opening recaptures the regularity and exhilaration of no. 5, but is in F sharp, the key of no. 6. Thus the work concludes in a key firmly established earlier. The music eventually reaches what the composer describes as 'a glorification of the love-theme'. A fast and brilliant coda then concludes the work, the piano contributing its percussive excitement and the Martenot its high trills.

MOZART

1756–91

That music does not 'advance', but exhibits successive peaks in an unending range, is shown by the continuing veneration which the musical world gives to Wolfgang Amadeus Mozart, and by the way in which each generation creates its image of him. 'Your son is the greatest composer known to me,' declared Haydn (nearly twenty-five years his senior) to Leopold Mozart. The system of patronage by court, aristocracy and church failed to find a secure place for him after he had abandoned his native Salzburg for Vienna, where his life was that of the practical musician of theatre and concert.

Beethoven, Chopin and Liszt wrote variations and other works on melodies from Mozart's operas. Tchaikovsky looked back on Mozart's age as one of delicacy and innocent pleasures, enshrined in the words *rococo* or *galant*. Until the mid-twentieth century, however, the Mozart repertory was only a small, concentrated selection from the total output. Today, exploration is vastly wider. All the piano concertos are cultivated, sometimes with the sound of the period's original pianos, or replicas of them. Recordings give access not merely to the celebrated last three symphonies, not merely to a few more, but to virtually every note of Mozart's orchestral works. What we now call the 'Viennese classical' forms and the types of melody and harmony that go with them proved an infinitely flexible matrix for genius to operate in. That *Little Serenade* for strings (1787) which in British usage retains the German name of *Eine kleine Nachtmusik* is only one of several lighter works which, as it were, surround Mozart's weightier output in symphonic and concerto forms.

But his immediate rewards were scanty. Throwing off the demeaning conditions of his early employment by the prince-archbishop of Salzburg, he chose the more competitive and more cosmopolitan environment of Vienna, Austria's imperial capital. But he found no secure patronage there, achieving only a modest livelihood from his freelance career (performing and teaching as well as composing). His begging letters and his burial in an unmarked grave are now famous testimonies to the public neglect of genius.

Mozart's works are indexed by 'K' (Köchel) numbers, a system of reference originated by the nineteenth-century scholar Ludwig Köchel. It preserves approximate date-order. So a 'high' K number (the numbering ends at 623a) denotes a late work.

The symphonies

Mozart wrote his first symphony at the age of eight in London – helped, it may be, by J. C. Bach (eighteenth of the great Bach's twenty children) who had taken up residence in London and become one of its leading musicians. He developed the 'classical symphony' (see p.12) from something which is delightfully entertaining to something which is profound but *still* delightfully entertaining. His instrumentation grew richer as the fuller forces offered by Mannheim, Paris and Vienna became available. Rarely did he omit the minuet and produce a symphony in three rather than four movements; and only twice did he write a symphony in a minor key.

A minimum orchestra for the symphonies is shown in the note on the first of his symphonies included here.

Symphony no.29 in A major, K201

>Allegro moderato
>Andante
>Minuetto
>Allegro con spirito
>Duration: 20–26 minutes

After a visit to Vienna (he was not yet living there), Mozart was again in Salzburg when he composed this symphony in 1774, very near the date of his 18th birthday. The date of its first performance is unknown.

It displays what may be called the irreducible minimum of the symphony orchestra in Haydn's and Mozart's day: two oboes and two horns in addition to the four-part strings – first violins, second violins, violas, cellos, with double-basses almost invariably reinforcing the cello line an octave lower. Occasionally, as in requiring two trumpets for his preceding symphony (no.28 in C, K200),

Mozart had already gone above this minimum and he was regularly
to do so later.

A soft opening for the first movement is deceptive. Soon the
theme, with its octave leap downwards, is repeated in the expectedly
loud, assertive way, with the wind instruments joining in. A more
placid theme is offered for contrast. The exposition has its conventional repetition after establishing the new key of E; and similarly
there is a repetition (today not usually observed) for the second and
longer 'half' comprising development and recapitulation, concluding in the original key. We may call these halves A and B. But after
B, unusually, there is a short extra tail section or coda, in which the
original octave-jumping theme makes a final assertive reappearance.

A gentle second movement in D follows, with the violins muted
until the last few bars. Thirdly comes a minuet in the expected form
with contrasting central Trio: the oboes and horns are rhythmically
prominent in the minuet proper, but confined in the trio to softly
sustained single notes.

The finale, like the first movement, is in two repeated 'halves'
with coda. Observe, after the first three notes of the lively melody, a
little upward scale: it grows to acquire a playful importance with a
clinching whole bar to itself just before the end.

Symphony No.35 in D major (Haffner), K385

> Allegro con spirito
> Andante
> Minuetto
> Presto
> Duration: 17–20 minutes

The wealthy Haffner family of Salzburg, who had commissioned an
orchestral serenade from Mozart in 1776, wanted a new work from
him for a family festivity in 1782. Again it was to be a serenade – that
is, in the terms of that time, a composition in several movements
beginning with a march. Once the festivity was over, he detached
the opening march, removed one of the minuets, added two flutes
and two clarinets to the scoring (pairs of oboes, bassoons and horns
were already present, as were two trumpets, kettledrums and
strings). He launched it as a symphony at a concert in Vienna
attended by the Emperor on 3 March 1783. This is the *Haffner
Symphony*, as it is now known; the name *Haffner Serenade* attaches to
the earlier, quite different work.

The most remarkable feature of the opening movement is Mozart's use of a single main theme instead of two contrasting ones (rare for him, common for Haydn). But there is an assertive 'extra' theme (bassoons, horns and lower strings) to clinch the ending of the exposition in A and to function similarly in D as the second part of the movement ends. The added wind instruments are omitted from the slow movement, with its graceful figurations for the violins, and from the following minuet, but return to invigorate the fast finale, which the composer said should be as fast as possible. The principal tune of this finale, heard at the outset, borrows from a song allotted to the comically villainous Osmin in *The Seraglio*, the opera Mozart had just finished.

Symphony No.38 in D major (Prague), K504

   Adagio – Allegro
   Andante
   Presto
   Duration: 24–30 minutes

Mozart set out from Vienna to superintend performances of *The Marriage of Figaro* in Prague and to launch his new opera, *Don Giovanni*, there. (The city of Prague and the whole of what is now Czechoslovakia formed part of the Austrian emperor's domain until after the First World War.) With him he took a newly composed symphony which he presented amid great enthusiasm on 19 January 1787. The orchestration is for two each of flutes, oboes, bassoons, horns and trumpets, with kettledrums and strings. This highly successful visit is commemorated by the attachment of the name 'Prague' to this robust but deeply probing music. Uniquely among Mozart's later symphonies it has no minuet, but it has a compensating extra – a slow introduction to the opening movement, a structural feature less often found in Mozart than in Haydn.

   This introduction, with its weighty drum-rolls and harsh discords, leads into a softly throbbing opening for the main tempo, with the sound of strings alone. Almost immediately, the violins embark on a phrase of repeated notes with a little 'turn' (musical ornament) before the final beat. In due course a smooth theme in A is presented on strings alone as the second subject, and in this key the exposition ends on a climax of sound with trumpets and drums. The strings similarly have the subject when it returns in D as the movement approaches its end.

The slow middle movement of clinging intensity, in A, reveals delicate detail on strings and woodwind, while horns sustain the texture and trumpets and drums are silent.

The scampering finale, in D, starts softly before emerging with force. It is in sonata form, the development offering witty interchanges between pairs of instruments. Prague music-lovers might have spotted that the opening theme of the last movement quotes from *Figaro*, the opera they had vociferously welcomed only two days before. The quotation is from the orchestral accompaniment to 'Aprite presto' in act 2.

Symphony No.39 in E flat major, K543

> Adagio – Allegro
> Andante
> Minuetto: allegretto
> Allegro
> Duration: 25–33 minutes

Mozart, in the (partial) catalogue he made of his own works, gave dates of completion for the last three symphonies: no.39, 26 June; no.40, 25 July; no.41, 10 August, all in 1788. The common statement that they were all written within six weeks is thus wrong as a simple matter of arithmetic, since even with Mozart we do not suppose that he began no.39 on the day he finished it. None the less the concentration is extraordinary, and likewise the differentiation of feeling between the symphonies. Strangely, there seems to be no clear record of the first performance of any one of them.

Exceptionally, no.39 calls for no oboes: a pair of clarinets replaces them, and there is a single flute, with two each of bassoons, horns and trumpets, plus timpani and the usual strings. All the instruments take part in the opening solemn introduction, so that a complete contrast follows when the main tempo begins – with a change of pulse (4/4 to 3/4), a smoother melody, and a stripped-down scoring. After a full-orchestral entry the music again quickens for the principal second subject on smooth violins and violas over *pizzicato* cellos and double-basses. A short but powerful development leads back, through a single bar's complete silence, to the recapitulation.

An emotional slow movement in A flat follows, with some intense clashes of melodies in counterpoint before an ending which recalls the opening. In contrast comes the extrovert minuet: in its central trio, the two clarinets have an enjoyably prominent duet which

Mozart could not have given to two oboes (the oboe does not go low enough).

The finale begins with the modest sound of violins only, working up to a display of Mozart's most passionate style. The processes we usually call development (adventures of the themes, with departures to remote keys) start even within the first section ('exposition'), and the end of the music is dramatic, almost abrupt.

Symphony No.40 in G minor, K550

Allegro molto
Andante
Minuetto: allegretto
Allegro assai
Duration: 24–28 minùtes

The concert-goer encounters two alternative orchestrations of this celebrated symphony. Originally, along with 2 horns, 2 trumpets, kettledrums and strings, he specified the woodwind as a single flute and pairs of oboes, bassoons and horns. He later added two clarinets and changed the oboe parts. The second version is now considered as an option, not as ruling out the first.

The huge majority of eighteenth-century symphonies are in a major key, symbolizing confidence, enjoyment, stability. Of Mozart's, only two are in a minor key, and it is the same key: the 'Little G minor' (no.25, K183, dating from 1773, not so often played) and the present work which ranks high among all favourite works of the concert-hall. Composers often seem to fix characteristics to keys, partly on individual preference and partly on an inheritance from the past: for Mozart, G minor seems to carry a special pathos as seen in his string quintet in that key and in a famous sorrowful aria of the heroine in *The Magic Flute*.

This pathos is not conveyed merely in slow music: the opening of the present symphony, with its passionate drive, presents it too. Before the violins embark on the main theme, the divided violas momentarily but significantly establish the insistent rhythmical pattern. A second subject in B flat, in dialogue between strings and woodwind, provides some escape, but the opening figures and the opening G minor hang in the wings as the exposition closes. Similarly at the end of the movement, the second subject has achieved G major but the minor-key end makes no compromise.

The E flat major of the major key of the second movement

suggests a move to another area of feeling, but it is still one of emotional tension. The minuet, though it has the usual pulse, no longer suggests the traditional courtly dance: the music is punched through by bold syncopations and harmonic clashes. It keeps the minor key, relaxing only for a deliberately naïve major-key trio.

The *very fast* marking of the finale (*allegro assai*) points up the relentlessness of the first subject: the contrast of a softer second subject is offered later by violins and violas only. Sonata-form is followed, with abrupt, questioning phrases at the beginning of the development and an unrelenting impetus to the end. Both 'halves' of the movement are marked to be repeated.

Symphony No.41 in C major (Jupiter), K551

Allegro vivace
Andante cantabile
Minuetto: allegretto
Allegro molto
Duration: 28–33 minutes

Where the nickname 'Jupiter' was coined and by whom is unknown: it may have originated with the London music-publisher (and composer) J. B. Cramer. But if the origin is in doubt, the meaning and the appropriateness of the nickname is clear. This is a godlike image in music, as though a Michelangelo were quarrying from his own nature the attributes of Jove himself. The notion of this as supreme among symphonies gains from triple coincidence: it is Mozart's last symphony, it is in C major (a 'basic' key, as musicians think of it), and it concludes with an unparalleled display of contra-puntal skills within the classical symphonic form.

The scoring adds trumpets and kettledrums to oboes, bassoons, horns and strings. Mozart opens the first movement with conven-tional figures of emphasis: the stateliness is not just an introductory gesture but persists, though the direction *Allegro vivace* underlines liveliness of spirit in addition to the normal fairly fast tempo. The exposition embraces a rich assortment of short themes, re-encountered with still greater force in the recapitulation. Muted violins and violas lead the delicate tracery of the slow movement in F, with woodwind and horns subtly reinforcing. A minuet follows, not sharply angled like that in no.40 but with a light, relaxed spring.

And then the crown – the majestic finale with which Mozart quits the world of the symphony. The four long notes with which the first violins open the finale (C,D,F,E, a phrase that ascends, then turns back) form a well-known 'tag' or formula. Mozart uses this and four other short melodic ideas in combination: a web of sound which, apart from its internal ingenuity, takes the path of a sonata-form movement from the home key to the intermediate key (C to G), then back, each 'half' repeated. After that, a coda clinches the matter, every thematic element in perfect place and every instrument making a distinct contribution. The two bassoons take one theme apiece.

The concertos

Mozart's concertos not only include some of his greatest works, but also enshrine the model of the 'classical' concerto, traceable in later composers' works right up to the mid-twentieth century, such as Richard Strauss's Horn Concerto no.2 (1943). Where a later composer breaks from the model, as Brahms did with four movements for his Second Piano Concerto, it is felt definitely to *be* a break.

Mozart's five violin concertos are early works with many beautiful ideas. He wrote four horn concertos, pleasant display-pieces for their instruments; a bassoon concerto (there are few such!), a flute concerto, another concerto for either flute or oboe, yet another for flute and harp, and various other works for soloist and orchestra. The rare combination of violin and viola with orchestra inspired an unusual work, treated below. But none of these works sustained the profundity of his piano concertos and specifically the last 14 (out of 23), all written in the seven last years of his short life; only one non-piano concerto, that for clarinet, comes from this period and is of equal stature.

In all these later works the 'classical' orchestra is used for the accompaniment – one or two flutes; pairs of oboes, bassoons and horns; sometimes a pair of clarinets and sometimes a pair of trumpets and their companions the kettledrums. The piano soloist in a concerto in Mozart's time would be expected to play throughout the work, supplementing the harmonies (the old *continuo* role – see page 370) and marking the rhythm for the orchestra to follow.

Standard first-movement form, mentioned above (and further discussed on page 11) is used:

> an opening presentation of themes (first ritornello),
> an entry of the soloist with some older material but also something new;

a move to the dominant key (or the relative major, if the
movement is in a minor key), at which point a second
ritornello will restate at least some of the original material;
a development;
a final ritornello in which orchestra and soloist reassert the new
key in reviewing the original material;
a cadenza for the soloist; and
a coda.

The second movement is slow and contemplative, following a
simple but free form; for the rondo and variation forms favoured in
the finale, see page 12.

Concerto for clarinet and orchestra in A major, K622

Allegro
Adagio
Rondo: Allegro
Duration: 27 minutes

By common consent the greatest of clarinet concertos, this is the last
of all Mozart's works in concerto form. It was not written for today's
standard clarinet, not even for its predecessor with the same range
but fewer keys than the modern instrument. Mozart's friend, the
admired clarinettist Anton Stadler, owned a specially built instrument which was capable of descending a few notes lower than the
standard instrument. Though the composer's manuscript does not
survive, it is clear that the concerto was written with use of these
extra low notes.

In the 1980s, leading soloists increasingly preferred to achieve
fidelity to Mozart by acquiring an instrument built specially to be
capable of such an extended range – sometimes called nowadays by
the confusing name of 'basset–clarinet'. (It is not a basset–horn, a
still lower instrument of the clarinet family, also used by Mozart.)
Performances on the normal instrument remain feasible, however,
with a few substitutions of notes.

The first performance took place in Vienna on some day in
October 1791, with Stadler playing under Mozart's direction. Only
a small orchestral force is required: 2 flutes, 2 bassoons, 2 horns and
strings. The clarinet's rich colour shines through them all. Indeed,
the custom of the time (now not generally observed) would have had

the clarinet playing throughout, doubling the violins where no special solo part was provided.

The orchestral opening is a long one, abundant in melody. The first solo entry puts the clarinet above the first violins, which support it as in a singers' duet. Then the soloist soars away, presenting some new material and exploiting the instrument's characteristic capacity for leaps between high notes and the dark-coloured lower register. The pathos of a theme in E *minor* surprises before the movement reaches an expected midway close in E major. Mozart's usual concerto structure is adapted to spacious, long-breathed eloquence.

The slow movement in D major is a gentle song for the solo instrument, framed by the orchestra as it displays its voice-like qualities of solo expression.

The finale, in rondo form, is at once suave and merry. The soloist begins it and is soon engaged in lively up-and-down figurations. As in the first movement, minor-key passages deepen the pathos – but a coda extends the movement to end in gaiety and exhilaration.

Concerto for piano and orchestra in D minor, K466

Allegro
Romanze
Allegro assai
Duration: 30 minutes

On 11 February 1785, in Vienna, Mozart himself was soloist at the first performance of this concerto – apparently without any rehearsal of the orchestra (which uses only one flute and excludes clarinets). It has an unusual passion and urgency. Its key of D minor, prominent also in *Don Giovanni*, is one which Mozart favoured for such a mood. The opening, in which the violins have a throb rather than a tune while the cellos and double-basses mark a firm rhythm, is particularly remarkable. The contrasting theme in F major is given out by oboes and bassoons. The piano's entry starts by launching a new theme; soon the 'throbbing' orchestra is heard again. The form is regular but the effect of agitation is strong as the piano's oscillating octaves strive towards the limits of the power available on Mozart's instrument. The ending is hushed.

Under the unusual heading of Romance (in German *Romanze*), Mozart begins his slow movement by presenting a regular, memor-

able tune for the piano in B flat. The music seems to be enclosed in a
serene, untroubled spirit, but (while the beat remains unchanged) a
more agitated motion is set up by a new section in G minor – the
bassoon part, high in its register, bringing an unusual touch. Then
comes the return to the serene opening strain.

The mood of passionate urgency returns as the piano leads off the
rondo which is the final movement. After the orchestra has joined in
and ended its statement, another D minor theme from the piano
continues the mood. Eventually a lighter touch arrives in the shape
of a whistleable 'street tune', as we may call it, piped out by
woodwind in octaves. The movement's biggest climax leads to a
cadenza and to a sudden, sunny turn to D major. In this key the
'street tune' returns. A cheeky little interpolation by horns and
trumpets launches the piano on its final flourish.

Concerto for piano and orchestra in A major, K488

Allegro
Andante
Presto
Duration: 26 minutes

With Mozart himself as soloist, this concerto was presumably
performed in Vienna soon after the date of completion which the
composer noted – 2 March 1786. Unusually, and happily for posterity, he included in the surviving manuscript score his own cadenza
for the first movement. The other movements require none. This is
sunny yet profound music, sharing the key of A major (and,
interestingly, sharing the first two notes) with two other works of
similar disposition – the Clarinet Concerto (see p.246) and the quintet
for clarinet and strings.

This concerto, too, is a 'clarinettish' work. Very unusually, the
score has no oboes, the pair of clarinets therefore being relatively
more important and contributing their warm tone to the colour of
the whole. Other than the strings, the only other requirement is a
single flute, 2 bassoons and 2 horns.

As usual, the orchestra opens the work – but unusually, the piano
when it enters has no decisive new theme. What it does is to put into a
new key, E major, one of the themes the orchestra presented in A.
Then, after the customary long trill on the piano has confirmed that

key of E, there is a further, folding-in theme (also in E) on the strings, which is developed into remote keys – but not for long. When the recapitulation arrives the 'folding-in' theme naturally slips with the rest into the home key of A.

The slow movement, gently undulating in the unusual key of F sharp minor, displays the solo instrument in one of Mozart's tenderest melodies. The musical thought leads to A major, after which the opening recurs identically but this time reposes in the original key.

Unbuttoned cheerfulness infuses the finale, which is in Mozart's favourite rondo-form. The piano gives out the opening theme and later another in the same key, A. Newer melodies flow, and Mozart's genius even turns to gold what seems a beginner's simple run up and down the scales.

Concerto for piano and orchestra in C minor, K491

Allegro
Larghetto
Allegretto
Duration: 30 minutes

Mozart himself was the soloist at the first performance – in Vienna on 7 April 1786. Like the other minor-key concerto discussed above, the C minor is one which seems more full of 'feeling' in the Beethoven-and-after sense than Mozart's concertos in major keys. The orchestra this time includes a pair of clarinets as well as one flute and two each of oboes, bassoons, horns and trumpets, together with kettledrums and strings.

A good example of feeling is encountered at the very opening – the rising figure is presented quietly, in unison, without harmony, chords being gradually added by the wind instruments before the theme is forcefully restated, fully harmonized, with kettledrums solemnly marking the rhythm. This orchestral opening is long. The piano, on its entry, presents brief new material before joining in the re-formation of the first themes. The music is led via the usual trill into the new key, E flat. Now, in the central section of the movement, the piano takes the lead in the passionate development of the themes, later seeming to delay the eventual return to the opening. Even after the soloist's cadenza, there is little sense of relaxation; the piano's passionate expression continues to the end.

The slow movement in E flat is begun by the piano in a way that suggests a refuge of serenity after what has gone before. But this proves deceptive. The entry of a quartet of wind instruments (flute, two oboes, bassoon) stirs more complicated emotions. That suggestion continues, even though the piano and its original theme are allowed to end the movement decoratively.

The finale brings the expected lively pace, but strikes a serious mood, exemplified by the drum-taps in the opening bars. The movement begins in the form of a theme and variations – the theme itself, and each succeeding variation, being divided into two halves, each half being repeated or itself varied. Emotion intensifies with the prolonged concentration on the key of C minor until the clarinets and bassoons begin an interlude in the contrasting key of A flat major. The soloist turns back to the opening material, but another contrasting episode in C major intervenes, with a further return to C minor for the pianist's cadenza. After the cadenza, despite the lightening of a rhythmical change to 6/8 time, the intensity of mood and of the original key of C minor continue to the end.

Concerto for violin and orchestra in A major, K219

> Allegro aperto
> Adagio
> Tempo di minuetto
> Duration: 30 minutes

The arresting feature of this concerto is the playfully wild episode of its finale – an imitation of the 'Turkish' vein of music, which had become known in Austria from Turkish military bands. The oriental setting of Mozart's opera *The Seraglio* prompted him to a similar pastiche, and yet another occurs in the well-known 'Turkish Rondo' (*Rondo alla turca*) of his piano sonata in A major, K331.

It is the last of five violin concertos which the youthful composer produced in Salzburg in 1775. Mozart himself was an accomplished violinist, but these concertos seem to have been intended for his Salzburg colleague Antonio Brunetti – who found the *Adagio* of this one 'too artificial'. Mozart obligingly wrote a substitute movement for him – now catalogued separately as K261 and not usually included in performances of the concerto.

The melodies pour out of the opening movement, sounding fresh and impassioned – though presented with a waywardness and irregularity which contrasts with the classical poise found in the more mature piano concertos already discussed. In the movement's heading, the word *aperto* ('open') apparently denotes a broad, unbuttoned style.

The slow movement in E major makes an immediate and ingratiating melodic appeal, to be deepened with the later appearance of more melancholy harmonies.

Returning to A major, an easy-going, memorable rondo-theme begins the finale. The Turkish 'explosion' comes later and the concerto ends by summoning a carefree atmosphere once more.

Sinfonia concertante for violin, viola and orchestra in E flat major, K364

> Allegro maestoso
> Andante
> Presto
> Duration: 30 minutes

Paris was the musical centre where this kind of double or multiple concerto was chiefly favoured. So the French form of title 'Symphonie concertante' is more strictly correct, if not commonly used for this Mozart example. The original score does not survive, nor do we know when the first performance took place, but the work seems to have been written in Salzburg in 1779.

From the early printed edition we note that the viola part is written a semitone lower than it is required to sound. The viola-player tunes the instrument *up* by that half-tone, so that the special resonance of the open strings, instead of being brought into play for the viola's normal C, G, D and A, occurs on D flat, A flat, E flat and B flat – notes more likely to be emphasized in a work in the present key. The normally 'weak' viola is thus helped to match the power of the violin, which does not re-tune and has no special resonance on those notes.

Oboes, horns and strings are all the orchestral instruments required. The two soloists are supposed to join respectively with the orchestral first violins and violas when not playing as soloists, a convention not generally observed in modern performances. In the following description, the music ascribed to 'soloists' refers to their special 'solo' sections.

The opening movement takes regular concerto form. An orchestral *tutti* presents several themes but does not leave the home key.

The soloists enter successively, establishing their character with new material. As the music moves to B flat, a strikingly declaimed theme is heard high on the violin, and then passes to the viola. Eventually a big orchestral climax in the new key leads to more meditative exchanges. The firm recapitulation is at first identical with the opening, but in the return of the declaimed theme in E flat the viola is now heard first. A cadenza, fully written out, features both soloists.

A minor-key slow movement, rare in a major-key work of this period, brings an emotional and even melancholy mood. After an orchestral opening, the main theme is intensified by the soloists. The orchestra now produces an enfolding theme which takes the music to a serene E flat, in which key the soloists again pursue the main theme. The enfolding theme also reappears. Later, a suspenseful passage in C minor leads to a shared cadenza (again, fully written out) and a short, resigned coda in that key.

The indication *Presto* signals a rapid, merry movement in E flat. A bustling tune for strings is followed by one for the horns, taken up by oboes. Solo violin, followed by solo viola, presents a new, sharp-edged theme. A further, upward-climbing theme is also given to the soloists. They eventually arrive, almost by surprise, at the opening (originally orchestral) theme in its original key. The horn-and-oboe tune also reappears, after which the course is clear to the final bars.

Overture to The Magic Flute

Duration: 7 minutes

In 1791 Mozart gave to the world both the last of his serious operas, *The Clemency of Titus*, and that unique blend of fun and philosophizing, *The Magic Flute*. Its first performance took place in Vienna on 30 September. The opera uses, as a symbol of wisdom, certain references to the Freemasons' order, to which the composer (and his librettist, Schikaneder) belonged. Among these symbolic references is threefold repetition – applied to notes and chords besides physical objects on stage.

Hence the overture, otherwise in regular sonata-form, is impregnated by solemn wind-chords in groups of three: in the opera they are associated with the temple of wisdom to which the hero will be admitted by its high priest, Sarastro. The participation of trombones (here as in the opera) lends a special solemnity. The orchestra is otherwise Mozart's symphonic one – 2 each of flutes, oboes, clarinets, bassoons, horns and trumpets; kettledrums and strings.

MUSORGSKY

1839–81

One work, the opera *Boris Godunov*, suffices to give immortality to
Modest Musorgsky. A bold type of dramatic declamation is reinforced by a harmonic language so stark, so disdainful of traditional
progressions that a revised and much smoother version by Rimsky-
Korsakov long held sway. Now that the original has been restored to
favour, Musorgsky can be relished for the force of his orchestral as
well as vocal writing.

Musorgsky left unfinished another opera, *Khovanshchina* (The
Khovansky Affair); Rimsky-Korsakov completed and orchestrated
it, and the opening prelude, depicting dawn over the river Moscow,
makes an effective concert work. Another piece, known as *Night
on the bare mountain*, or in America as *Night on Bald Mountain*, is a
free re-working by Rimsky-Korsakov of Musorgsky's materials.
The Musorgsky original, when (rarely) heard, is sometimes
distinguished as *St John's Night on the bare Mountain*.

But the music of Musorgsky is most often represented in the
orchestral concert-hall by the following brilliant transcription from a
piano original.

Pictures at an Exhibition (orchestrated by Maurice Ravel)

> . . . Promenade
> Gnomus (The Gnome)
> . . . Promenade
> Il vecchio castello
> . . . Promenade
> Tuileries
> Bydło (Cattle)
> . . . Promenade
> Ballet of the chickens in their eggshells

Samuel Goldenberg and Schmuyle
Limoges: the market-place
Catacombae: sepulchrum romanum (Catacombs: Roman
  sepulchre)
Cum mortuis in lingua mortua (with the dead in a dead
  language)
The hut on fowls' legs
The great gate of Kiev
Duration: 30 minutes

In 1874 Musorgsky composed this set of musical images to correspond to ten paintings by his friend Viktor Hartman. The extra element of a 'promenade' round the exhibition is cleverly added and the music of the final 'picture' seems to have risen from the theme of the 'promenade'. The painter had recently died when these paintings were shown at an exhibition which the composer visited. On title ('Samuel Goldenberg and Schmuyle') in fact represents two pictures, both of which were owned by Musorgsky and lent to the exhibition.

In the original scoring for piano solo (not published till after Musorgsky's death) they have had only limited currency; Ravel's orchestration, which propelled them to popularity, was commissioned by Serge Koussevitzky before he established himself in Boston (see p.43) and was first given under his baton in Paris on 3 May 1920. An alto saxophone is an unusual constituent of the large orchestra, which otherwise comprises: 3 flutes (one doubling piccolo), 3 oboes (1 doubling english horn), 2 clarinets and bass clarinet, 2 bassoons and double-bassoon, 4 horns, 3 trumpets, 3 trombones, tuba, kettledrums, other percussion (snare drum, bass drum, cymbals, triangle, rattle, whip, xylophone, glockenspiel, tubular bells), celesta, 2 harps and strings.

Promenade. The spectator makes his way round the gallery, attracted by various pictures in turn. A pronounced 'walking' theme is heard, with the brass prominent.

Gnomus (***The gnome***). The painting is sometimes said to have been of a dwarfed creature walking awkwardly on deformed legs. But an apparently more authoritative source claims that it was of a nutcracker in the shape of a gnome. The abrupt, angular music has many pauses and changes of rhythm.

Promenade. A new scoring, as though to suggest a new point of interest for the spectator.

Il vecchio castello (The old castle). A singer is stationed outside the Italian castle. The 'song' is given principally to the alto saxophone.

Promenade. Again a new scoring.

Tuileries. An impression of the famous park in Paris, with children and their nursemaids. High woodwind represents the children's chattering, both at the beginning and at the end of the piece.

Bydło. A Polish peasant wagon with enormous wooden wheels is seen, drawn by oxen (the word 'bydło' is Polish for 'cattle'.) A solo tuba makes the point of heaviness, and the music suggests the disappearance of wagon and beast into the distance.

Promenade. The theme is now more tranquil, and begins smoothly with high flutes and clarinets. It leads straight to . . .

Ballet of the chickens in their eggshells. The painting appears to have shown a child dressed up as a chicken with its limbs poking through the shell of an egg. A clucking little scherzo movement is heard. The first part is repeated; a central part (trio) begins with sustained soft trills for the violins; finally comes a shortened repeat of the first part.

Samuel Goldenberg and Schmuyle. The two Jews, one rich and the other poor, are vividly contrasted: a heavy self-satisfied theme is followed by a whining, supplicating utterance on a muted trumpet.

Limoges: the market-place. The picture depicts the gossiping market women. Scurrying themes on woodwind and strings are enlivened by triangle, tambourine, and cymbals. The music passes dramatically, without interruption to . . .

Catacombae: sepulchrum romanum. These catacombs (a Roman burial place) are not in Rome but in Paris, where the painter depicted himself with a friend and a guide. A sense of mystery is conveyed by solemn brass notes in long pauses. Apart from the double-basses, the strings are strikingly silent.

Cum mortuis in lingua mortua (with the dead in a dead language). A continuation of the preceding scene. The composer commented: 'The creative spirit of Hartman leads me towards the skull; he addresses them and they become gradually lit from within.' The theme of the Promenade is recalled.

The hut on fowls' legs. The artist had shown a clock in the form of a hut belonging to Baba-Yaga, the Russian witch who eats human bones and rides through the sky. Her ferocity is indicated by the heavy down-strokes for the strings, reinforced by percussion and other instruments. Later a whirling figure is set up by the flutes; the heavy music returns. We are led directly to . . .

The great gate of Kiev. Contrary to many listeners' supposition, this is not an actual gate. It was one imagined by the artist and his submission for a competition for a gateway to be erected in commemoration of the escape of Tsar Alexander II from assassination in 1866. A dome took the form of an ancient Russian helmet, the horses in the picture no doubt giving the composer the idea of a processional piece. The music in fact combines procession and hymn tune. Tubular bells and tam-tam make their first entry into Ravel's brilliant orchestration.

NIELSEN

1865–1931

Little celebrity came in his lifetime to the composer now regarded as Denmark's greatest and one of the leading symphonists after the era of Brahms and Bruckner. Carl Nielsen worked (as violinist, conductor and composer) almost exclusively in Copenhagen. His varied range of compositions won a posthumous international recognition in the 1950s: as well as six symphonies, they include a flute concerto and a clarinet concerto.

Often compared with Sibelius, Nielsen is unlike him in attaching titles to most of his symphonies (no. 2 is *The Four Temperaments*; no. 4 is *The Inextinguishable*). A symphony with two solo voices (no. 3, the 'Sinfonia espansiva') also sets him apart from Sibelius's practice. Nielsen's Symphony no. 1 (1891–2) begins in one key and ends in another – the first symphony to effect this break with convention. Bold harmonic clashes and broad, song-like themes are characteristic of his work.

Symphony No. 5, opus 50

Tempo giusto – Adagio non troppo
Allegro – Presto – Andante un poco tranquillo – Allegro
Duration: 35 minutes

On 24 January 1922, nine days after completing the score, the composer conducted the first performance of his Fifth Symphony in Copenhagen. Built in only two movements, its most remarkable feature is a solo for snare drum 'to be played as though intended at all costs to disrupt the flow of the music' and continued as an improvisation by the solo drummer. The other orchestral requirements are 3 flutes (one doubling piccolo), 2 each of oboes, clarinet and bassoons; 4 horns, 3 trumpets, 3 trombones and tuba; celesta; kettledrums; and strings.

The first movement proceeds from uncertainty to affirmation. Its first (faster) part seems to have no key centre; but the succeeding *Adagio* settles into G major with a serenely flowing song tune. Although the snare drum combats it, the serenity is eventually re-established. The music then ebbs in a cadenza for solo clarinet while the snare drum's sound vanishes in the distance.

An energetic theme in triple time dominates the *Allegro* which opens the second movement. A scherzo-like section follows, then an *andante*, both these sections gaining intensity from the fugue-like overlapping of their melodies. Then the *Allegro* is recapitulated, with no impediment to its drive to a final E flat major. Triumphant brass plays its traditional role, and in place of the disruptive snare drum the kettledrums give a solid, reinforcing beat.

POULENC

In the 1920s, when Jean Cocteau was a leader of literary life in Paris, when Picasso was active there and the Diaghilev ballet had made Paris its home, French music blossomed. Of composers younger than Ravel, Francis Poulenc achieved distinction with ballets, piano pieces, songs and chamber music. He himself, as an excellent pianist, was one of the best exponents of his own works. Orchestral music (apart from the ballet) occupied him little, nor did he essay opera until after the Second World War.

He did, however, compose four concertos, all for keyboard instruments. The earliest (1928) was for harpsichord, fancifully titled *Concert champêtre* with allusion to the open-air musical diversions in paintings by Watteau; another was composed for two pianos and another (1949) for piano solo. None of these has been so enthusiastically received into the orchestral repertory as the work discussed here.

Concerto for organ, strings and kettledrums in G minor

> Andante – Allegro giocoso . . . (and further changes to tempo)
> Duration: 20–22 minutes

What need of wind instruments in the orchestra when the solo part is entrusted to the grandest wind instrument of all? Such a consideration may have been in Poulenc's mind in scoring this one-movement concerto. Composed in 1938 and privately performed in the following year, it received its first public performance in wartime Paris on 10 June 1941, under the restricted conditions of concert life permitted under German occupation. The conductor was Charles Munch and the soloist Maurice Duruflé (himself a noted composer), whom Poulenc thanked in his score for assisting in the specification of organ stops to be used.

Its single movement is crafted in a masterly way to form a unity despite its many changes of mood and speed. It avoids hymns and fugues, two of the kinds of music most routinely associated with the organ, but nevertheless pays tribute to Bach as the great master of the instrument. A big, Bach-like, declamatory opening is given to the solo instrument. The first section of the work is serious in tone and is heavily concluded by drums and organ.

The strings then launch into a more agitated section. The soloist joins in. Soon, behind a powerful, long-held chord of C major, may be heard a quick, ascending four-note figure many times repeated – B, C, D, E. The music comes to a complete halt and the organ resumes in quieter vein, beginning the central and longest section of the work with varied moods flowing into one another. There is a notable moment of suspended motion when a full chord of A minor slides to A major. Much later, when the emphatic chord of G minor recalls how the work began, it similarly 'brightens' to G major. In that new key the four-note ascending figure becomes the theme of a new section of fast and happy music.

Over-happy – perhaps hysterically happy? Indeed so. It disappears as the full weight of the Bach-like opening flourish returns in the more sober G minor. The concerto ends slowly, reflectively.

PROKOFIEV

1891–1953

The Russian composer Sergey Prokofiev won particular fame in orchestral and piano music – especially if we include, in the former category, his ballet scores. Of these both *Romeo and Juliet* (1938) and *Cinderella* (1945) have established themselves in the concert-hall. From one of Prokofiev's operas comes one of the best-known pieces of our century: the cheeky, grotesque march from *Love for Three Oranges* (1921).

Prokofiev's early reputation was that of a composer of violent, barbarous music who could nevertheless produce such a lyrical and witty tribute to the past as the *Classical Symphony*. A brilliant pianist, he left Russia under its new Soviet government but returned to live there from the 1930s. The Soviet pressure towards a simpler style produced, among other works, the popular *Peter and the Wolf*. But there were later severe clashes between the adventurous composer and a culturally repressive government. Besides seven symphonies, he left two violin concertos (testimony of his long association with David Oistrakh) and five piano concertos, no. 4 for left hand alone.

Classical Symphony *(Symphony no. 1 in D)*

Allegro
Larghetto
Gavotta: non troppo allegro
Molto vivace
Duration: 15 minutes

The Soviet revolution was not yet one year old, nor had Prokofiev himself quite reached his 27th birthday, when the composer conducted the first performance of this work in Petrograd (the future Leningrad) on 21 April 1918. Wholly individual, it can nevertheless be seen as one manifestation of a broad musical trend. After experiencing the free forms and outsize orchestral scores of the early 1900s, of which Stravinsky's *The Rite of Spring* is now the most famous, several composers decided to re-explore the forms and sounds of the eighteenth and early nineteenth centuries. The label 'neo-classical' is widely given to such explorations, but Prokofiev was the only well-known composer actually to incorporate the word 'classical' into his title.

Elegance and wit are its features. Though the general model is the Haydn or Mozart symphony, the expected minuet is replaced by a gavotte, a dance favoured in an earlier (Bach–Handel) period. The orchestration is precisely 'classical' (double woodwind, 2 each of horns and trumpets, 2 kettledrums and strings), but the usage of the instruments is often modern and individual: for example, the two drums are struck simultaneously in the gavotte, and the violins' melody in the finale is coloured by the use of 'harmonics' (see p. 373). The symphony is in D major – all movements being in that key, except for the second in A.

The first movement follows, with a few twists, the classical sonata-form pattern, with a first subject in D, a second in A (with pronounced leaping from high to low by the violins); after a complete bar's pause, a development follows, and a recapitulation.

After a few bars setting the rhythm in moderately slow time, the second movement presents a sunny, spacious tune. A contrasting tune shows itself in low notes on a single bassoon with cellos and double-basses, after which the first section returns.

The gavotte's steady rhythm takes in the characteristic musical feature of the dance, a start with two unstressed beats before the first down-beat. The first section is vigorously accented, the middle section (with a change of key from D to G) quieter and smoother, after which the return of the first section brings the surprise of a slightly slower pace and a quiet ending.

The fast finale displays the strong rhythms and cheerful spirit expected from eighteenth-century precedent. It follows sonata-form – the first subject heard immediately on the violins, the second with rapid articulations of a high note in the flutes. The exposition is marked to be repeated (as was not the case in the first movement). The development is brief; when the exposition returns, it is the flutes which now present the original opening tune.

Symphony No.5 in B flat major, opus 100

Andante
Allegro marcato
Adagio
Allegro giocoso
Duration: 44 minutes

It was with the first performance of this work that Prokofiev made his last appearance on the conductor's rostrum on 13 January 1945, in Moscow. The new symphony signalled the composer's reappearance in the capital after the ravages of war – a war whose end was now in sight. Immediately welcomed for its sense of confidence and noble aspirations, it has survived as an outstanding example of how genius can take hold of the traditional symphonic form and fuse it with intensely individual and modern expression.

A piano makes a distinctive contribution to the orchestra, and five players besides the kettledrummer are required to handle the large array of percussion, with wood-block, tambourine and tam-tam as well as snare drum, bass drum, cymbals and triangle. A harp is also required, the other instruments being 2 flutes and piccolo, 2 oboes and english horn, 2 clarinets with 1 high clarinet and 1 bass clarinet, 2 bassoons and double-bassoon; 4 horns, 3 trumpets, 3 trombones and tuba; and strings.

The movements follow a familiar Russian sequence, the scherzo coming second and the slow movement third. The rather pensive principal theme of the first movement is briefly recalled at the opening of the finale – with the effect of a reminiscence swiftly banished by the new joyful (*giocoso*) mood.

The first movement is itself unusual, being conceived in a kind of modernized sonata-form but in slow rather than fast tempo. The gentle, upward-tending first subject, in 3/4 time, is worked to a climax and then succeeded by the contrast of a new tune (at first on flutes and oboes) in 4/4. A development starts as the cellos and double-basses softly repeat the opening phrase, and at the recapitulation the same phrase is blazed forth by the brass. After the second theme has also returned there is the surprise of an extra section in a martial but solemn spirit. Bass drum and tam-tam lead the full percussion as the movement's opening theme is expanded in mighty fanfares.

The second movement, though a scherzo in supplying a lighter element to the symphony, is longer and more diverse than that label might imply. A main section in D minor presents grotesquely dancing figures (solo clarinet, oboe, violins) which later induce a chattering of snare drum and wood-block. In contrast (like a trio in the classical scherzo form), a new section displays a slower, rather wistful melody in D major for woodwind against horn accompaniment: this in turn takes off, then returns in the original woodwind-and-horn colouring. A transition soon brings back the original strain with even rougher vigour to the end.

A slow movement in F major is fervently lyrical: the emotional heart of the symphony. It develops melodically, moving into E major for a warm statement on the strings, then into different keys. Over repeated notes on the piano a more threatening air enters; a climax of great stress erupts but suddenly clears as the strings regain the opening melody in its original key and the full orchestra embraces it. The music takes no easy escape in reaching a final peaceful chord.

A fast finale is preluded by a slow introduction: here the cellos, divided into four, give a harmonized reminiscence of the first movement's main theme. Then, over a regular-rhythmed accompaniment, a solo clarinet thrusts forward the new and joyous main theme – ascending, cavorting downwards, then pointing up again. Much contrasting material follows, including a lyrical theme and a sombre one (rising from the lower strings), but eventually the perky main theme returns on solo flute and english horn, two octaves apart. The end of the symphony is exuberant.

Concerto No.3 in C major for piano and orchestra, opus 26

> Andante – Allegro
> Theme and variations
> Allegro ma non troppo
> Duration: 26 minutes

Prokofiev was in the habit of 'collecting' materials, as they occurred to him, for inclusion in future works. As early as 1911 he had evolved part of the material which found its way into the present work, completed ten years later and first given on 16 December 1921 in Chicago. The composer was the soloist, with Frederick Stock as the conductor.

The concerto was to establish itself as a standard work, thanks to its combination of a vigorous, attacking style with some appealing, almost sentimental melodies not far from the Rakhmaninov model. There is none of the deliberate barbarity of some of Prokofiev's other works of the period. In the orchestrations, perhaps the only surprise is to find castanets along with other percussion: snare drum, bass drum and cymbals, as well as the usual kettledrums. Full brass (4 horns, 2 trumpets, 3 trombones) participate with double woodwind and the usual strings.

The traditional three movements are presented and the key of C major is specified. A solo clarinet quietly opens the work with a song-like theme carrying a hint of A minor, but immediately the orchestra places it in full C-major dress. The tempo quickens to *Allegro*, where vigorous and busy music is shared by soloist and orchestra. Against the tap of castanets, an oboe gives out a more sustained, contrasting tune. At a climax the slower, song-like tune of the opening returns. The *Allegro* material is resumed and worked to a brilliant conclusion.

A slow movement in E minor, beginning like a cousin of the *gavotte* in the *Classical Symphony*, consists of a theme (orchestra alone) and variations. The piano enters with a trill to begin the first variation. A cymbal clash marks the change to quicker tempo for the second and third variations, where the piano's strenuous activity (with triplets in the third variation) is countered by orchestral reminders of the theme. A slow fourth variation and a faster fifth lead into a restatement of the theme itself – but now at half-speed, the piano's chords rippling round the melody.

The finale opens with a melody given unexpectedly to two bassoons in unison. As with the opening of the first movement, there is a hint of the key of A minor – but, after an intervention by the piano, the lower strings place the theme firmly in C major. Extended vigorous musical argument followed. It yields eventually to a flowing, Rakhmaminov-ish theme in slower tempo (woodwind first, then strings): the piano answers with another theme, then joins in. But the sentimental impulse does not last. The opening theme returns in its own faster tempo and the piano hurtles and hammers its way to an exciting finish.

Symphonic suite, Lieutenant Kizhe, opus 60

The birth of Kizhe
Song
The wedding of Kizhe
Troika
The burial of Kizhe
Duration: 21 minutes

In a satirical tale by the nineteenth-century Russian author Yuri Tynyanov, a military clerk creates by a slip of the pen an officer called Lieutenant Kizhe ('Lieutenant That', more or less). Such is the power of bureaucracy that when the Tsar noted the presence of this person, a military and private career had to be invented for him. The tale was made into a Soviet film for which Prokofiev composed the music in 1933. Four years later, in Paris, on 20 February 1937, Prokofiev conducted a suite from the film which remained among his most popular works.

A lively score parodies both military music and sentimental song. Two numbers (the second and fourth) have a solo baritone voice, but the composer provided alternative versions for orchestra only which are generally performed. No.2 is often headed 'Romance' in concert programmes but this is a mistake: that word in both its French and Russian forms corresponds simply to 'Song' in English. A French usage has also made familiar the spelling of the surname as 'Kijé'.

The orchestration has prominent parts for a solo cornet (which begins and ends the work with a military fanfare off-stage) and a tenor saxophone. The other orchestral requirements are 2 flutes and piccolo, 2 each of oboes, clarinets and bassoons; 4 horns, 2 trumpets, 3 trombones and tuba; celesta and piano; percussion which includes sleigh-bells as well as kettledrums, snare drum, bass drum, tambourine, cymbals and triangle; and strings.

RAKHMANINOV

1873–1943

One of the great concert pianists of his time (by no means confining himself to his own works), Sergey Rakhmaninov stands also as one of the principal Russian composers. Even though he chose to live outside Russia after the 1917 Soviet revolution, latterly living in California and acquiring US citizenship a few weeks before his death, his work retained its original Russian focus. Many songs, many piano pieces (the famous prelude in C sharp minor being an early work, 1892) and a choral work *The Bells* (on a Russian version of Edgar Allan Poe's poem) show his art in characteristic form.

His three symphonies and a late set of *Symphonic Dances* (1941) did not gather the instant and sustained interest attaching to his works for piano and orchestra, but the Second Symphony (1908) is now increasingly performed and admired. Indeed, even the First Symphony, which the dissatisfied composer destroyed in its original full score, has been reconstructed and performed. He wrote no concertos for instruments other than the piano, and he himself gave the first performances of all the piano concertos.

The concertos

Rakhmaninov's four piano concertos, plus the *Rhapsody on a Theme of Paganini* which may be placed with them, constitute a substantial and distinctive part of the musical repertory. The early First Concerto (1891), revised in 1917, is rarely heard; no.4 was considered a failure when first given (Philadelphia, 1927) and even in its revision (1941) has hardly established a hold. But both the second and third remain among the most played of all concertos, with the *Rhapsody* hardly less popular. In all these three works a characteristic combination of surging melody, rhythmic excitement, and brilliant pianistic display carries the composer's unmistakable and personal stamp.

Concerto No.2 in C minor
for piano and orchestra, opus 18

> Moderato
> Adagio sostenuto
> Allegro scherzando
> Duration: 46–48 minutes

The story of the genesis of this concerto fulfils, almost like fiction, the Romantic fantasy of the artist with a creative power he can hardly control. Rakhmaninov was treated for depression by Dr N. Dahl, a Moscow physician and hypnotist who repeatedly told his half-asleep patient: 'You will begin to write your concerto . . . you will work with great facility . . . the concerto will be of an excellent quality . . .'

To Dahl the concerto was eventually dedicated. It was given complete in Moscow on 9 November 1901 (eleven months after a performance of just the second and third movements), the composer being the soloist and Alexander Ziloti conducting. Double wood-wind, 4 horns, 2 trumpets, 2 trombones, tuba, 3 kettledrums and strings are used, with bass drum and cymbals added in the finale.

Bell-like chords, subtly changing, ring out from the piano to open the first movement. Violins announce the swaying first subject. After the first big climax the soloist presents the rising and falling second subject in E flat. A seamless development follows, with the piano constantly active in melody or in rippling accompaniment. The main theme's eventual return, at full strength on the violins, is triumphantly reinforced by the march-like insistence of the piano. A softly playing horn brings back the second theme (in A flat). The music then seems to seek repose in C major, but C minor is re-established and a sudden animation on the piano ends the movement.

Muted strings work a soft transition from the preceding C minor to the key of the new movement, E major (a transition like that which leads to the *Largo* of Dvořák's *New World* symphony.) The piano accompanies while woodwind instruments construct a curling theme. The piano itself takes over in a 'singing' melody, then passes to a slightly faster tempo to present new material in partnership with a bassoon. Later the orchestra's motion halts for a solo cadenza, after which the 'singing' theme returns.

Once more the new movement (finale) starts with a transition of keys – this time, a rum–ti–tum rhythm moves from the preceding E major back to C minor. A full-orchestral explosion and a solo cadenza precede the vigorous main theme on the solo piano. The pace slackens as the violas plus a solo oboe present a smooth, yearning tune which is to be this work's most memorable melody; the piano takes it over. The quicker pace returns, itself quickening to *presto*; an agitated orchestra is 'calmed' by the piano. The yearning tune now returns gently on the piano, in D flat. In that 'remote' key the music cannot end; after further interchange between solo and orchestra, an altered version of the theme in C major leads to an optimistic conclusion.

Concerto No.3 in D minor for piano and orchestra, opus 30

> Allegro ma non tanto
> Intermezzo: Adagio, *leading to*
> Alla breve
> Duration: 35–42 minutes

With the same orchestration as for his Second Concerto (except for the addition of a snare drum), Rakhmaninov's Third Concerto is much in the earlier mould. It had its first performance in New York at the start of Rakhmaninov's first American tour – on 28 November 1909, with the composer as soloist and Walter Damrosch conducting. For the substantial cadenza required in the first movement, the composer published two alternative versions – each, however, concluding with the same impassioned chordal proclamation leading to the wind instruments' interventions. The material of the first movement lingers, transformed, in the other movements.

Against a quiet but firm orchestral rhythm, the pianist enters with the first subject, which curls round the keynote D. A gentle, *staccato* figure on the strings leads into a smoother, slower theme for piano, in B flat. To this theme, with its 'yearning' sentiment so typical of the composer, bassoon and other instruments add their contributions. Development begins with a sudden switch back to faster tempo. After a climax it dies away towards a cadenza (see above): towards the end of this, a solo flute steals in with a reminder of the opening theme; other wind instruments do likewise. A recapitulation of both main themes leads to a soft ending.

The second movement, though starting afresh, takes the chord of

D minor just heard and breathes a new theme which starts from that key. The movement's own key, F sharp minor, is reached as the piano enters. The soloist's rhapsodizing now dominates the music. Then, surprisingly, over the most delicate piano figurations a waltz tune is heard from woodwind instruments. The more soulful rhapsodizing returns but shifts – via fierce exclamations from the piano – directly into . . .

. . . the finale. A persistent march-rhythm in D minor is like a reinforcement of the opening of the first movement. Vigorous exchanges between soloist and orchestra lead to a dramatic new theme in a new key (C major) – a theme which rises in big chords stamped out on the piano. Later comes a kind of skittish, *scherzando* interlude, with piano against muted strings. Reminders of the first movement are strongest with a slow (lento) section that follows, the piano again 'yearning'. Eventually the quicker beat of the opening march-rhythm returns and then (with a cymbal-clash!) the opening key of D minor. The 'stamping' theme quickly follows, more majestic than ever, and the conclusion works up with force and speed to *presto*.

Rhapsody on a Theme of Paganini, for piano and orchestra, opus 43

Duration: 22–24 minutes

The theme of an unaccompanied *Capriccio* by the great violinist–composer Paganini (1782–1840) was made the subject of a set of variations by Brahms (1886). The same theme served Rakhmaninov for *his* set of variations, to which he gave the title *Rhapsody*. The theme has also been borrowed by at least two later composers, the German Boris Blacher and the Pole Witold Lutosławski.

The composer was the soloist, and Leopold Stokowski the conductor, at the first performance on 7 November 1934, in Philadelphia. Glockenspiel and harp, not present in either of the two famous concertos discussed above, lend their colour to the orchestra, which otherwise uses double woodwind plus piccolo and english horn; 4 horns, 2 trumpets, 3 trombones and tuba; kettledrums, bass drum, snare drum, cymbals. Important in the work is a quotation from the Roman Catholic chant, *Dies irae*, referring to the terrors of the Day of Judgement. Berlioz in the *Fantastic Symphony* quoted it parodistically, alluding to a Witches' Sabbath (see p.81); for

Rakhmaninov, here and in other works, it is almost a personal signature.

Unusually in a set of variations, the theme does not come first. The key of A minor is set by the opening flourish in which the orchestra suggests what is to come, the piano merely punctuating. Then comes Variation 1 (the entry of the snare drum is conspicuous); then the theme itself on violins alone, immediately followed by Variation 2, the tune passing to the piano with reinforcement of certain notes on horns and trumpets. The *Dies irae* enters in Variation 7 in slow chords on the piano while cellos and a bassoon have the theme melody. Soon afterwards (Variation 10), while the clarinets in a low register deliver an angular distortion of the theme, the piano once again pronounces the *Dies irae*, this time in slow, spaced-out octaves.

This variation fades on two high notes of the piano, ending the first section of the work. After a slight pause the second section begins. A more dreamy mood is established: over *tremolo* strings the piano reflects on the theme, and shortly launches a cadenza in which the harp joins. Later variations give much contrast of rhythm; in no. 16 a rather wistful version of the theme is heard on a solo oboe in a far-away key, B flat minor. Prolonged through the next variation, that key then yields to D flat major for the emotional climax of the work – Variation 18 (marked *Andante cantabile*). The piano begins it.

Pizzicato strings snap the mood, the key returns to A minor, and the third section (Variations 19–24) follows. A final climax comes when the brass thunders out the *Dies irae* theme which seems to drag Paganini's theme down with it. The percussionists join in a combined orchestral exclamation and leave the piano to whisper the end.

RAVEL

1875–1937

To say that Maurice Ravel was a supreme colourist of the orchestra is true enough. That facility is evident in the skill with which he orchestrated some of his own piano pieces, and in the resources he brought to the treatment of Musorgsky's *Pictures at an Exhibition*. Often in his own music the sense of movement or illumination comes equally with the patterning of notes and the kaleidoscope of tone-colour.

His works *originally* written for orchestra are few: even the well-known *Pavane for a dead infanta* is an orchestration of an early piano piece. The *Tzigane* (i.e. a piece in gipsy style) is, however, original in its violin and orchestra form, the piano accompaniment being an alternative. The two piano concertos are confusingly titled: the latter (1932) is 'in G'; the one for left hand alone (below) bears no indication of key. In general, Ravel shares some traits with his compatriot Debussy (but with detectable differences, and by no means as a disciple). If sometimes an 'impressionist', exhibiting a swirl of outlines and tiny points of light, Ravel at other times values a sharp-edged clarity linked to a cultivation of eighteenth-century French forms.

Concerto for piano (left hand) and orchestra

Duration: 17–18 minutes

The concerto is one of several works, by Richard Strauss, Britten and others, for the Austrian pianist Paul Wittgenstein, who lost his right arm in military action during the First World War. He gave the first performance of the work in Vienna on 27 November 1931. It has three parts, the middle one jazzy. The orchestration is for 3 flutes (one doubling piccolo), 2 oboes and english horn, 2 clarinets and high clarinet in E flat, bass clarinet, 2 bassoons and double-bassoon,

4 horns, 3 trumpets, 3 trombones and tuba; kettledrums and other percussion (triangle, snare drum, bass drum, cymbals, wood block, tam-tam); harp and strings.

Bolero

> Duration: 15–17 minutes

'Seventeen minutes of orchestral fabric without music' was Ravel's tongue-in-cheek description of his *Bolero*, with its single *crescendo* which has made it one of the most famous of twentieth-century works. It was first performed as a ballet for solo dancer, in Paris, on 22 November 1928. Proceeding from the faintest drum-taps it rises cumulatively to full orchestral force with one enormous sideways key-change (C to E).

Two snare-drums lead the important element of percussion (with cymbals, kettledrums and tam-tam). Unusual additions to the orchestra are 3 saxophones and the Bach-period 'oboe d'amore'. The remaining orchestration comprises 2 flutes (1 doubling piccolo), 2 oboes and english horn, 2 clarinets plus high clarinet in E flat and bass clarinet, 2 bassoons and double-bassoon, 4 horns, 4 trumpets, 3 trombones, tuba and strings.

Suites from the ballet, Daphnis and Chloe

Diaghilev's famous Russian ballet in Paris gave the first performance of *Daphnis and Chloe* on 8 June 1912, with Pierre Monteux conducting. The story of two lovers united by the goodwill of Pan is taken from the ancient Greek author Longus, but Ravel declared that he was 'less concerned with archaism than with fidelity to the Greece of my dreams, which is close to that imagined and painted by the French artists of the eighteenth century'. Detailed directions for the action of the dance are given throughout the score.

Ravel's orchestration, exceptionally large for ballet, includes a wordless chorus as well as triple or quadruple woodwind, 4 trumpets, 2 harps, a large percussion section, celesta and wind-machine. The inclusion of the alto flute is characteristic of the composer. In the concert-hall, even with the chorus omitted, this music has enjoyed much success – either in its complete form or as represented by two suites (selections which were actually published as 'symphonic fragments'). The wind-machine occurs only at the opening of the first.

Suite no. 1

> Nocturne
> Interlude
> War–Dance

> Duration: 12 minutes

The scene is a sacred grove. At the point at which the suite begins, the shepherd Daphnis has been thrown into despair because his beloved Chloe has been abducted by pirates. It is dark, but in an unreal light the statues of three nymphs now come to life. At the first orchestral climax a kind of suspended oscillation is heard like a solemn nature-call. The nymphs dance to a swaying figure on three flutes plus alto flute. They comfort Daphnis (theme on violas and clarinets) and invoke the god Pan, whose form begins to show.

An interlude with slow-moving wordless voices (or their orchestral replacement) is interrupted by urgent calls on horn and trumpet. The scene changes to the pirates' camp and their war-dance begins in successive waves of full-orchestral sound. Over a continuing excited beat a quieter strain arises from a piccolo, and finally this is itself absorbed in the strenuous dance.

Suite no. 2

> Dawn
> Pantomime
> General Dance

> Duration: 18 minutes

Chloe has been rescued from the pirates by Pan. (The music for this falls between the two suites.) The scene is the grove once more: Daphnis lies prostrate. Dawn breaks with bird-song – richly imitated on the woodwind. A warm theme on a clarinet, related to that by which the nymphs comforted Daphnis, suffuses the music. Shepherds awake Daphnis: he searches for Chloe who at last appears (climax of the 'suffusing' theme). A crown on her head signifies Pan's divine intervention.

An old shepherd explains that Pan was moved by the memory of his own love for the nymph Syrinx. In a 'pantomime' (i.e. a mime-play, the original meaning of the term), Daphnis and Chloe now represent Pan and Syrinx: the god's melancholy playing of his reed-flute is heard as a high flute solo. At the climax of the representation they fall into each other's arms. To the sound of the 'nature-call' (see the Suite no. 1) they pledge their troth. An animated general dance with dazzling orchestration and intoxicating changes of rhythm ends the ballet.

Choreographic poem, **La Valse**

Duration: 11–13 minutes

Intended to be used in a ballet but refused by Diaghilev (which caused a rupture between the composer and the impresario), *La Valse* had its first performance in the concert-hall instead – on 12 December 1920, conducted by Camille Chevillard. None the less this exaltation of the Viennese waltz retains its designation as a 'choreographic poem' and carries on its score the stage picture he envisaged of an Austrian imperial ball about 1855: 'Intermittently, through rifts in a cloud, waltzing couples may be glimpsed. The clouds gradually disperse to reveal a huge ballroom filled with whirling dancers . . .'

The sound-picture is conveyed by a large orchestra with tripled or quadrupled woodwind instruments, full brass, 2 harps and a rich assembly of percussion: included are gong, glockenspiel, castanets, and crotales (small 'antique' cymbals tuned to definite notes). The initial mist is suggested by the muffled sound of double-basses and low notes on the harps.

A waltz melody rises to be heard on the violins, playing with their mutes on and with their bows 'over the finger-board', giving a tone like a ghost of normal violin sound. Then gradually, one by one, the players change to normal, rich tone . . . and at the point where, in Ravel's direction, 'the full light of the chandeliers bursts out', a vigorous Viennese waltz tune takes possession of the whole orchestra. Among later tunes is one which might also have been given to strings but is artfully allotted to solo trumpet. Over the insistent beat the music finally becomes wilder – to the point of explosion.

RIMSKY-KORSAKOV

1844–1908

The emergence of a school of Russian nationalist composers who at times had to pursue other occupations – Musorgsky a civil servant, Borodin a professor of chemistry, Rimsky-Korsakov a naval officer – is one of the striking events of nineteenth-century musical history. Almost self-taught, Rimsky-Korsakov became established as a composer and conservatory teacher of the greatest importance, and a recognized master of orchestration: his textbook on that subject contains examples only from his own works.

A fondness for Russian subjects and Russian folk-melody is found in many of his works – including his Symphony no. 2 (*Antar*) and the well-known *Russian Easter Festival Overture*. But it is typical of such nationalist composers to be interested not only in 'their own' music but in other strongly characterized national traits: hence Rimsky-Korsakov's *Spanish Caprice* (more usually given the hybrid title of *Capriccio espagnol*) with its vivacious orchestral rhythms. The universally known *Flight of the Bumble-bee* may emerge at orchestral concerts as part of a suite drawn from the opera *Tsar Saltan*, which is its original source.

Symphonic Suite, Scheherazade, *opus 35*

Duration: 46 minutes

Memorable melody and brilliant orchestration have made this work a perennial favourite. It springs from the fascination of Eastern tales for Rimsky-Korsakov and other Russian composers. The listener's fantasy is invited to soar from the music to the fancied scenes of the *Arabian Nights*. That collection of stories gave rise to the inscription on the score:

> The Sultan Shahriar, convinced of the falsehood and inconstancy of all women, had sworn an oath to put to death

each of his wives after the first night. However, the Sultana Scheherazade saved her life by arousing his interest in the tales which she told during the 1001 nights. Driven by curiosity, the sultan postponed his bloodthirsty design.

The composer labelled his four movements separately: 'The sea and Sindbad's ship; the narrative of the Kalender prince [Kalenders were an order of mendicant dervishes]; the prince and princess; festival at Baghdad – the ship dashed against the rock'. Later, not wishing the listener to seek for too much detail, he cut out the headings. But they remain a useful guide. As a title of this Russian work, the spelling *Sheherazada* would be more logical but the German form *Scheherazade* is commonly found in British and American use.

The composer himself conducted the first performance at St Petersburg on 3 November 1888. The picturesque effects gain from the enlarged percussion section of the orchestra – snare drum, tambourine, triangle, cymbals, bass drum, requiring five players; the orchestra is not large: strings, 2 flutes plus piccolo (or, sometimes, 2 piccolos and one flute), 2 each of oboe, clarinet, bassoon, 4 horns, 2 trumpets, 3 trombones and tuba.

The two pervasive themes are heard immediately: fiercely threatening (trombones prominent) for the Sultan, sweetly coaxing (violin solo) for Scheherazade. In symphonic terms, the presentation of these themes makes a slow introduction in E minor. The main section of the first movement follows in E major: the Sultan's theme becomes its first subject, with a quicker pair of themes (woodwind) as second subject. Scheherazade's theme re-enters in the development; there is a symphonic recapitulation, and a quiet ending which shows that the Sultan is thus far appeased.

The second movement in B minor is begun with Scheherazade's cajoling violin solo. She launches on a new tale (bassoon solo). At length the impatient Sultan interrupts. His theme takes on a threat as a solo trombone is answered by solo trumpet over *tremolando* strings. The story-telling becomes mixed with the menaces of the Sultan and the pleading of Scheherazade. Finally the Sultan's theme is pushed down to a protesting role on the bass instruments.

There is no conventional 'slow' movement. The third movement, in G, begins with a violin theme which is both a new 'tale' and an obvious emanation from Scheherazade's own theme. An up-and-down feathery effect (in a clarinet solo at first) is notable. A dance-rhythm is set up by the tambourine and the theme takes a new, swaying form in a solo clarinet. Lightly, other percussion instruments enter with their own different rhythms. Scheherazade's own theme (violin and harp) is later heard and the tale is further developed – with the Sultan silent.

The fourth movement opens to a recurrence of the Sultan's threats and Scheherazade's pleading. The new tale begins: over an insistent rhythm on the strings, a whirling theme on a solo flute grows in excitement. Rapid, repeated figures come from horns and trumpets against a pattering snare drum. The 'swaying' theme from the previous movement re-enters. Fragments of the Sultan's theme return on the trumpets. Finally, at a climax, the music proceeds in huge sweeps: the Sultan's theme is presented grandly but no longer angrily, and the concluding E major is reached. One of the quieter themes from the first movement briefly appears. Scheherazade's violin solo ascends to the instrument's fragile, high harmonics. Her serenity ends the work.

ROSSINI

1792–1868

The legitimacy of taking operatic overtures out of the theatre and into the concert-hall becomes obvious in the case of Rossini: some half-dozen of these works are among the most enjoyed of short orchestral items. They feature what is known as 'the Rossini *crescendo*' (though he was not quite its first user) – a long, gradual, full-orchestral wave of increasing sound. Rossini's name also attaches to six juvenile sonatas for strings which sometimes stray into orchestral concert programmes, but which are really chamber music.

Gioachino Rossini began his chain of operatic successes in his native Italy at the age of 18 with *La cambiale di matrimonio*; he ended that chain in France with *Guillaume Tell* (the original French title), which, though little performed today, is one of the most important operas of its period. In French opera the ballet was a required element, and the ballet music from *Tell* was to be a concert-hall favourite too.

The Overtures

Rossini's overtures are short, vivacious orchestral pieces, usually without musical reference to the opera. The orchestral style is direct and clear, the catchy melodies supported by strong, regular harmonic changes. But there are occasional surprises in the use of individual instruments: a side-drum roll begins the overture to *The Thieving Magpie*, more than once deceiving a British audience into thinking it the start of the national anthem. The form is regular and unproblematic. A slow and spacious opening section (too substantial to be called an introduction) is followed by a fast movement in a kind of compressed sonata-form. Two main tunes are presented, the second in a new key; then, with no development but only a few bars of transition, the first subject returns, and eventually the second – this time in the main key.

Overture, The Barber of Seville

Duration: 7 minutes

No overture is more famous than that of *The Barber*, though originally Rossini used it for an earlier work which failed. *The Barber* itself, originally taking a title from its tenor hero ('Almaviva, or the Useless Precaution'), was first heard in Rome under the composer's direction on 20 February 1816. The overture has a conventional scoring for its time: 2 each of flutes, oboes, clarinets, bassoons, horns and trumpets; kettledrums and bass drum; and strings.

The slow section in E major achieves an elegance with a violin melody above other strings *pizzicato*. The ensuing fast movement first engages us with a mischievously starting tune in E minor; an oboe presents the second subject in G major, which will make a more fully scored return in E major.

Overture, The Italian Girl in Algiers

Duration: 8 minutes

The East-Meets-West comedy formula, this time with a comically stupid Algerian prince outwitted by the Italian woman he has captured, animates this opera – first produced under the composer's direction in Venice on 22 May 1813. The overture has an unusual orchestration (but is often heard in corrupt versions). The authentic requirement is for a piccolo (no flutes), 2 each of oboes and clarinets, 1 bassoon, 2 horns and 2 trumpets, and bass drum (no kettledrums) with strings.

It is in C major. An oboe is the main solo instrument in the slow section, and in the fast section the graceful second subject has two charming presentations – by oboe and clarinet one octave apart, and later by piccolo and bassoon two octaves apart.

SAINT-SAËNS

1835–1921

No French composer enjoyed higher international esteem than the long-lived Camille Saint-Saëns. He was welcomed in Germany (where he was himself the soloist in the first performance of his First and Third Piano Concertos) and in England, where Cambridge University gave him an honorary doctorate of music. He conducted his own works in the United States and, at the age of 81, in South America. His opera *Samson and Delilah* had to overcome the resistance of those who thought it blasphemous to put a biblical episode on stage, but became universally known.

His orchestral sound is rich, ingratiating, and dedicated to the effective presentation of melody. He was indeed a highly individual melodist and it is not surprising that he disliked the newer style represented by Debussy, in which melody in its traditional sense plays little part. But little in Saint-Saëns's formidable catalogue of orchestral music (including five piano concertos, three violin concertos and two cello concertos) is regularly heard. The great violinists, however, cherish the *Introduction and Rondo Capriccioso* with its brilliant contrast between the smoothly lyrical and the lightly fantastic. It was written for Sarasate (see the reference under *Lalo*).

Symphony no.3 in C minor (Organ Symphony), opus 68

> Adagio – Allegro moderato – Poco adagio
> Allegro moderato *and* Presto (alternating) – Maestoso
> Duration: 30–36 minutes

The nickname 'Organ Symphony' merely points to an unusual ingredient of the orchestra – the organ is given no extended solo role. An even rarer presence is a piano, first with a single player and then with two. Otherwise the orchestration of this symphony – which had its first performance in London, on 19 May 1886, under the composer's direction – requires 3 flutes (1 doubling piccolo), 2 oboes and english horn, 2 clarinets and bass clarinet, 2 bassoons and double-bassoon, 4 horns, 3 trumpets, 3 trombones and tuba, kettledrums, bass drum, cymbals and triangle; and strings.

The two-movement symphony embraces an unusual plan. What promises to be a first movement in regular sonata-form is not formally concluded but leads straight into what could well serve as a self-contained slow movement. Similarly, the symphony's other movement starts as a regular scherzo with contrasting section (trio) but moves straight into the equivalent of a full finale, beginning *maestoso* and changing to a faster tempo. The symphony is unified by a transformation of themes from one movement to another, but what makes it so attractive is its energy, indeed exhilaration.

After a few preliminary slow bars (pregnant with future developments), the main opening movement is launched with a swift-running theme on the strings. In various altered guises it will dominate the symphony. At length a smoother theme is heard in D flat major. The two themes, in combination and in alternation, maintain a vigorous onward flow which leads to a return of the opening and later dies to a bar's silence and the quiet first entry of the organ. A sustained slow section now begins in D flat with an unmistakable air of earnest aspiration. Note the tiny, one-and-a-half-bar solo for double-basses *pizzicato* – the same sequence of notes as the 'swift-running' theme above!

The second movement begins in C minor with a fast-driving theme and the bite of a traditional scherzo. A change to C major and an even faster tempo (*Presto*) brings a new the pulse and introduces the brilliant tinkle of the piano for the first time. The initial music returns, and so does the *Presto*, but soon a steadier flow leads to a sudden loud organ chord of C major. The equivalent of a finale has now begun. The strings intone a hymn-like strain against the halo of the piano duet. After joyous fanfares, the music assumes new vigour (*Allegro*): a fugue subject rises (from strings and woodwind at first), which represents a further transformation of the fast opening theme of the symphony. A blazing peal of brass presents a new exhilaration (again generated from the same theme!) and organ and kettledrums clinch the ending.

Carnival of the animals

Introduction and royal march of the Lion
Cocks and Hens
Mules
Tortoises
The Elephant
Kangaroos
Aquarium
The Cuckoo in the depths of the forest
The aviary
Pianists
Fossils
The Swan
Finale
Duration: 24 minutes

Composed in 1886, this 'grand zoological fantasy', as he called it, was considered by the composer as a frivolity for private hearing only, and during his lifetime he permitted public performance only of 'The Swan'. But on 25 February, 1922, two months and nine days after Saint-Saëns's death, it was unveiled at a Paris concert conducted by Gabriel Pierné (himself a composer of some standing) and has since won the hearts of the public. It is indeed one of the few 'funny' pieces in the repertory, the fun being controlled by a highly sophisticated musical imagination.

The scoring gives a leading role to two pianos, who are joined by flute (doubling piccolo), clarinet, harmonium (doubling celesta), xylophone and strings. The inclusion of 'Pianists' among the animal-titles makes an extra joke, mocking the practising of scales by not-so-skilled performers. The other picturesque touches can be easily appreciated, and the rippling beauty of 'The Swan' for solo cello and two pianos is undimmed in its inspiration.

Some passages are parodied or quoted from other music, as follows. 'Tortoises' borrows the can-can and another tune from act 1 of Offenbach's operetta *Orpheus in the Underworld* – very fast, hectic music ridiculously slowed down. In 'The Elephant', the 'Dance of the Sylphs' from Berlioz's *The Damnation of Faust* is heard – music for fairy creatures here lumbering along on a double-bass. 'Fossils' quotes three traditional French songs, 'J'ai du bon tabac', 'Ah, vous dirai-je, maman' and 'Partant pour la Syrie', Saint-Saëns's own

Danse macabre, and the heroine's 'Una voce poco fa' from Rossini's *The Barber of Seville*.

Danse macabre, *opus 40*

Duration: 7 minutes

The title is unique, but the idea of representing a 'dance of death' in music is not: Berlioz's *Fantastic Symphony* and Mahler's Fourth yield examples. An inspiration of Saint-Saëns's was to use the dry chattering tones of the xylophone – an instrument developed from a 'folk' original which here enters the concert repertory for the first time. The orchestration is otherwise normal: 2 flutes and piccolo; 2 each of oboes, clarinets, bassoons; 4 horns, 2 trumpets, 3 trombones and tuba; kettledrums, bass drum, cymbals and triangle; and strings. A solo violinist is used, playing an instrument deliberately mis-tuned – the high E-string is lowered to D sharp.

Its impact on audiences is immediate, and it stands indeed among the cleverest of those 'characteristic' or descriptive pieces which occupied so many nineteenth-century French composers. It was first performed (and encored) at a Paris concert on 24 January 1875, conducted by Edouard Colonne. Saint-Saëns's original approach to the subject was a setting of words by Henri Cazalis, but he threw over the words in favour of this orchestral work. Three couplets from the poem nevertheless give the clearest indication of the basis of the music:

> Death plays a dance-tune at midnight
> (Zig and zig and zig!) on his violin . . .

> Zig and zig and zig, everyone shakes,
> The dancers' bones are heard to rattle . . .

> But psst! Suddenly the dance breaks off–
> Jostling, they all flee, the cock has crowed!

SCHOENBERG

1874–1951

Along with Stravinsky, Arnold Schoenberg was the most influential
of composers who, from about 1910 onwards, split open the older
conventions of tonality (the major/minor key system) rather
as Picasso and Braque overturned conventional perspective.
Schoenberg was the oldest composer of the so-called 'second
Viennese school' – Schoenberg, Berg, Webern, so grouped as a
supposed parallel to Haydn, Mozart, Beethoven. From his work in
an 'atonal' (keyless) style he evolved his particular innovation – the
12-note system, according to which the composer takes steps to a
mathematical equality of all the notes of the octave.

But unlike Stravinsky, Schoenberg has not become a staple of the
concert-hall. His strongly intellectual innovations, though they
inspired other composers the world over, were not matched by the
creative gift of communication. Ironically, his best-known orchestral works (below) date from before those in which he adopted the
12-note method, which include a violin concerto (1936) and a piano
concerto (1942). By that time, the composer was living in California,
a Jewish refugee from Nazi Germany and Austria. In some of the
music of his last years, Schoenberg reverted to tonality.

Five Pieces for Orchestra, opus 16

    Premonitions: *molto allegro*
    Yesteryears: *andante*
    Colours (Summer morning by a lake): *moderato*
    Peripetia: *molto allegro*
    The obligatory recitative: *allegretto*
    Duration: 17 minutes

Composed in 1908, this famous set of pieces was one of the first to
introduce 'atonal' (key-less) music on a large, orchestral scale. It

became the first work of Schoenberg's to be heard in Britain when Henry Wood included it in a Queen's Hall promenade concert on 3 September 1912 – the first performance of the work. An outsize orchestra was required, as in many other composers of the period (Richard Strauss, Stravinsky, Skryabin), the requirement being: 3 flutes (one doubling piccolo) and one extra piccolo; 3 oboes and english horn; 3 clarinets and bass clarinet; 3 bassoons and double-bassoon; 6 horns, 3 trumpets, 4 trombones, 1 tuba; kettledrums; bass drum, tam-tam, xylophone; celesta, harp and strings.

Late in life, to facilitate performances by orchestral managements reluctant to engage extra players, Schoenberg reduced the scoring. His revision, published in 1949, eliminates one each of oboes, clarinets and bassoons, and cuts the horns down to 4 and the trombones to 3 (the normal strength). The orchestration in any case is less remarkable for size than for its venturesome extremes of instrumental expression that are called for: the 'flutter-tongue' required of the brass-players (giving an attack like a sort of rolled *r*) will be noticed in the first piece. At the end of the fourth piece a percussionist keeps up a long sound on the cymbal by stroking it with a cello bow – an effect still received as a supposed novelty in compositions of the 1960s and later.

It is not usually pointed out that the pieces have a perceptible interconnection in performance. Despite their atonal (key-less) construction they sometimes suggest the note A as a point of destiny or rest. Such a point is felt at the end of the second piece, on an A-minor-ish chord taken up strikingly by the first chord of the next piece. The 'impressionistic' titles do not appear in all references to the work but were Schoenberg's own and are helpful in giving a clue to mood. These come across, indeed, as powerful mood-pieces even when the strict thematic construction may be difficult to follow.

The first piece (*Premonitions*) is fast and fleeting, built on a tiny five-note theme which timidly ascends on muted cellos and passes to a trill on a solo clarinet. At a climax, the rest of the instruments are cut off to leave a 'flutter-tongue' effect from all brass – playing with their mutes on, but *fortissimo*. A gong-stroke leads to a section of heavily emphasized notes and a feeling of emotional descent. The 'flutter-tongue' for brass recurs at the end as the repeated phrases for cellos and double-basses suddenly cease.

A tiny theme in muted cello tone (this time a solo instrument) also opens the slow *Yesteryears*. The theme passes to the woodwind, ascending. After a moment of apparent standstill a new section, tenderly flowing, arrives on a solo viola (also muted). Yet another section exposes repetitive figures on the celesta, with two flutes accompanying. The oboe voices a yearning feeling as it recalls the opening theme. An emotional climax is reached. The celesta's figures recur, but with other material stealing across it in counterpoint, before the final dying-away chord.

Perhaps the most remarkable of the pieces is the third: the changing colours of a sunlit lake are represented by slow-changing instrumental colours while the same chord persists. The chords change little; the listener is hardly conscious of more than the flow of tone, plus tiny flecks of decoration (a function in which the harp is conspicuous).

The title of the fourth piece, *Peripetia*, should really signify 'violent reversal'. But, with one central and one final climax, the music does not seem to pivot on any such single point. Very fast, it presents a series of aggressive, explosive themes in contrasted tone-colours. The upward-leaping woodwind figure at the very opening becomes the downward figure shouted by trombones and tuba at the end.

Likewise a puzzling title is *The obligatory recitative*: the adjective 'unending' (which Schoenberg once suggested) would seem a better choice. A winding theme descends on oboes, violas and cellos, then passes again to clarinet, then moves to the violins, and so on in an unceasing succession of instrumental colours. (It is as if the process applied in the previous piece to *chords* is now applied to *melody*.) Against this continuing theme is heard a complicated web of subsidiary themes. Two piccolos unite themselves to the violins to top the sound as a climax is reached, thick with different simultaneous strands. The texture falls suddenly sparse. Muted cellos (again, that tone-colour!) lead to the hushed ending.

Transfigured Night (*Verklärte Nacht*)

Duration: 29 minutes

One of Schoenberg's earliest works, and the first to make him famous, *Transfigured Night* (*Verklärte Nacht*) was originally written for string sextet and first given in that form in Vienna on 28 March 1902 (not 1903 as usually stated). The composer issued it for string orchestra in 1917, adding double-basses, and made minor modifications in 1943. It had been an almost unique example of chamber music with an external 'programme' (based on a poem by Richard

Dehmel) and is now best known in its orchestral dress. Its emotional language makes it seem like an epilogue to Wagner (especially, because of its subject, Wagner's *Tristan and Isolde*) rather than a forecast of Schoenberg's later music.

It begins in D minor with a prominent falling phrase which recurs later. Though the correspondence of music and poem cannot be exact, the reappearance of the phrase near the end parallels the near-repetition of the words. The emotional transformation – from deceit and anguish into acceptance and love – is signified by a rapt, suspenseful passage in D major in which a high violin solo is heard above a web of bowed and plucked sounds, and in the progress of the whole work from D minor to its final D major.

From the poem, printed as a preface to the score, the following translated extracts indicate the course of the narrative:

> Two mortals walk through a cold, barren grove. The moon above sails with them. A woman speaks. She confesses a sin to the man at her side: she is with child, and he is not its father. Having lost belief in happiness, and longing for life's fullness and for motherhood, she had surrendered herself, shuddering, to a stranger's embraces. Now life had avenged itself upon her, by giving her the love of the man she addresses. She staggers onward. A man speaks. Let her not burden her soul with thoughts of guilt. See, the moon's sheen enwraps all. 'You will bear the child to me – from me.' Their breaths kiss in the air. Two mortals wonder through the wondrous moonlight.

SCHUBERT

1797–1828

Not a single note of Franz Schubert's orchestral music was published in his lifetime. Incredible as that may now seem for a composer judged to be among the world's greatest, it reflects Schubert's failure to gain any firm recognition in his native Vienna beyond a devoted but narrow circle of personal admirers. Within his short span of life (he was born more than a quarter of a century after Beethoven, but died only one year after) he tried and failed to become established with opera and other theatrical work.

Apart from the late symphonies (see below), a few other orchestral works have won posthumous fame. Some charming ballet music is among the eleven pieces he wrote for the play *Rosamunde* (1826). There is also a piece which is now generally called the *Rosamunde* overture but was composed earlier (1820) for another play, *The Magic Harp* (Die Zauberharfe). Two concert overtures, in C and D, both bear the subtitle 'in the Italian style' (not, perhaps, the composer's own words) meaning 'in the style of Rossini'. Three early works for violin and orchestra are of slight importance. A weightier contender for attention is Liszt's transcription for piano and orchestra of Schubert's so-called *Wanderer* Fantasy, written originally for piano alone.

The symphonies

Schubert began writing symphonies early, in the manner of a young Viennese composer conscious of the models of Haydn and Mozart; he ended as the great artist whose two final symphonies breathe the new Romantic spirit and foreshadow another great Austrian symphonist – Bruckner.

The two late symphonies now so well known (below) had their first performances only after his death; of six youthful symphonies, the composer heard no. 5 at a private performance in 1819 and may not have ever heard the others. Between the group of six symphonies and the well-known pair comes no. 7 in E, existing in a draft of which completions have been offered by several later musicians – most recently by the British scholar Brian Newbould. In 1978 the musical world was surprised by a further discovery in manuscript in Vienna: three sketched movements intended for a further four-movement symphony, dating from the last months of Schubert's life. This symphony (no. 10) has also had its completion by Newbould.

In his orchestral works Schubert does not refer directly to songs as he does occasionally in chamber music (the 'Death and the Maiden' quartet, the 'Trout' quintet), but his melodic gifts as a song-writer are often recalled in the more lyrical themes of the symphonies.

Symphony No. 8 in B minor (Unfinished)

> Allegro moderato
> Andante con moto
> (missing?)
> (missing?)
> Duration: 23–25 minutes

The pathos of this work, grave but never overbearing, has made it a favourite and has attached to the label 'Unfinished' a rather tragic overtone which is not really warranted. In 1822, six years before his death, Schubert completed the first two movements: why he never brought his symphony to completion is not known. He gave the manuscript of these movements to a friend (who seems to have forgotten about it!). He had begun a third movement, a *scherzo*, sketching out most of the structure in piano score, and had even orchestrated the first few bars.

Perhaps even his projected finale exists, redesignated by the composer for another function. A whole movement in the correct key of B minor, and of appropriate length and scoring, appears as an *entr'acte* in Schubert's music to the play *Rosamunde*. Since a completion of the *scherzo* has now been made by Brian Newbould (1982), it has become possible to follow this by the *Rosamunde* extract and so to perform Schubert's no. 8 as a reconstructed four-movement work.

Using this scheme, the two question-marked movements above should be filled in as: 'Scherzo [Allegro] and Trio' and 'Allegro molto moderato'. Most commonly, however, the opening two movements are performed on their own – however unsatisfactorily to ears accustomed to 'think through' a classical symphony, which necessarily begins and ends in the same key. In this form the *Unfinished* was first performed under Johann Herbeck in Vienna on 17 December 1865, after lying undisclosed in private hands for about forty years. To a basically classical scoring (double woodwind only) Schubert adds trombones, using them for soft, dark reinforcement of sound as well as for the customary emphasis.

The opening movement in B minor presents its main theme on solo oboe and clarinet over a string background. The contrasting second subject in G major, arriving gently on the cellos, is later taken by the violins. In classical pattern, this exposition section is repeated. Tension mounts in a development section, then subsides as the oboe and clarinet theme returns in the home key. The contrasting theme follows, but in an unexpected D major; there is a second development before this theme finds a final statement in B major. Even then, this 'happy' turn to the major key is rejected: pathos marks the end.

A downward *pizzicato* scale on the double-basses (not to be overlooked!) begins the second movement. The violins deliver the smooth, consoling principal theme in E major. The first theme to offer a contrast comes from the clarinets (in C sharp minor). A varied discourse allows the consolatory theme a final authority, with the downward *pizzicato* to seal it in quietness.

Symphony No.9 in C major

> Andante – Allegro ma non troppo
> Andante con moto
> Scherzo: Allegro vivace
> Allegro vivace
> Duration: 50 minutes

Unrecognized in his lifetime as a symphonic composer, Schubert had no opportunity to bring his last, longest and greatest symphony to performance. Finished in the year of its composer's death, it remained unheard for another eleven years – until the enthusiasm of Schumann and Mendelssohn led to its performance at Leipzig, under Mendelssohn's baton, on 21 March 1839.

In deploys the standard four movements of the Viennese symphony at a 'heavenly length' – Schumann's phrase. As in the 'Unfinished', a trio of trombones joins the orchestra and assumes bold, melodic role as well as assisting the grandeur of the full orchestral sound. Otherwise the instrumentation conforms to

Viennese—classical norms: 2 each of flutes, oboes, clarinets, bassoons, horns and trumpets; kettledrums and strings.

The opening horn-call is of that 'Romantic' type which is so often connected explicitly to heroic adventure or to enchantment – as in Weber's *Oberon* overture or the nocturne of Mendelssohn's *A Midsummer Night's Dream* (see pages 231 and 363). So begins the slow introduction to the symphony. After a climax, the main faster section sets strings and woodwind exchanging insistent phrases. A strong, march-like beat is established, continuing even when a new thought comes with a theme in paired notes from oboes and bassoons. It is in E minor, moving to G major; a shift to E flat then makes room for a new 'calling' theme on the trombones over dancing strings. The key of G major is regained and concludes the exposition (marked to be repeated).

The development, again showing the trombones in their new role, is short but powerful. Recapitulation begins quietly on the strings, the themes appearing in a newly defined order of keys, ending in the 'home' C major. An increase of speed brings a long coda, in which the horn-call from the slow introduction reappears as a triumphant conclusion.

The slow movement, in A minor, begins on the strings like a subdued slow march (a reminiscence of the slow movement of Beethoven's Symphony no.7, in the same key?). Over it the oboes deliver a melody which eventually turns in a very Schubertian way to A major (clarinet). A new sustained 'song' leads to a passage of Romantic tenderness: the horns repeat a high D while the harmonies of the strings change beneath. When the oboe's tune is heard again, a trumpet provides a soft, pattering counter-theme. The second 'half' of the movement (actually the slightly longer part) has now begun, restating the earlier material – the F major 'song' now moving to A major. But the movement ends in A minor as it began.

In shape, the third movement in C is a scherzo of the standard kind with enclosed central Trio (that is, A–B–A). But the 'A' itself is a sonata-form in miniature: – its 'second subject' being an appealingly lyrical tune in which the cellos 'chase' the violins. The Trio changes the mood: it is a rustic waltz (*Ländler*) in A major, with a more leisurely motion. The *Scherzo* proper is then repeated in full and unaltered.

March-rhythm, already experienced in the first and second movements, overwhelms in the finale. Waves of excitement succeed one another until, after a sudden silence, four identical notes from the horns lead to the second subject (itself beginning with four repeated notes) on the woodwind. Further waves of sound finally sink as this very long exposition (364 bars) ends. The development allows the trombones to seize thrillingly on the 'four repeated notes' idea. A long–built–up preparation for the return of the opening theme brings a surprise: the theme arrives not in C but in E flat. Fast in pace but unhurried in span, the recapitulation unfolds – the second subject being again the property of the woodwind. The end of the movement (1154 bars!) arrives with no lessening of pace and excitement.

SCHUMANN

1810–56

The identity of Robert Schumann as a 'Romantic' composer – one whose music appeals for its suggestion of particular, individualized feelings – is enhanced by the well-known story of his personal and musical courtship of Clara Wieck. Against her father's will, they were married in 1840, a time when the composer's ardour over-flowed in his most famous songs, including the set entitled *Dichter-liebe* (Poet's Love). As a pianist Clara was (and remained after his death) Schumann's most celebrated interpreter.

As well as the piano concerto which has remained such a favourite, he left an admired cello concerto and a highly unusual *Concert Piece* (Konzertstück) for four horns with orchestra. A more problematic work is a violin concerto, composed at a time when he was liable to mental instability (1853), and not performed until 1937. His symphonies (see below) are large-scale works standing at the other end of his art from the songs and the miniatures for piano, including the pictures-in-music which make up the *Carnival*.

The symphonies

Unlike his contemporary, Chopin, Schumann was one of those Romantics who felt throughout his life the pull of the standard large orchestral form, the symphony. A German composer does not easily discard that heritage! Warm in their Romantic sentiment, the four symphonies of Schumann are not as often performed as those of Brahms which followed. Yet their songful or assertive themes are absorbed into balanced structures which sympathetic conductors can make much of. Although he did not go as far as Liszt in replacing separate movements by a wholly continuous structure, Schumann shared the Romantic impulse to suggest the 'wholeness' of a work by other processes linking the movements.

The Second Symphony was first performed in 1846; the third (the so-called *Rhenish* symphony, though its connection with the

Rhineland is not specific) in 1851. The latter, in five movements, is the only symphony not in the usual four. Additionally, Schumann wrote a kind of 'symphony without slow movement' under the title *Overture, Scherzo and Finale* which has claims to be better known.

Symphony No.1 in B flat major (Spring), *opus 38*

Andante un poco maestoso – Allegro molto vivace
Larghetto, *leading to*
Scherzo – Molto vivace
Allegro animato e grazioso
Duration: 28–32 minutes

A Romantic composer here offers deliberate 'freshening' of the symphonic form. The orchestra is a 'romantic' one also. Trombones play a notable role – they have tunes as well as solid chords! – and a triangle takes part in the first movement. Importantly, there are three kettledrums, not the 'classical' two; in the first and last movements, one of the drums is tuned to the note G flat so that it can join in more remote, out-of-key harmonies.

The fanfare which opens the first movement is not a military one; it is a call to attention which corresponds in rhythm to a line of poetry by the composer's friend Adolph Boettger. With corresponding stresses, an English version might be 'Today the valley blooms with spring'; hence the nickname of 'Spring' Symphony for this work. The slow introduction does not come to a halt as in most classical examples, but quickens until the pace of the *Allegro* is reached. The main theme of the *Allegro* is the fanfare theme itself, speeded up and continued. A gentler theme from clarinets and bassoons, against a rustle in the violas, leads to a climax. The whole exposition (i.e. from the beginning of the *Allegro*) is marked to be repeated.

The development gives some exciting back-and-forth exchange of themes. The return of the main theme occurs unexpectedly in long-held notes, sounding like a re-evocation of the slow introduction. Near the end of the movement (in a Romantic departure from classical form) a new, smoother theme is heard. There is a festive conclusion.

The dreamy *Larghetto* in E flat which follows is plainly an evocation of a countryside scene, on the precedent of Beethoven's *Pastoral* Symphony. The opening tune later recurs in the richly coloured tone of solo horn and solo oboe. The hushed entry of the trombones (their tone, and that of the trumpets, has been hitherto

silent in this movement) leads to a chord of D minor, the key of . . .
. . . the third movement. The Beethoven plan of 'scherzo and
trio', with the scherzo itself in two parts each repeated, is followed,
but with a difference. There are *two* trios so that the plan is: scherzo; a
much faster trio I in D major (with interchanges between strings and
wind at first); scherzo again; trio II (theme rising from cellos and
double-basses); abbreviated scherzo; coda in D major based on trio I.
The stamping rhythm of the scherzo makes it unmistakable as the
movement's unusual pattern unfolds. A few final bars in quick time
include a single, soft stroke for kettledrum solo.

With the fourth movement, there is a return to the striding,
optimistic style of the first. Here again is an opening fanfare – like
figure; here again follows an *Allegro* with the first part repeated.
Within this, the second subject (switching to G and then to F)
reintroduces the opening fanfare of the movement. In the development section, the trombones hint at the opening figure of the *first*
movement, and this development ends with the unique feature – a
kind of cadenza built from a horn call and a solo flute's high warbling
(last signs of spring!). A recapitulation follows immediately,
reasserting the themes and concluding with reinforced vigour.

Symphony No.4 in D minor, opus 120

> Un poco lento – Vivace
> Un poco lento
> Scherzo: Vivace, *leading to*
> Lento; Vivace
> Duration: 28–32 minutes

Only nine months separate the first performances of Schumann's
Symphony no. 1 and the present work, which was in fact his second
symphony. But after the first performance on 16 December 1841 at
Leipzig (Ferdinand David conducting) Schumann was dissatisfied
and withdrew the work. He then went on to compose two other
symphonies before returning to this one – relabelled as no. 4 for its
appearance at Düsseldorf on 3 March 1853, with the composer
conducting. Pursuing the Romantic inclination to unify a long
work, Schumann provided thematic interrelationships between the
movements and directed that the symphony be played without
pause.

In a slow introduction, a winding theme in D minor grows in
intensity and then is quickened to reach the speed of the main section
of the movement, which pursues its vigorous way on a novel plan.

The exposition, moving from the home key of D minor to F major, is built on a single, ardent theme. This whole section is then repeated. Only afterwards during the development arising from this theme do we encounter a strongly contrasting lyrical theme, softly given out by the violins in F major. The music continues to develop freely. There is no formal return to the opening, but the lyrical theme in a more resolute rhythm and in full-orchestral scoring bursts out in D major to lead to the conclusion of the movement.

The heading 'Romance' (in German 'Romanze') seems here to denote nothing but a tender expressiveness. A solo theme on the oboe, in A minor, is followed by the 'winding' theme from the first movement, soon embellished by a violin solo. The oboe returns, its melody sweetened by an ending in A major.

The lively *Scherzo* in D minor is of a traditional emphatic vigour. In contrast, a gentler *Trio* for a reduced orchestration recalls the winding theme from the introduction to the first movement. In traditional pattern, the *Scherzo* is repeated. Rather unexpectedly the *Trio* also returns, but this time passes without pause . . .

. . . into the Finale, which begins in hushed tones with a quotation of the main allegro theme of the first movement. There is a strong counter-theme from the trombones. Tension grows, to culminate on a long, loud chord. With a switch to D major, the main section of the Finale begins. Sonata-form is followed, but with Schumann's characteristic freedom. Within the first section (exposition), the trombone theme from the introduction is heard again. After a repeat of this section, development begins and brings a strong new theme on the horns. Eventually the key of D major is reasserted with some of the older material (but the beginning of this faster section never returns). A quickening and a final presto section proclaim the most vigorous aspects of this symphony once again.

Concerto for piano and orchestra in A minor, opus 54

> Allegro affettuoso
> Intermezzo: Andantino grazioso, *leading to*
> Allegro vivace
> Duration: 28–31 minutes

The composer's wife, Clara, was naturally the soloist in the first performance of this concerto at Dresden on 4 December 1845, when Ferdinand Hiller conducted. Strangely, in view of the later popularity of the work, the first movement (composed as an independent piece in 1841) was considered difficult to understand and was refused by several publishers. The other two movements are contrasted with the first, but thematically related to it. The beginning with its flourish for the piano alone seems characteristic of the Romantic composer's idealization of the performer's feeling. The scoring is that of the classical orchestra, i.e. with pairs of woodwind instruments (including clarinets), 2 horns, 2 trumpets and kettledrums. Trombones do not invade this work as they do Schumann's symphonies. Not permitting the intrusion of any one else's cadenza, Schumann composed his own for the first movement. In the finale he avoided a cadenza altogether, though providing the performer with the necessary fireworks to excite an audience.

After the soloist's opening flourish, the oboe announces the theme which is to pervade the whole of the first movement – first in A minor then in C major, and later when a new, dreamy expression and a change of key to A flat brings a dialogue between the piano and the solo clarinet. The opening flourish returns, extended. In a recapitulation, the key of A major is reached, but the cadenza reverts to A minor and is followed by a brisk coda which transforms the rhythm of the main theme.

In entitling the slow movement 'Intermezzo', the composer perhaps indicated that he was aiming at a light, delicate expression, rather than profundity. The figure of four rising notes, which opens the movement in dialogue between the piano and strings, is derived from a sequence of notes within the main theme of the first movement. The slow movement is in F major, moving to C major for an expansive theme on the cellos. The opening theme duly returns. But something unexpected happens: the music comes to a point of stillness and the theme of the first movement is insinuated by the woodwind. But only briefly. With a quickening of pace we are launched on . . .

. . . the finale. With its cheerily swinging pace, this movement derives its theme from that which pervaded the first movement. In its new guise, the theme becomes the main element in a freely treated rondo structure, with episodes in between. One of these episodes, heard quietly on the strings, has a syncopation across the beat in a manner Schumann particularly made his own. It first appears in E major and later returns in A major. The piano (given no cadenza) sweeps on, over a series of trills, into a coda in which the key of A major is joyously asserted.

SHOSTAKOVICH

1906-75

Dmitry Shostakovich remains the pre-eminent figure of Soviet music. Unlike Prokofiev his creative life was spent entirely in the Soviet Union, save when he travelled as its distinguished representative abroad. Though his music never embraced the 12-note method or other western radical tendencies, it was modern enough to involve him twice in conflict with the official Soviet guardians of art – in the 1930s, after his 'shocking' opera *Lady Macbeth of Mtsensk*, and in 1948. By tact, an inner stubbornness and artistic persistence he survived with honour. Soviet Russia's leading violinist and cellist, David Oistrakh and Mstislav Rostropovich, championed his concertos: there are also a concerto for piano with trumpet and strings and a second piano concerto.

The symphonies

Shostakovich's main achievement, paralleling that of his fifteen string quartets, is that of his fifteen symphonies – works of wide variety, no.2 (virtually unknown) having a choral ending, and two well-known later ones (nos.13, 14) also with vocal participation. Enigmatic quotations from Rossini's *William Tell* overture and from Wagner's *Die Walküre* leave a question mark over the final symphony.

Shostakovich proceeds by thematic musical argument, like the great classical and Romantic symphonists; like them he generally (but not always) presents four movements of equal weight and clear contrast, with extremes of whirling scherzos and intense slow unfoldings. The framework often seems conservative, but the content deeply personal.

Symphony No.1, opus 10

> Allegretto – Allegro non troppo
> Allegro
> Lento – Largo, *leading to*
> Allegro molto
> Duration: 28–33 minutes

The youthful genius of Shostakovich was made clear when his First Symphony was unveiled while he was still four months off his 20th birthday. It was conducted in Leningrad by Nikolay Malko on 12 May 1926; next year Bruno Walter conducted it in Berlin, to be followed by Leopold Stokowski in Philadelphia. Emotional tension is achieved by modern dissonances within an overall classical symphonic structure. Though not so labelled, the symphony is in F minor, turning at the end to F major. The slow movement comes third, as in some earlier Russian examples, and the key–centres of the successive movements are F–A (minor)–D flat (major)–F, a progression nearly but not quite the same as Brahms chose for *his* First Symphony (see p. 104).

The orchestration is striking – from the richly divided strings in the first movement (with 8 soloists from the violins and 4 from the violas) to the sharply individual percussion. A distinctive contribution to the second and fourth movements is made by a piano. The other requirements are 2 flutes and 2 piccolos (3 players suffice), 2 each of oboes, clarinets and bassoons, 4 horns, 3 trumpets, 3 trombones and tuba, kettledrums and 4 other percussionists sharing snare drum, bass drum, cymbals, triangle and tam-tam.

A muted trumpet launches the introduction, hinting at what is to come. The main faster section is begun by a solo clarinet enunciating the jerky first theme over a shadily rhythmical accompaniment in 4/4 time. An unexpected change to waltz-time brings the smoother second subject on a solo flute. Development, beginning quietly, becomes fierce, the trumpets taking up the theme which opened the introduction. The waltz-tune subject is recapitulated, again on the flute, and then the first subject reappears with new force. The material of the introduction quietly seals off the movement.

The second movement is in effect a scherzo – with an introduction, a main section with an angular, quick-moving melody (the piano prominent) and then a contrasting trio where a triangle and then a snare drum accompany a pair of flutes. The main section was in 4/4, the trio in 3/4 – but after the scherzo theme has returned (again with piano), both themes are simultaneously heard, that of the trio now being transformed into 4/4. Loud solo chords from the piano initiate a coda.

Shostakovich's eloquence in lyric melody shines in the slow third movement – at first with a long-drawn oboe solo, taken up by the full orchestra. At a slightly faster pace the strings begin a firmly treading theme to which the oboe adds a counterpoint. The first theme reappears on a solo violin, then on full strings, with the brass making urgent interruptions (in a rhythm which will be powerfully re-used in the finale). The slightly faster material also reappears. The movement seems about to conclude in a mood of resignation, on a widespread chord of D flat major for divided solo strings, but a snare drum roll pushes itself forward and leads directly into . . .

. . . the final movement, which is to crown the symphony's grandeur and intensity. Like the first movement, it has a slow introduction. Its main section is begun almost in a frenzy by a solo clarinet accompanied by clashing cymbals and followed by the piano. A new theme is screamed out but soon takes on quieter form as a violin solo. The frenzied pace returns and violence erupts. A dramatic silence is broken by the kettledrums in a characteristic rhythmical figure borrowed from the previous movement. The drums sound loud, then soft, then softer still (muffled with a cloth). Mournful strings interpose, anchored in F minor. But with an inner strength the music swells and reaches F major on the full orchestra, *fortissimo*. A quickened ending confirms that triumphant arrival.

Symphony No.5, opus 47

> Moderato
> Allegretto
> Largo
> Allegro non troppo
> Duration: 42 minutes

'A Soviet artist's reply to just criticism' is the composer's own supposed self-description of this work – though the words do not appear on the published score. There is no doubt that its first performance – conducted by Yevgeny Mravinsky in Leningrad on 21 November 1937 – served to rehabilitate the composer's 'official' reputation. But though the symphony marks an assertion of the traditional values of tonality and sonata-form structures, it is anything but a retreat in personal terms. It shows the composer combining passionate melody with a fierce clarity of texture in a way that releases his most powerful utterances. A strong link with older symphonies is established by the driving rhythms of the first and last movements, separated by a triple-time scherzo and an intense slow movement. Though not given a key label, the symphony is in D minor, turning finally to D major – another traditional and immediately effective procedure.

A xylophone is prominently used for rhythmical emphasis and colour; the celesta's repeated scales as the ending of the first movement are also remarkable. Two harps are asked for, but playing the same music. As often with Shostakovich, a piano is included in the orchestral forces, the other requirements being 2 flutes and piccolo, 2 oboes, 2 clarinets and high clarinet, 2 bassoons and double-bassoon, 4 horns, 3 trumpets, 3 trombones and tuba, kettledrums, snare drum, bass drum, cymbals, triangle, tam-tam and strings.

The opening is urgent, even aggressive – the upper strings, in D minor, chasing the lower. The theme becomes an accompaniment as the first violins deliver a descending second theme. The main contrast arrives, however, when a chord on the harps ushers in a new key (E flat): here a calm theme in long notes is unfolded above a regular, pattering rhythm. The development involves a speeding-up, so that when the aggressive theme returns (the strings now reinforced by woodwind) it is nearly twice as fast. The insistence continues until, signalled once again by a harp chord, the smooth theme now returns in D major on flute and horn. With the sense of a goal achieved, the music fades.

The second movement (in A minor) is a scherzo, though not so named. An oom-pah-pah rhythm provides the driving force, sometimes grotesquely, for a contrast of high clarinet and bassoon, is followed by the more solid sound of the horns and a perky solo violin tune which might be by Mahler. A soft but insistent *pizzicato* for strings provides a brief contrast, after which the rougher material returns.

For the third movement the brass is silent and the strings are unusually divided – the violins into two, the violas and cellos into three. From this rich texture of strings, a close-knit pattern of sound is unfolded, with an initial ascending theme and (still on strings only) a high, descending theme. The opening is in F sharp *minor*; through various developments and passionately discordant climaxes the music eventually wins its tranquillity on a long-sustained, trembling high F sharp (first violins) and a dying-away chord of F sharp *major* for all the stringed instruments.

The finale blazes up in a brass-and-drums march in D minor continued by the other instruments. The tempo gradually quickens. Over rushing strings and woodwind, a solo trumpet makes a proclamation which other instruments turn into a sweepingly grand tune. The music suddenly breaks off at a climax with mighty strokes on cymbals and tam-tam, but a new impetus (based on the opening theme) takes over immediately. Later the 'grand tune' is heard in subdued form on a solo horn. But soon the tempo is re-animated – the rhythm is jerked from march-time into 3/4, then back again. In a final climax, brass and drums restate the original theme in a version triumphantly changed to D major.

Symphony No.14, opus 135

Duration: 53 minutes

From its first performance in Leningrad on 29 September 1969 (with Rudolf Barshay conducting), many of the composer's admirers must have wondered in what sense this work could be called a symphony. Its eleven movements take their moods and forms from the poetic texts on which they were founded, rather than from traditional symphonic models. But it is a remarkably compelling work, not least in the concentration of the texts on a single theme: Death. The work is dedicated to Benjamin Britten, who conducted the first Western performance (Aldeburgh, 14 June 1970).

A symphony written for the limited forces of a chamber orchestra is unusual, and this work is unique among the composer's fifteen symphonies. The orchestration calls only for strings, celesta and a highly selective array of percussion. The percussion instruments required are castanets, wood block, 3 tom-toms, whip, tubular bells, vibraphone and xylophone; the strings are precisely specified as 10 violins, 4 violas, 3 cellos and 2 double-basses. The instruments are used with sharp individuality and sometimes with a kind of irony: the 'trumpet-call' introducing no.5 is heard on the xylophone (the 'Dance of Death' instrument since the famous usage of Saint-Saëns: see p.284).

A soprano and bass soloist, united only in two of the numbers, deliver a set of poems by four writers. One, a Russian with a German name, Wilhelm Küchelbecker (1798–1842), is unfamiliar to Westerners; the others are Apollinaire (1880–1918), Lorca (1898–

1936) and Rilke (1875–1926), whose verses are translated from the French, Spanish and German originals into Russian for the composer's setting. The printed score also bears a German text, an evident sign that the composer contemplated performances in the vernacular for audiences not speaking Russian. Indeed for the Rilke poems the composer provided an alternative musical line to provide a closer match for the German text.

Leaders (. . .) at the end of a movement indicate direct links to the subsequent movement, without pause.

1. ***De Profundis*** (Lorca) – bass; a poem lamenting the dead of the Spanish Civil War.
2. ***Malagueña*** (Lorca) – soprano: the traditional Spanish dance-rhythm is ironically set to a description of a personified Death going in and out of the taverns . . .
3. ***Lorelei*** (Apollinaire) – soprano and bass: dialogue between the river-nymph and a bishop who comes to 'redeem' her, falls in love with her, but is rejected by her in favour of her true lover . . .
4. ***The Suicide*** (Apollinaire) – soprano: a song of three lilies (the words 'Tri lilii' recur) blooming on the suicide's grave.
5. ***On the Alert*** (Apollinaire) – soprano: a woman prepares to receive a soldier who will shortly die, 'my loved one and brother' . . .
6. ***Madam, Look!*** (Apollinaire) – soprano and bass: 'Excuse me, haven't you lost something?' 'Nothing! – only my heart, ha, ha!' . . .
7. ***At the Sante Jail*** (Apollinaire) – bass: 'They dragged me here to die: God, have mercy, remove this crown of thorns!'
8. ***The Zaporozhian Cossacks' Reply to the Sultan of Constantinople*** (Apollinaire) – bass: 'You worse than Barabbas, you companion of Beelzebub, you filth-eater, celebrate your sabbath without us!' . . .
9. ***O Delvig, Delvig!*** (Küchelbecker) – bass: 'Oh, my friend! despite persecution, immortallity rewards virtuous deeds'.
10. ***The Death of a Poet*** (Rilke) – soprano: 'The dead poet's face was like that spaciousness which now wraps him' . . .
11. ***Conclusion*** (Rilke) – soprano and bass: 'When we think ourselves in the middle of life, Death dares to weep within us'.

SIBELIUS

1865–1957

Britain and the United States embraced the music of Sibelius between the two World Wars: in Britain, after the death of Elgar (1934), he was the most admired living symphonist. Vaughan Williams dedicated his own Fifth Symphony 'without permission' to him. Yet by this time Sibelius had long ceased to be an active composer: the remarkable sequence of seven symphonies was complete by 1924, and some of the other much-admired works date from around 1900. Nevertheless he remains Finland's best-known composer.

Still under Russian rule till after the 1917 Soviet revolution, his country had nevertheless maintained its own culture. Though as a young man Sibelius had studied in Berlin and Vienna he nevertheless, like his Danish contemporary Carl Nielsen, felt the national stimulus. The famous *Finlandia* (1899) represents national aspirations at a time of insurgent feeling. The collection of national Finnish legends, the Kalevala, provided titles for many of Sibelius's compositions, but he gave no explicit story to the orchestral work called simply *A Saga* (or in Swedish, Finland's second language, *En Saga*).

Following a fashion of his youthful years he adopted the French forename Jean instead of his own Johan, and a similar convention accounts for the title of his well-known *Valse triste*, 1903, from music for a Finnish play.

The symphonies

To his admirers the symphonies of Sibelius are sufficiently numerous, sufficiently varied, and yet sufficiently stamped with one man's musical fingerprints to constitute a major cycle in the way that Beethoven's or Mahler's do. Unlike Mahler, Sibelius did not push chromatic harmony to its limits of agonized expression; nor did he venture, as Mahler and Nielsen did, on a symphony which should begin in one key and end in another. Unlike Mahler again, he did not expand the orchestra beyond the received dimensions nor add vocal texts.

In such respects he is a conservative symphonist. Most of his symphonies are in the standard four movements; no. 3 has three only; no. 7, exceptionally, is in one movement but elements of four movements are discernible. A Romantic feeling not far from Tchaikovsky's is signalled in the Symphony no. 1 and even in no. 2, but later a remarkable individuality takes over, with a particular way of presenting a group of musical ideas fragmentarily at first, then coming together.

Symphony No. 2 in D major, opus 43

> Allegretto
> Tempo andante ma rubato
> Vivacissimo, *leading to*
> Allegretto moderato
> Duration: 41 minutes

With clear thematic outlines and a swinging last-movement tune, this symphony was to win particular appeal. Sibelius himself conducted the first performance in Helsinki on 3 March 1902. The scoring is for double woodwind, 4 horns, 3 trumpets, 3 trombones, tuba, kettledrums and strings. The outer movements in D major have the contrast of a second movement in D minor and a third in B flat.

The opening in the strings, which seems simply to set up a rhythm, will actually come to play a thematic role as the music unfolds. The main theme of the first movement, however, is that which follows in perky *staccato* notes on oboes and clarinets. Among associated themes is a strongly sweeping one which is given to the violins unaccompanied. A speeding-up leads to the contrasting material ('second subject group') beginning with a long-sustained note and falling figure in the high woodwind. A development is followed by a recapitulation: this time, the 'perky' woodwind theme is announced without its preceding pulsing figure on the strings. This figure, however, ends the movement – quietly.

The sparse texture which opens the second movement – a drum-roll, a single *pizzicato* line begun on the double-basses, a mournful tune in slow octaves from the bassoons – is a typical Sibelius sound and one which commentators can hardly refrain from comparing to the barren, flat Nordic landscapes of their imagination. The sound becomes fuller and more impassioned with much interchange, question-and-answer fashion, between sections of the orchestra. The sparse opening texture does not return, but the end is again slow and heavy.

The third movement reproduces the classical scherzo pattern: a fast-moving main section embracing a contrasting central section. The main section builds up on scurrying strings. After a series of pauses there is a marked change of key (B flat to G flat), a new, slower tempo, and an oboe melody beginning with the same note nine times over. The main, scurrying section is repeated; the oboe starts its G-flat melody again but the music gradually takes on a more assertive character, moving over a drum-roll to . . .

. . . the fourth movement. The rising tune on the strings, punctuated by kettledrums and with a trumpet-call as its pendant, treads a triumphant way. Next, over rapidly moving lower strings, an oboe announces a further tune, also bearing the mark of decision. Each of these tunes is heard again. Finally after a solemn trombone-call the first tune ends the symphony with a waving of banners.

Symphony No.5 in E flat major, opus 82

> Tempo molto moderato, *leading to*
> Allegro moderato, ma poco a poco stretto
> Andante mosso, quasi allegretto
> Allegro molto
> Duration: 30 minutes

It was in London that Sibelius conducted this symphony on 12 February 1921 – apparently the first performance of the symphony in a final, revised version. The original version was first heard in Helsinki on 8 December 1915 (the composer's 50th birthday) under Robert Kajanus, a Finnish conductor closely associated with Sibelius. The orchestration is that of the Symphony no.2 (above) with a significant difference: from his Third Symphony onwards, Sibelius dropped the tuba, considering it awkwardly heavy and not blending well with the trombones.

The score published in 1921 places over the correct points the tempo titles as listed above but does not print them as headings for separate movements. Though the second tempo takes over from the first without a break, the music of the second tempo is so fresh that the listener registers a division of the symphony into four movements rather than three.

The first movement prominently uses an ascending, fanfare-like theme – B flat, E flat, F, B flat. In contrast comes a more pathetic, drooping theme on the high woodwinds. Later comes a bassoon solo marked 'mournful' (*lugubre*). As the music becomes broader, the home key of E flat is reasserted and both main themes are re-heard. The pace is speeded for a transition to . . .

. . . the second movement, a scherzo in dancing 3/4 time. It is led off by flutes and clarinets, in the new key of B major. But that proves deceptive: the horns' long-held B slips down to B flat and the dancing theme has moved to the key of E flat, the key of the opening movement. A new theme rings out confidently on a trumpet. The key is further disturbed but settles in E flat, the harmony becoming more solid and the pace quickening. Thus the first two movements together form a key-unit, E flat returning to E flat.

A fresh start in G major gives the simple-seeming main tune of the third movement. It is extended in a kind of continuous variation, with a 'wrong' note which recurs (high on the flutes) in both the opening and closing sections to add a special savour. In a slower middle passage a prominent double-bass theme, rising and falling, anticipates the big tune of the finale.

The finale returns to E flat and crowns the work. Under the light-fingered violins, the violas spin out the first theme. Then, as the strings continue busily, a big tune rings out on the horns (a tune in thirds, the horns playing characteristically in pairs). The original viola theme later returns with the mysterious sound of much-divided muted strings (the violins split into eight parts instead of two) and the symphony receives its triumphal end when the big tune, now on the trumpets, peals forth against drum-rolls. No, not quite the end: six irregularly spaced hammer-blows finally fall in unison on the keynote.

Concerto for violin and orchestra in D minor, opus 147

Allegro moderato
Adagio di molto
Allegro ma non tanto
Duration: 34 minutes

It has grown to be one of the most popular of twentieth-century violin concertos, but it was not always so. Nor was the composer at first satisfied with it. After the first performance on 8 February 1904 in Helsinki, with Victor Nováček as soloist and the composer conducting, he revised it, bringing out in 1905 the new version which is now current. Following Tchaikovsky's example it exploits a soulful song-style in its middle movement and the fiery, furious style of violin playing in its finale. The opening of the whole concerto – into which the soloist plunges forthwith – is an arresting feature.

The technical difficulties, particularly in octave playing and harmonics, are formidable. Here Sibelius had the assurance of his own early professional work as a violinist. The orchestration is conventional for its period, with double woodwind, 4 horns, 2 trumpets, 3 trombones and tuba, kettledrums and strings.

Mendelssohn, long before (p.229), had begun his violin concerto by simply establishing an orchestral chord and a rhythm and letting the soloist begin the principal melody. Sibelius goes further. The strings (muted and *tremolando*, giving a faint and eerie sound) strike the chord in an undefined rhythm. The soloist, who enters *against* the chord (with the note G against D minor) establishes rhythm as well as melody. The first theme is extensively spun out. A short cadenza for the soloist leads to a more soulful theme – in the orchestra first, then on the solo instrument in D flat; a faster, more insistent theme follows in B flat minor with a swaying, syncopated after-theme. In a long cadenza, then with the orchestra, the soloist meditates on this material and develops it, eventually making a restatement of the soulful theme in a high register and in D major. But this is no final arrival, and the other themes re-establish a sombre D minor to end the movement.

A questioning interchange between the woodwind instruments opens the second movement, leading to the soloist's measured theme in B flat on the dark lower strings of the violin. The theme gathers force; the violin soars high and passionately, then returns to its dark brooding.

The finale in D major has the 3/4 rhythm of a *polonaise* and suggests a kind of savage or brutal dance. The main theme is relieved by others but finally returns, the soloist all the while exerting a headlong leadership with forceful 3-note chords, flashing scales and other resources of the virtuoso performer.

Legend, The Swan of Tuonela, *opus 22, no.3*

Duration: 9 minutes

The *Kalevala*, the Finnish national epic which is of ancient origin but reached printed form only in the ninteenth century, inspired several of Sibelius's works. At one time he considered an opera based on it, to which the present work was conceived as a prelude. It appeared instead as one of four short 'legends'. Originally conducted by the composer himself at Helsinki on 13 April 1896, it was twice revised, the definitive version dating from 1900. Early editions of the score carried this explanatory note: 'Tuonela, the kingdom of Death, the Hades of Finnish mythology, is surrounded by a broad river of black water and swift current. On it, in majestic course, floats and sings the Swan of Tuonela'.

The orchestration is unique and distinctive: an english horn solo, with oboe, bass clarinet, 2 bassoons, 4 horns, 3 trombones, kettle-drums and bass drum, harp and strings. (No flutes, no standard clarinets, no trumpets are used in this dark palette.) The violins are divided into eight to give a special sonority; all the stringed instruments are muted, except the double-basses.

The music rises mysteriously from a chord of A minor (the key of the work) to a remote G minor where the swan in the voice of the english horn begins its song. A long, plaintive utterance is rounded off by the entry of two horns. The english horn begins a new paragraph of its song, this tune rounded off by the harp. The stringed instruments launch their own, more urgent theme, then stand as if motionless (playing *col legno*, with the back of the bow) as the english horn takes over their theme. The vision fades: the music dies away.

SKRYABIN

1872–1915

Around 1900 a number of composers sought to push musical expression further by means of an expansion of the symphony orchestra, particularly its wind sections. Mahler and Richard Strauss furnish the most obvious examples. In the case of the Russian composer Alexander Skryabin (accent on the *ya*) this orchestral expansion was placed at the service of a definite, though elusive, religious creed. The evocation of a creative spirit is found in such large-scale works as *The Divine Poem* (otherwise Symphony no. 3) and *Prometheus: The Poem of Fire*. For the latter, the composer had formulated a correspondence between sound and colour, and a 'colour organ' or 'keyboard of light' was to make appropriate projections. Practicality, however, dictated a first performance (Moscow, 1911) without any such addition.

Not all his music (most of which is for piano) carries 'philosophical' or otherwise allusive titles. All of it, of course, is intended to make its point self-sufficiently.

The Poem of Ecstasy, *opus 54*

Duration: 24 minutes

Originally conceived as a four-movement symphony, *The Poem of Ecstasy* was the musical fulfilment of a literary poem written by the composer himself. It celebrates an ego-centred universal bliss, ending:

> And the universe resounds
> With the joyful cry, 'I am!'

The composer did not print the poem in the score, which is left as musically self-fulfilling. But its interpretation is guided by various emotional directions for performance, e.g. 'with desire'. The score proved too complicated for the conductor of the intended first performance in Leipzig, and was first heard in New York on 10 December 1908, under the Russian emigré musician, Modest Altschuler. The work is scored for a vast orchestra – quadruple woodwind, 8 horns, 5 trumpets, 3 trombones and tuba, 2 harps, organ, celesta, kettledrums and supplementary percussion, bass drum, cymbals, tam-tam, triangle, tubular bells and a single heavier deep bell and strings.

The opening, in which a solo violin answers a solo flute (both marked 'with languid desire'), displays a sinuous, ingratiating theme. In contrast comes a faster pace which the composer marks *allegro volando* ('flying') with prominent woodwind and cymbal-rolls. The 'languid' mood returns, but a faster tempo provides a summons by four horns which leads immediately to the entry of a solo trumpet ('imperious') – soft at first, but then joined by another trumpet in a new theme of deliberately ascending fourths. This is the main generating material of the work. The trumpet theme will return ('with a noble and joyous emotion') on four trumpets in unison.

In the beginning the shape of the prevailing melodies was such as to leave the tonality uncertain, but at the mid point a resounding climax focuses on a prolonged chord of C major over the sustained low note G. After more interplay of themes comes the final section: the trumpet theme returns to provide the apotheosis of the whole work, and C major again swells forth in full richness of the orchestra including bells. This time the keynote C is firm as rock below. The organ's entry, deferred until now, crowns the effect of sensual power. The composer's comment may be recalled: 'When you listen to *Ecstasy*, look straight into the eye of the sun!'

SMETANA

1824–84

For nineteenth-century national cultures striving to assert themselves, opera was an obvious ready-made form. The story could convey a definite message, folk-music had a legitimate place, and a popular audience could be collected more easily than through a symphonic work. Hence the success of Smetana's *The Bartered Bride* produced in Prague in 1866 and recognized as a Czech national opera. (Though under Austro–Hungarian sovereignty, the Czech region, known as Bohemia, had by then been granted a certain cultural expression.) No other opera by Bedřich Smetana has won such celebrity, nor has penetrated the concert-hall through its overture and dances.

German being the dominant language of the Empire, Smetana himself did not speak Czech. Nor is it often pointed out that he honoured the Austrian emperor's marriage with a *Triumph Symphony*. But Czech nationalism shows not only in his operas but in some of his admirable piano pieces and in the set of symphonic poems to which belongs *Vltava* (below). Equally important in their own field are his two string quartets.

Symphonic poem, Vltava

Duration: 13 minutes

As an ardent Bohemian patriot and nationalist, Smetana enshrined his love and loyalty in the cycle of six symphonic poems collectively entitled *Má Vlast* (My Fatherland). Of these, *Vyšehrad* was the first (named after a mountain fortress overlooking the city of Prague). *Vltava* (named after the river which flows through Prague) was the second and was first performed on 4 April 1875 in Prague, conducted by Adolf Cech. Though not at the time the most acclaimed of the cycle, it has now become by far the best known. The descriptive character of the music is perfectly realized in a self-contained musical form. The orchestral force required comprises piccolo, 2 each of flutes, oboes, clarinets, bassoons; 4 horns, 2 trumpets, 3 trombones, tuba; kettledrums, triangle, bass drum, cymbals; harp and strings.

An inscription on the score makes clear the way in which the music represents the course of the river from its beginning in two mountain streams (2 flutes, E minor). The river gathers force in a broad, surging melody. A hunt is taking place in a forest on the river bank (horns); a peasant wedding is suggested by a polka (woodwind and strings in G major). By moonlight, nymphs are dancing (the flutes' initial theme is developed against long-held chords on muted strings). The broad tune in E minor returns and eventually transforms itself majestically into E major (full orchestra, including triangle). To mark the river's arrival at Prague with its fortress of Vyšehrad, the wind instruments add a theme from the symphonic poem of that name. Then 'the river vanished far beyond the poet's gaze'.

Overture, The Bartered Bride

Duration: 7 minutes

The finale to the second act of this three-act opera gives a lively scene in which the hero deliberately gives the false impression that he is selling his claim to the heroine's hand. From this comes part of the music of this popular overture with its syncopated opening and its merry theme chased around the various sections of the strings. The scoring is for standard large orchestra (but no tuba to go with the trombones). The opera was first heard in Prague, under the composer's conductorship on 30 May 1866.

The syncopated opening and the 'chasing' theme are followed by an exuberant, full-orchestral tune. All these recur; and when what seems to be the final climax is over, there is a gentle extension (tune on two oboes in thirds) and a still more emphatic strain in conclusion.

STRAUSS, JOHANN

1825–99

Son of another celebrated musician of the same name, the 'Waltz King' is sometimes known as Johann Strauss II. His waltzes brought the dance to a new elegance and sumptuousness and the dance orchestra which he led (as violinist-cum-conductor) was itself a Vienna institution. His most famous waltz, *The Blue Danube*, is almost never heard with its original and exceptional chorus part, but this and half a dozen other waltzes, including the *Emperor Waltz* with its majestic introduction, and the sweet-toned *Tales from the Vienna Woods*, plus some of his polkas, are much-loved features of the orchestral repertory today. The famous *Radetzky March*, however, is his father's composition.

He embarked also on a career as operetta composer. (The story that he was personally encouraged to do so by Offenbach, on a visit to Vienna, is fanciful.)

Hardly any of them except for *Die Fledermaus*, and occasionally *The Gipsy Baron*, are now to be encountered, but the former manages to fuse a highly amusing light comedy with the composer's musical inspiration at its most lively and seductive.

Overture, Die Fledermaus

Duration: 8 minutes

Die Fledermaus or *The Bat* was the rather odd choice of title for this popular three-act operetta: a bat costume had been worn to a fancy dress ball by one of the characters on whom a practical joke was played, and the operetta itself narrates this character's comic revenge. The overture itself is built on tunes from the operetta, which the composer himself conducted at its first performance in Vienna on 5 April 1874. The orchestration of the overture is for 2 flutes (1 doubling piccolo), 2 oboes, 2 clarinets, bassoons, 4 horns, 2 trumpets, 3 trombones, kettledrums, snare drum, bass drum, a bell (a single note, E) and strings.

The famous waltz–rhythm breaks in with a whirling tune from the finale of the party scene (Act 2); later a polka anticipates a comic trio of the first act – to which the words of Christopher Hassall's translation, 'Oh yes, oh yes, it had to be/It's just a sad necessity', can easily be fitted. Both these tunes, originally in other keys, recur in the home key of A major in a joyous impetus to the end of the overture.

STRAUSS, RICHARD

1864–1949

Unrelated to the Strauss dynasty of Viennese waltz-kings, Richard Strauss left his mark on the repertory of the orchestra as on that of the opera. Indeed one could argue that the revolutionary one-act operas *Salome* and *Elektra* (1905, 1909) took over a dense-packed narrative style from where the symphonic poems left off.

He wrote in a considerable variety of orchestral forms. Born and brought up in Munich, son of a famous horn-player, he left two horn concertos (and an oboe concerto and other works with soloist). He wrote a famous set of *Four Last Songs* with orchestral accompaniment. But his chief fame is for story-telling through the orchestra – whether the result was called a symphony (*An Alpine Symphony*, 1915) or was given some other label. To this task he brought an unsurpassed handling of orchestral instruments, both for their solo qualities and for their massed effects, and often used an unusually large complement of instruments to do so.

His later years brought, as with some other composers, a partial withdrawal into simpler, less grandly imposing music. Throughout his career he was a distinguished conductor as well as composer.

Symphonic poem, Don Juan, *opus 20*

Duration: 17 minutes

The composer himself conducted *Don Juan* at Weimar on 11 November 1889 – and with it, established himself as the most important figure to emerge in German music since Wagner's death (1883). He was twenty-five. If the most famous treatment in music of the legendary seducer and blasphemer is that of Mozart's *Don Giovanni*, this perhaps comes next. Strauss's immediate literary source was a dramatic poem by the Austrian writer Nikolaus Lenau (1802–50), three extracts from which stand at the head of the score.

In this version Don Juan, after his successful pursuit of so many women, does not die defiant; disillusioned, he allows himself to be killed in a duel.

A full orchestra with triple woodwind and harp, and a glockenspiel among the percussion, is used to brilliant effect. Much of the opening section yields later development. But memorably, perhaps uniquely, the famous horn-tune which seems best to depict the hero does not come until about half-way through the work.

The opening (in E major) is ardent and athletic: Don Juan himself. Eventually a tender tune in B major (clarinet and horn, taken up by violins) introduces the portrayal of the hero's new love. A solo violin becomes prominent. Don Juan breaks away (recall of opening theme). A new love is seen: passionate in the violas and cellos, 'weeping' (*flebile* in the score itself) on a solo flute. With the long-spanning oboe melody in G it would seem almost as if the hero were satisfied.

But suddenly a fresh principal theme, on all four horns in unison, gives a new representation to the hero. He plunges into festivity, the new theme prominent on trumpet and glockenspiel. From revelry he is suddenly thrown down (trombones; long kettledrum-roll). Faint recalls of previous love-music are heard.

The concluding section of the work now begins – in formal terms, a recapitulation, with the opening material in its original key. In narrative terms, it will take Don Juan to another excitement, but thence to his fatal duel. There is a climax, a bar of total silence, then a curtain of sound which is shut off from the top downwards. It is over.

Symphonic poem, Till Eulenspiegel, *opus 28*

Duration: 14 minutes

Of all Strauss's examples of descriptive music, none better shows his orchestral virtuosity than *Till Eulenspiegel*, as it is universally known. The full title is *Till Eulenspiegel's Merry Tricks*. The hero is a legendary rogue and perpetrator of practical jokes, whose adventures first appeared in print around 1500. Strauss's work was first performed on 5 November 1895 in Cologne, under Franz Wüllner. The composer later identified some of the most important references to the material of the tales, and these musical references are used in the following analysis.

The sound owes much to the composer's employment of quad-ruple woodwind instruments – piccolo as well as three flutes; english horn as well as three oboes; high clarinet in D as well as two standard clarinets and a bass clarinet; three bassoons and double-bassoon. In addition to writing for the usual four horns, three trumpets, three trombones and tuba, Strauss provided for the optional use of four more horns and three more trumpets. There are the usual strings and a modest array of percussion – kettledrums, snare drum, bass drum, triangle and cymbals.

The composer himself described this work as a rondo, alluding no doubt to the way in which the two themes representing the hero recur as each new episode of his adventures is narrated. The smooth, coaxing theme which opens the work on the strings corresponds to the story-teller's 'Once upon a time . . .' Two themes chiefly characterize Till: one heard immediately on a solo horn, impudently ascending and then dropping right down to a low note, and one which, after the first big orchestral climax, is piped out by the high clarinet. The two themes are energetically developed to suggest some unspecified escapade. After a whole bar's silence and a short transition, an amiable, jog-trot theme represents Till's disguising himself as a priest, followed shortly by a rather grotesque sound – a foreboding of a sticky end? He banishes such thoughts, however, with a slide from a high note on a solo violin right down to its lowest. His cheeky theme returns (originally on the high clarinet, now on the oboe) as he begins an amorous pursuit: the desired woman rejects him. After a stormy climax of orchestral sound, the four horns alone cock a snook at the world.

Bass clarinet, bassoons and double-bassoon now represent some stupid peasants among whom Till finds himself. Again Till is foiled and vents his feelings in a great grimace trilled out on the woodwinds and sustained by horns and trumpets. But not for long – he is merrily off again (tune on the violins) to vent his mischief elsewhere. The ensuing mix-up expresses itself in the most sustained of orchestral climaxes. Justice and malice catch up with him. Suddenly the combined orchestral sound is cut off, and only the sound of a snare drum roll continues. Heavy chords proclaim a sentence of death. The squeaky clarinet protests, but there is no hope. A return of the 'foreboding' theme leads to Till's inevitable end with the heavy, downward-moving jump of two notes. Silence. The gentle 'Once upon a time' theme returns, with a final reminder of Till's own themes to end the work.

Metamorphoses *for 23 solo strings*

Duration: 24–27 minutes

The title (in German, *Metamorphosen*) refers to the changes or continuous variations to which Strauss subjected a well-known theme from the Funeral March of Beethoven's *Eroica* symphony. But we are left to wonder whether the ageing composer was also meditating on the changes in the destiny of Germany. He wrote it at his Bavarian retreat when Hitler's Reich was crumbling in March and April 1945. The composer then sought hospitality in Switzerland, and the first performance took place in Zurich on 25 January 1946, under the distinguished Swiss conductor Paul Sacher and his Collegium Musicum (chamber orchestra) to whom the piece is dedicated.

The unusual scoring requires 10 violinists, 5 violas, 5 cellos and 3 double-basses. The piece develops in a single long span. After a short introductory section for cellos and double-basses, two violas enter with the theme – one note twice repeated, followed by a falling phrase from the Funeral March (and in the key of that march, C minor). Slow at first, the music grows passionate with various changes in the complex string texture. Is there a hint of Strauss's earlier *Ein Heldenleben* ('A Hero's Life') in an upward-leaping phrase which is later prominent? On the final page, in a slow and deliberate manner, cellos and double-basses give the Beethoven quotation in longer form (and without the three introductory notes). Here, in the printed score, the words 'In memoriam!', with exclamation mark, add a personal comment from the composer as his work draws to its end in C minor.

STRAVINSKY

1882–1971

Russian by birth, then successively French and American by adoption, Igor Stravinsky captured the concert-hall in an unparalleled range of styles and textures. No composer has seemed so deliberately to try now this, now that – veering from brilliant fullness to skeletal sound, from long symphonic development to the tiny dimensions of his *Movements for piano and orchestra* (1960, almost his last orchestral work). The recourse to very small dimensions and tight cellular patterns followed Stravinsky's late adoption (under the posthumous influence of Webern) of the 12-note method of composition.

But his chief fame still arises from earlier works. He was only one of many composers who worked in Paris for the Russian impresario of ballet, Diaghilev, in the era beginning just before the First World War; but of these he was the only one to make three ballets into three classics of the concert-hall. Not to be confused with the first of these, *The Firebird*, is the earlier (non-ballet) composition, *Fireworks*, which shows a link with Stravinsky's teacher, Rimsky-Korsakov. His nomenclature is not always clear or consistent: a work of 1940 is called *Symphony in C* (it has four movements), and its successor is the *Symphony in Three Movements* with no specification of key. A piece dating from 1920, dedicated to the memory of Debussy, is called *Symphonies of Wind Instruments* (not 'A symphony for wind instruments').

A piano concerto (with wind instruments, double-basses and percussion), a capriccio for piano and orchestra and a violin concerto are among Stravinsky's considerable catalogue of other orchestral works.

Symphony in Three Movements

♩ = 160 *alternating with* ♩ = 80
Andante, *leading to*
Con moto
Duration: 21–24 minutes

Perhaps uniquely in the history of orchestral music up to this point
(the date of the first performance was 24 January 1946), Stravinsky's
symphony begins with a movement which carries only a metronome mark for its heading. The composer himself was the
conductor of that first performance, in New York.

Exciting in itself, the work seems to span Stravinsky's great arch
of creativity from *The Rite of Spring* of thirty-three years before to
the opera *The Rake's Progress*, still to come. The orchestral sound
likewise has its characteristic Stravinsky flavour. A piano contributes
remarkably to the orchestral sound, which otherwise calls on 2 flutes
and piccolo, 2 oboes, 3 clarinets (one doubling bass clarinet), 2
bassoons and double-bassoon, 4 horns, 3 trumpets, 3 trombones and
tuba, kettledrums, bass drum, harp and strings.

In a programme-note for that first performance, Stravinsky said
that, while this symphony was 'absolute' music (not linked to any
external 'programme'), it contained traces of experiences coloured
by 'this our arduous time of sharp and shifting events, of despair and
hope, of continual torments, of tension, and at last cessation and
relief'. The reference was to the final stages of the Second World
War. He later revealed the influences of film images on the first and
third movements, in particular.

The first movement was prompted by a documentary film of
'scorched-earth' tactics in China; the beginning of the third movement was partly a reaction to newsreels of goose-stepping Nazi
soldiers; and the latter part of the movement (from the fugue
onward) was associated with the rise of the Allies after the overturn-
ing of the German war machine. The second movement arose quite
differently: it was salvaged from an abortive project of incidental
music for the scene of the apparition of the Virgin in the film *The
Song of Bernadette* based on Franz Werfel's novel.

This second movement now stands as a lyrical island between two
harshly dynamic structures. The first movement is in C, the second
in D; the third opens in C – with an unexpected ending not in that
key but in D flat. In the composer's own words: 'the final, rather

too commercial D–flat–sixth chord in some way tokens my extra exuberance in the Allied triumph'.

The first movement is headed by *two* metronome marks to indicate an alternation of tempos. In the opening of the first section there are pronounced upward 'skirls' leading to the main notes: this is music massive in sound and aggressive in impact. A quiet transition leads to the second section at exactly half the preceding speed (♩=80): the texture is sparser, and the piano with only light orchestral accompaniment is treated almost as the soloist in a concerto. Material from the first section returns, then material from the second, each at its own tempo; then the emphatic 'skirls' reappear to signify the conclusion in the manner of the opening.

The second movement opens in lightly dancing tempo as an oboe solo descends over a springing accompaniment from the strings. The movement is delicately restricted to woodwind, two horns and strings only. After some diversion the oboe's theme returns. A moment's silence and a seven-bar 'interlude' (as the score calls it) lead the music to . . .

. . . the finale, opening with an urgent pace and heavy strokes. The notes of the chord of C major (C, E, G) are hammered out, but a later section 'contradicts' with an emphasis on the key of D flat. When the impetus slackens, a couple of isolated notes from a solo trombone introduce a fugue – the piano delivering the first full entry of the subject, followed by the harp (here, as rarely in orchestral music, a melody-instrument in its own right). Activity increases and the opening urgency returns. A fast-pulsing end (in D flat and not C) celebrates powerfully but briefly, urged on by trombones.

Suite from the ballet, The Firebird

> Introduction – the Firebird – her dance
> Round-dance (*khorovod*) of the princesses
> Infernal dance of King Kashchey, *leading to*
> Lullaby (*berceuse*), *leading to*
> Finale
> Duration: 29 minutes

The performance of the ballet *The Firebird* on 25 June 1910 at the Paris Opera made Stravinsky a celebrity. It was conducted by another composer, Gabriel Pierné. The story is drawn from Russian legend – the firebird being a benevolent supernatural being who assists the young Tsarevich to liberate and marry one of the princesses enslaved to the monstrous king, Kashchey. In 1911 the composer drew from his ballet score a suite of five numbers, retaining the very large orchestral forces used in the ballet itself – including high clarinet in D, bass clarinet, two double-bassoons, and three harps. The energy and vivid colouring of the music, with its strong contrasts, were sufficient to make an immediate conquest in the concert-hall.

The composer's skill also enabled him to make the music accessible to a smaller orchestral force with not too much sacrifice. A new suite (1919) not only reduced the orchestration but entailed some re-ordering of the numbers. In this suite, which is described here, only one harp is required, and only two players of each type of woodwind instrument – one of the flutes being interchangeable with piccolo, one of the oboes with english horn. The standard brass is required (4 horns, 2 trumpets, 3 trombones, tuba), as are piano, kettledrums, a more restricted range of extra percussion than before (bass drum, tambourine, triangle, cymbals, xylophone) and strings.

In 1949 Stravinsky compiled yet another suite for reduced orchestra, comprising (in a different order) the present numbers and some others.

The 1919 suite begins (as do the other suites) with a nocturnal picture of Kashchey's enchanted garden – conjured up at first by undulating figures on cellos and double-basses over a soft roll on the bass drum. There is a flutter of harmonics on the strings like flashes of light. The undulating figures return. Suddenly there is an expectant *tremolo* on the strings and a new presence is announced by the fluttering of the woodwind: it is the Firebird. After a moment's pause she begins her dance – at first with clarinet, flute and piccolo above the strings. The animation and excitement increase.

In the next number a gentle, swaying motion leads to a tune on the oboe in B major. It is the round-dance of the captive princesses.

A sudden *fortissimo* explodes from the whole orchestra. It is followed by a kettledrum-roll and a jagged rhythmic figure on the horns, introducing the monster Kashchey himself. Trumpets in octaves hurl out a menacing theme. Kaschey's dance (the longest number of the suite) is extended with changes of rhythm between 3/4 and 2/4 but never loses its force and athleticism. Sweeps up and down the strings of the piano and harp make their contribution, as well as the varied impact of percussion. A sustained note in the oboes and horns, suddenly soft, leads to . . .

. . . the Lullaby (berceuse). With her magical powers, the Firebird casts the evil king into sleep. A drowsy tune is heard from a solo bassoon against the unearthly sound of harmonics on the harp. The drowsiness spreads through the strings and woodwind of the orchestra. With trembling strings, the music sinks down. Immediately . . .

. . . the Finale begins. A soft horn-call serves as a symbol of deliverance and a happy outcome. The tempo accelerates. Festive chords peal forth. Once again the tempo quickens and the texture becomes richer. A sequence of dazzling brass chords ends the music.

Ballet, Petrushka

Duration: 29 minutes

It was Stravinsky's own idea to centre a ballet on the traditional Russian puppet-figure of 'Petrushka' (a pet-name form of the Russian equivalent of 'Peter'). The story was worked out by Alexander Benois, who designed the scenery and costumes when the ballet was given by Diaghilev's company in Paris on 13 June 1911, with choreography by Fokine. A lasting success as a ballet, it also proved a favourite work of the concert-hall. The score vividly depicts Petrushka himself in a grotesque cry formed of the new chord-combination of C and F sharp (now known as 'the Petrushka chord').

It called for a very large orchestra, with quadruple woodwind (though not as large as would be required for *The Rite of Spring*!). Loopholes in the international law of copyright allowed this score of 1911 to be pirated in America – that is, to be printed and performed without fee to the composer. Partly for this reason, Stravinsky prepared a new version, published in 1947, playable by a smaller orchestra (with triple woodwind, but retaining a prominent piano part, as in the original). The 1947 version also makes various revisions to the musical text, and presents an alternative loud ending: it is more obviously a concert and is the basis of the following commentary.

The action takes place in the Shrovetide Fair at St Petersburg – the present Leningrad, and formerly Russia's capital. It concerns an old puppet-master, misleadingly called a Charlatan in the original synopsis, and his three puppets, Petrushka, a Moor, and a Ballerina, who come to life. There are four scenes:

Scene 1: The Fair

On a sunny winter's day, people of all classes are promenading among the stalls and entertainments. Outside his little theatre, the puppet-master blows on a pipe to attract attention (unaccompanied flute solo). His three puppets perform a vigorous Russian Dance. A rasp of drums leads without interruption to:

Scene 2: Petrushka

Petrushka (here a living being) is in his tiny room. Two clarinets utter his grotesque cry. The Ballerina enters (two bars of piano solo); he woos her but she scorns him. His cry recurs, even more stridently, on muted trumpets. Again the drums roll as the scene changes to:

Scene 3: The Moor

In his comfortable room, the Moor dances. The Ballerina enters with false daintiness (trumpet solo with side drum), then waltzes lovingly with the Moor. Petrushka tries to enter (theme on trumpets) but is pushed out. Drums lead to:

Scene 4:

The Fair. There is bustle as before. Nursemaids dance (a rapid, rustling tune from clarinets, bassoons, trumpets); a peasant enters, leading a tame bear (prominent tuba). Other dancing is halted by Petrushka's entrance – one trumpet, joined by two more in *crescendo*. The Moor pursues and kills him. The puppet-master, questioned by a policeman, demonstrates that Petrushka was only a puppet. The fuss should be over, but the puppet-master is terrified to see a phantom Petrushka on the roof-top (his theme once again strident on trumpets). The work ends softly with a shrug of doubt – or, as an alternative, loudly with an exclamation.

Ballet, The Rite of Spring

Duration: 33 minutes

Reckoned one of the landmarks of twentieth-century music, *The Rite of Spring* met with an appropriate baptism of fire when given by the Diaghilev company in Paris. Nijinsky was the choreographer. The first performance (conducted by Pierre Monteux on 29 May 1913) provoked physical disturbances among the audience. Even today, an impact is still made by the unusualness of tone-colours and violence of rhythm. The music is now more frequently given in concert than as a ballet, partly because the very large orchestra required is not always available under theatrical conditions.

The orchestral requirement indeed deserves to be listed: the following are the *instruments*, though some players take more than one (for instance, one instrumentalist plays only the piccolo, but another alternates between flute and piccolo):

    1 piccolo, 3 flutes, 1 alto flute
    4 oboes, 1 english horn
    1 high clarinet in E flat, 3 standard clarinets, 2 bass clarinets
    4 bassoons, 2 double-bassoons
    8 horns
    2 Wagner tubas
    1 small trumpet, 4 standard trumpets, 1 bass trumpet
    3 trombones
    2 tubas
    5 kettledrums
    bass drum, tam-tam, triangle, tambourine, *guero* (rasp), 2
      crotales (antique cymbals)
    strings

Subtitled 'Pictures from Pagan Russia', the music shows an ancient fertility rite in which a chosen virgin is sacrificed to placate the powers of earth. Stravinsky once said that *The Coronation of Spring* would be a better English rendering of his idea than the usual title (itself a translation of the French *Le sacre du printemps*). Short and rough-cut phrases, obsessive rhythms, and eruptive percussion all convey the primitive.

The work is divided into two large parts. Within each part the music is continuous, but titles indicate where a new section of the dance is envisaged, often with a change in the speed of the music. These titles are given below, with instrumental indications of their openings only:

Part One: Adoration of the Earth

Introduction (slow): Very high bassoon solo, one of the most remarkable instrumental innovations

Spring auguries: Dance of the adolescent girls (fast) heavy cross-rhythmed stamping on the strings

Game of the abduction (very fast): Sustained chord on horns and trumpets; shrill call from upper woodwind and trumpet

Spring rounds (slow): At first, woodwind only; high flute trills

Game of the rival cities (very fast): Interruption by trombones, tubas and kettledrums

Entrance of the wise man (fast): Repetitive march on tubas

Adoration of the earth: The wise man (slow); four mysterious, suspenseful bars

Dance of the earth (very fast): Bass drum alone leads to full orchestra

Part Two: The Sacrifice

Introduction (slow): Woodwind oscillations

Mysterious circles of the young girls (slow): Rich-textured strings without violins

Glorification of the chosen one (fast): High shrieks from flutes and piccolo

Invocation of the ancestors (fairly slow): Heavy repeated chords from woodwind and brass

Ritual action of the ancestors (slow): *Pizzicato* lower strings, english horn solo

Ritual dance of the chosen one (fast): (After bass clarinet duet) violent short phrases, full orchestra

TCHAIKOVSKY

1840–93

Tchaikovsky is one of the few composers (Beethoven is another)
who can be relied on to draw a large audience to a mixed programme
compiled entirely from his music. This suggests that, no matter how
easily the First Piano Concerto is described as hackneyed or the *1812
Overture* as trivial, Tchaikovsky's work is both strong and well
varied. Inventive melody is combined with rich harmonic resource
and vivid orchestration: indeed Tchaikovsky's use of rushing strings
and cutting brass is unmistakable. Extreme emotions are evoked and
contrasted – darkest gloom, exultant affirmation.

Although Pyotr Ilyich Tchaikovsky is usually considered less
'nationalist' than Rimsky-Korsakov, Borodin and their fellows, his
melodies have a distinctively Russian pattern and an occasional
quotation of traditional Russian music. He put his distinctive stamp
on the 'German' forms of symphony and concerto, but followed
Liszt into the newer descriptive field of the symphonic poem. A
story-telling element holds together Tchaikovsky's *1812 Overture*, a
tribute (1880) to his countrymen's defeat of Napoleon. With similar
patriotic purpose, four years previously, he composed a *Slavonic
March* – known also in the French form of the title, *Marche slave*, so
liable to mislead English speakers.

His scores for the ballets *Swan Lake*, *The Sleeping Beauty* and *The
Nutcracker* are a major contribution to the nineteenth-century heritage of orchestral music. A waltz-tune not from these ballets but
every bit as characteristic of Tchaikovsky's art is to be found in the
Serenade for string orchestra. Occasionally he brings out, in his
orchestral music as in his operas, an appreciative regard for the
charm which the nineteenth century saw in Mozart: hence the
'rococo' element in one of the works considered below.

The Symphonies

Tchaikovsky could be said to be the most important composer of symphonies outside the German–Austrian tradition. He encompasses the traditional multi-movement plan but makes it his own – using his mastery of the orchestral palette to cultivate the widest emotional range from frenzied liveliness to utter gloom, and preferring to 'throw' themes (or fragments of themes) at each other rather than seeking small, subtle transformations in Brahms's way.

His first three symphonies, from the period 1866–75, are of lesser status than the well-known three, but by no means negligible: no.1 in G minor (subtitled *Winter Reveries*), no.2 in C minor (known as the *Little Russian*, meaning Ukrainian) and no.3 in D (the nickname of *Polish* is unauthorized and misleading). Standing apart from these is the (unnumbered) *Manfred* Symphony of 1885, a descriptive work after a poem by Byron, in four movements: it is a considerable testimony to its composer's art and its neglect is hard to explain.

Symphony No.4 in F minor, opus 36

> Andante sostenuto – Moderato con anima
> Andantino in moda di canzona
> Scherzo: allegro
> Allegro con fuoco
> Duration: 39–42 minutes

'Our symphony has a programme', the composer wrote to his patron, Nadezhda von Meck, 'and I will tell you, and you alone, the meaning of the entire work and its separate movements. The introduction is the germ of the symphony, without question its central idea. This is *Fate*, that fatal power which prevents our striving for happiness from succeeding'. Tchaikovsky proceeded to give a detailed account of the music but in a postscript called it 'a confused and inadequate programme'. First performed in Moscow under Nikolay Rubinstein in 10 February 1878, it was slow to achieve its present firm popularity. Its scoring is for conventional large symphonic orchestra (with three trombones and tuba) plus bass drum, cymbals and triangle.

Horns, backed by bassoons, announce the Fate theme first of all: the menace of its rhythmical summons is unmistakable, and is reinforced when a new harmony suddenly supports it. The theme fades as the main section of the movement begins in a faster, swaying tempo (the composer actually calls it waltz-tempo). A flow of new themes is presented and developed, but 'these are only dreams: we are awakened by Fate' (the composer's words). The summons sometimes interrupts the flow, sometimes mingles with it.

'In the style of a song' runs the direction for the slow second movement, again in a minor key (B flat minor). The oboe's melody suggests, according to the composer, melancholy, reminiscence, passivity. But here too Fate bursts through on horns, trumpets and kettledrums.

The third movement turns to a happier feeling in F major. It is subtitled *pizzicato ostinato*: the string-players pluck their instruments throughout. A contrasting section for wind and drums only (Tchaikovsky's 'street song' and 'military music in the distance') is followed by a resumption of the *pizzicato* section into which the other instruments now insert their themes. This time there is no interruption by the summons of Fate.

The soft ending of the third movement gives way to the cymbal clash, full brass chords and swirling strings and woodwind which open the finale in F major. Flute, clarinet and bassoon announce an innocent folk-tune, and a strong, joyful vigour develops. Twice the folk-tune recurs in its simple state, twice more the jollity rises. ('Go to the people: see how they can enjoy life and give themselves entirely to festivity'.) Then, suddenly, the Fate theme reappears – with the same dramatic shift of harmony as in the introduction to the first movement. But it fades, and jollity takes the symphony to its end.

Symphony No.5 in E minor, opus 64

> Andante – Allegro con anima
> Andante cantabile, con alcuna licenza
> Valse: allegro moderato
> Andante maestoso – Allegro vivace
> Duration: 45–48 minutes

No 'programme' for this symphony was suggested by the composer, as it was for no.4. But there is a similar use of an overriding theme (this time present in all four movements, not three only) and the two symphonies can be listened to in much the same way – as a succession of varied moods and tempos all subject to a unifying idea. The Fifth is orchestrated without extra percussion.

The composer himself conducted the first performance in St Petersburg on 5 November 1888. Like the Fourth, it was slow to establish
its present position of popularity.

The unifying motto-theme is announced in hushed tones, low
down on the two clarinets. Only clarinets, bassoons and lower
strings are used for this sombre introductory section of the first
movement. The dark tone-colour hardly changes when the quicker
main section starts (solo clarinet and solo bassoon), but the music
soon rises to excitement. After a climax, a smoothly expressive
theme comes from violins, violas and cellos only, yielding to a more
sustained theme in D major – a slow waltz-tune of great passion.
Further climaxes follow, and the waltz-tune returns, but the movement ends as softly as it started (bassoons, kettledrum-roll, lower
strings) – without the return of the motto-theme.

The sustained tones of a horn solo in D major begin the soulful
appeal of the second movement. A rather faster tempo with clarinet
solo promises simply to provide a lyrical contrast, but now the
motto-theme intrudes alarmingly on the trumpets, and will intrude
again.

Against a gentle rhythmical background, the violins give out in A
major the graceful waltz which commands the third movement. A
lightly scampering tune (also on the violins) later offers a diversion.
But when the main theme returns, its progress to a happy ending is
interrupted by the mournful reminder of the motto-theme from
clarinets and bassoons.

The finale opens with the motto-theme itself: slow, as at the
opening of the symphony, but now majestic and transferred to the
major key – from gloom to confident hope, as it seems. This slow
introduction is long, ending on drum-roll from which the main,
faster section breaks out with its principal theme in E minor. Later,
the high woodwind introduce a brisk march. The mood is one of
stress – but the tension is finally broken after a dramatic pause of
expectancy, when the major-key version of the motto-theme is
thundered forth as a triumphal proclamation. Finally this theme
takes on a new, simplified rhythmic shape and is hammered home.

Symphony No.6 in B minor (Pathetic)

Adagio – allegro non troppo
Allegro con grazia
Allegro molto vivace
Adagio lamentoso – andante
Duration: 42–45 minutes

'Never in my life,' Tchaikovsky wrote to his publisher, 'have I been so contented, so proud, so happy in the knowledge that I have written a good piece.' The *Pathetic* Symphony (there is no good reason for retaining the French *Pathétique* in English-speaking use) had its first performance on 28 October 1893, in St Petersburg (Leningrad) under the composer's direction, but its success is held to spring from a performance on 18 November under Eduard Napravnik – twelve days after the composer's death.

Only a small minority of symphonies are in a minor key, and most of those end with a switch to the major: Dvořák's *New World* (p.144) brings off the effect marvellously. But Mozart's no.40 holds the minor, and so does this one of Tchaikovsky's – a Romantic composer's exploration of the most tragic expression. Doom is sounded by the tam-tam (gong), reserved for one single stroke in the finale. In other respects the orchestration is as for the Symphony no.5, with the addition of bass drum and cymbals. Conductors frequently add a bass clarinet to replace the bassoon at a moment of extreme softness in the second movement.

Pathos characterizes the opening movement. A short introductory section opens in the sombre colour of a solo bassoon. Equally striking, where the main faster section begins, is the rich four-part harmony of the urgent theme on divided violas and cellos. The principal contrasting theme is a consoling tune in D major on muted strings. The music fades to extreme softness (marked *pppppp* on a solo bassoon or bass clarinet) before an explosive bang starts the development. When the waves of strong feeling finally subside, a hymn-like solemnity is suggested by trumpets and trombones against the slow-marching tread of *pizzicato* strings, and the end is again subdued.

Escape from the shade comes with the second movement in D major – composed in 5/4 time, like nothing in any previous symphony. It starts with a lilt, like a waltz in disguise, but an ensuing section (still in the same rhythm) has a drooping theme, actually marked 'tearful', over a persistent slow kettledrum beat. The graceful strain returns, with fragmentary reminders of the other theme towards the end.

The third movement presents excitement and triumph. A catchy march theme carries irresistible impetus, and the various sections of the orchestra are displayed in brilliance and contrast. The third flute is exchanged for the shrill piccolo and the cymbals and their excited off-beat clashes.

Totally original is the finale in B minor, which returns the listener to the opening mood of the symphony – one of dragging despair. The strings lament; the music achieves one throbbing climax only to fall. Another climax, another fall: the tam-tam's stroke is followed by requiem chords from trombones and tuba, and the throb (now darkly on the double-basses) only takes the music to its extinction.

The concertos

In works for solo instrument and orchestra, Tchaikovsky was no less resourceful and successful than with symphonies. Indeed he exploits, as in the symphonies, the full force and dazzle of the orchestra along with the increased virtuosity of the solo performers of his day. In view of the conquering role of the Piano Concerto no.1, the merely modest success of a second piano concerto (first performed in 1881) is a little curious. In a remainder of a common practice of Bach's day, its slow movement is almost entirely 'chamber music' – a solo violin and cello joining the piano.

For cello, Tchaikovsky wrote no concerto, but his *Variations on a Rococo Theme* allow a concerto-like interplay between soloist and orchestra and have proved one of the best-loved works written for the instrument.

Concerto for piano and orchestra No.1 in B flat minor

Allegro non troppo e molto maestoso – Allegro con spirito
Andantino semplice – Prestissimo – Andantino, *leading to*
Allegro con fuoco
Duration: 33–35 minutes

What has become perhaps the most popular of all piano concertos began its career by being rejected by a distinguished Russian pianist of the day, Nikolay Rubinstein. Tchaikovsky dedicated it instead to the German pianist Hans von Bülow, who took it on his scheduled American tour and gave its first performance on 25 October 1875 at Boston, under the baton of a local musician, Benjamin Johnson Lang. Its success was immediate.

Later, the composer made considerable alterations, only then arriving at the final form of the piano's thunderous opening. The pianist confronts a challenge of force, agility and endurance as the solo instrument contends with the full display of Tchaikovsky's large orchestra, used with the composer's characteristic virtuousity. The scoring requires 2 each of flutes, oboes, clarinets and bassoons; 4 horns, 2 trumpets, 3 trombones, kettledrums and strings.

The opening horn-call, the chords which march majestically up the piano keyboard, and the sweeping tune in the strings which these chords accompany – all these are powerful elements in the impression left by the concerto. Yet the whole of this first section of the first movement sets a puzzle. It is 106 bars long (out of 667 bars) and seems no mere introduction. Yet it makes no return. It fades out, and what has to be regarded as the self-contained 'main' section of the movement starts. A rippling theme for the solo instrument in B flat minor (derived from a beggar's song which the composer heard!) is developed at some length. Woodwind instruments take over with a smooth, pleading theme in D flat major, confirmed by the muted strings. The piano asserts itself with bold passages in octaves, and later with an entirely solo passage – like a free, new development rather than a cadenza. Later still, after the 'pleading' theme has been brought back in B flat major, a further expanse of figuration leads to an alternation of chords between piano and orchestra and a cadenza proper (the composer's own), speeding and slowing down as if in improvisation, and dying away as a flute and clarinet recall what was earlier the muted strings' theme. The happier major key (B flat major) is sustained though a final burst of energy.

For the quiet middle movement in G flat major the orchestral strings put on their mutes, striking up a *pizzicato* rhythm over which the flute gives out a simple, gentle melody which the piano takes over. Later, this theme passes to two solo cellos while the piano supplies a decorative background. There is a 'full stop' and a change to a new, quicker, scherzo-like section in which a graceful waltz-tune in D major soon appears on violas and cellos (another 'borrowed' tune – this time a French popular song). The piano emerges from its background role for a brief meditation on its own, of which the climax is marked by a single loud chord (the full orchestra's only entry in the movement). The original flute tune, now transferred to the piano, gently returns.

The finale, a 'fiery' movement (*con fuoco*) starts with yet another borrowed tune, from a Ukrainian folksong. This fast, dance-like theme on the piano is followed by an even more vigorous, stamping utterance by the full orchestra (in G flat major). In quieter vein and in D flat major the piano gives out a lyrical, yearning tune which is destined to linger in the memory. Towards the end of the movement, majestically heralded by the soloist, this theme soars out on piano and full orchestra in the 'home' territory of B flat major, clinching the work and needing only a short, quick resumption of dance-like energy to finish.

Concerto for violin and orchestra in D major, opus 35

Allegro moderato
Canzonetta: Andante, *leading to*
Allegro vivacissimo
Duration: 30–33 minutes

Like the First Piano Concerto, Tchaikovsky's only concerto for violin had an initial rejection. On its completion in 1878 it was declared by the great St Petersburg violinist Leopold Auer to be 'un-violinistic' (he must have meant 'too difficult'!) and not until three years later did the young Adolf Brodsky give the first performance – at Vienna on 4 December 1881, under Hans Richter. The views of critics who attacked it there ('stinking music', wrote Hanslick) were negated by the esteem it later won from soloists and audiences. Auer himself later took up the work.

Trombones and tuba are excluded from the score, bringing Tchaikovsky's orchestration nearer to that of earlier violin concertos: 2 each of flutes, oboes, clarinets, bassoons; four horns, 2 trumpets, kettledrums and strings.

The orchestra enters first – but not with the usual long statement of themes. A brief introduction suffices and then the soloist takes command – passing from a preliminary flourish to the well-defined first theme. A climax, giving the first taste of the rapid exciting solo style required, yields to the second main theme – again from the solo instrument, with orchestral strings accompanying. It is notable that *both* themes have a 'singing' rather than assertive melody, the assertiveness arising from what happens later. A big orchestral entry with prominent brass now delivers the first themes in the new key of A major. Later the violin is involved in a 'contest', its strong rhythmical chords across three and four strings standing out against waves of orchestral sound. A brilliant cadenza (Tchaikovksy's own) leads to a recapitulation in which both main themes are now heard in the home key, D major. More solo 'fireworks' and a speeded tempo contribute to an exciting finish.

The attractive melancholy of the second movement shifts the key to G minor and establishes a quieter tone-colour. Trumpets, trombones and drums are silent; after a woodwind introduction, the violin with its mute in position delivers its song. ('Canzonetta' in this context implies a simple or folk-like song.) An elaboration of it is begun by a flute. A short, major-key melody, similarly given to the soloist, forms a contrast; the return of the opening melody receives a delicate accompaniment on the lower register of a clarinet. The woodwind introduction reappears but gives way to a direct move into . . .

. . . the finale. A loud first beat brings back the full orchestra again; soon the solo violin (discarding its mute) enters with a preliminary flourish and then delivers the main theme in D major – brisk and accented like a Russian dance (indeed, like the Russian dance in *The Nutcracker* – see below). The same dance-like characteristic is shown in a second theme (in A) delivered by the soloist over a repeated bass chord from the cellos. From these elements the music pursues its swift, energetic way – the violinist forcefully competing with the orchestra or soaring in delicate high harmonics (an unmistakable passage against woodwind only). The dance reaches a stamping, *fortissimo* conclusion.

Variations on a Rococo Theme, for cello and orchestra, opus 33

Duration: 16–19 minutes

Standing among the modest number of works for cello and orchestra by composers of the first rank, this is not formally a concerto. But it carries a similar range of expression and a similar demand for a virtuoso's precision, delicacy and fire. A theme of a supposedly eighteenth-century grace (hence 'rococo') is matched by an orchestra of eighteenth-century size – 2 each of flutes, oboes, clarinets,

bassoons and horns, with strings. There is thus no threat to drown
the cello's tone. The musical idiom, however, is no eighteenth-
century pastiche but represents Tchaikovsky's distinct emotional
style.

The work was dedicated to Wilhelm Fitzenhagen, a German cellist
active in Moscow's musical life. He gave the first performance on 30
November 1877 in Moscow, with Nikolay Rubinstein conducting.
After a short introduction ending on a solo horn, the cello soloist
enters with the theme itself (in A major), which is in two halves each
repeated. A little bridging passage follows, leading directly into the
first variation. The variations all observe the two-sectioned structure. In most performances seven variations are heard, with the
seventh extended by a 32-bar coda to make it much the longest. A
fully written-out cadenza precedes the sixth variation.

But this sequence, which until recently was universally accepted,
does not follow the composer's intentions. It has been shown that, in
preparing the published score, Fitzenhagen not only rewrote the solo
part (as he was supposed to do) to make it fully effective for his
instrument, but also took the liberty of exchanging the place of two
of the variations and scrapping another variation (intended as the
last) altogether! A modern Soviet edition has reconstituted the
authentic form. The sixth variation, which is in D minor and has an
appealing pathos, should really come third, along with its preliminary cadenza. Conversely, the waltz-movement in C major which
Fitzenhagen put as the third variation should really come seventh,
with a return to A major in a final variation which Fitzenhagen
omitted altogether (except for that 32-bar coda).

The neatness of the orchestral accompaniment, and the combination of eloquence and brilliance in the solo part, do not fail to make
their point in any case. The coda has some solo passages in octaves
(with the player double-stopping) which really test the virtuoso's
technique. It may take time for the authentic score to overtake the
more established other version, but it must surely happen.

Fantasy Overture Romeo and Juliet

Duration: 19 minutes

Perhaps the most popular of all orchestral 'narratives', *Romeo and
Juliet* did not immediately assume the form in which we now know
it. After the first performance, conducted in Moscow by Nikolay

Rubinstein on 16 March 1870, the composer revised it, substituting a new first opening (the section depicting Friar Laurence) at the urging of Balakirev, the older composer who had originally suggested the subject. In its revised version it was given in St Petersburg on 17 February 1872 under Edward Napravnik. This is substantially the version now known, though minor revisions were made later.

Romeo and Juliet is called a 'fantasy overture' – probably indicating its 'free' assembly of themes: it does not follow the strict form of a symphonic first movement which so many composers had adopted for an overture. Here an introductory section in slow time in F sharp minor precedes the principal fast section of the movement (from the beginning of the 'feuding' music) which progresses from B minor to B major. 'Overture' itself does not imply that it was intended for use in conjunction with a theatrical performance of the play, but only that it is a substantial, single-movement work. The orchestration uses double woodwind plus piccolo and english horn, standard brass (2 horns, 2 trumpets, 3 trombones and tuba), harp, percussion (bass drum and cymbals in addition to the kettledrums) and strings.

The events of the play are not followed literally. The slow opening evokes Friar Laurence (Romeo's confidant, who performs the ill-fated marriage) on the organ-like tones of clarinets and bassoons. A further calm passage suggesting benediction (with sequences of *arpeggio* chords on the harp) changes to agitation and a new, swifter tempo. Jagged, angry music represents the feud of Montagues and Capulets. At length the tumult is quietened for the love-theme in D flat – at first on english horn solo against sparse accompaniment, then swelling into throbbing, full-orchestral expression.

A central section corresponding to symphonic development represents the conflicts and their fatal consequence. Friar Laurence's theme is involved in the tension. When the return of the love-theme is suggested, an unrest continues beneath. But for an ecstatic moment the love-theme soars forth in its passionate full-orchestral form, now in D major. A further destructive outbreak leads to catastrophe: a kettledrum-roll thunders out, then quietens. In slower tempo over a relentless bass note the tragedy is emphasized, with the harp *arpeggio* figures returning to offer a consolation as the violins deliver a last, sad version of the love-theme.

Suite from the ballet The Nutcracker, opus 71a

Miniature overture
March
Dance of the sugar-plum fairy
Russian dance: Trepak
Arabian dance
Chinese dance
Dance of the reeds
Waltz of the flowers
Duration: 20–22 minutes

Produced in St Petersburg on 18 December 1892, the two-act ballet with choreography by Petipa has yielded some of the best known of Tchaikovsky's music. Yet the composer took on the work with some reluctance and considered the result 'far weaker than *The Sleeping Beauty*'. The ballet is founded on a children's tale by E. T. A. Hoffmann, with the heroine a little girl and the nutcracker turning into a handsome prince. The concert suite from *The Nutcracker* represents only a selection from it, mostly from the second act in the Kingdom of Sweets: here the Nutcracker Prince welcomes Clara to a banquet and a danced *divertissement*.

The *Overture* is 'miniature' only in the sense of its restricted, almost toy-like scoring – the product of a master-orchestrator. The only strings used are violins and violas, with 2 flutes and piccolo, 2 each of oboes, clarinets, bassoons, horns – plus triangle. Full-orchestral sound bursts forth in the *March* (with 4 horns, 2 trumpets, 3 trombones, tuba and cymbals). But still there are surprises to come: the *Dance of the sugar-plum fairy* introduces the tinkling of the celesta (newly invented in Tchaikovsky's time!) and the bass clarinet; the kettledrums enter at last in the vigorous Russian dance, the *Trepak*, and so do english horn and tambourine. In marked contrast comes the veiled sound of the *Arabian dance* (note the special role of the tambourine).

Yet another instrument, the glockenspiel, adds its tones to the *Chinese dance*, where the pattering of the bassoon underpins the exclamations of flute and piccolo. The flutes have a different but equally striking role in the *Dance of the reeds*. Finally, one of the most famous of waltzes in the entire world of ballet: the harp (its first entry) takes a long preliminary curtsey, and the horns lead off the irresistible sequence of dance-melodies.

TIPPETT

born 1905

A long creative life, a willingness to embrace many different musical forms including opera, and a readiness to put forward non-musical ideas of a vague philosophical nature have given a special position in Britain to Michael Tippett – with some favourable repercussions in America also. Like Holst (his predecessor as musical director of Morley College, London) he drew inspiration from English music of the first Elizabethan period and borrowed too from the American tradition of spiritual, jazz and blues. A notable product of this is the treatment of spirituals in his pacifist oratorio, *A Child of Our Time* (1944).

In his orchestral music he has found continuing life in the older forms of symphony, concerto and variations. He made an apparently unique choice of instruments in composing a concerto for violin, viola, cello and orchestra (1979), the successor to a piano concerto (1953–5); other works include a *Praeludium* for brass, bells and percussion. A set of *Ritual Dances* from the opera *The Midsummer Marriage*, first staged in 1955, is also excerpted for orchestral concert use.

Symphony no.4

Duration: 31 minutes

Not many British symphonic works have had their first performances abroad, and it is a mark of Tippett's status that this symphony was commissioned by the Chicago Symphony Orchestra, with Sir Georg Solti as its musical director. He conducted the first performance at Chicago on 6 October 1977. Of all Tippett's four symphonies it is the only one in a single movement.

Unique, too, is its scoring, particularly in having six instead of the usual four horns and two tubas instead of one. Besides the kettledrummer, four percussionists are required for xylophone, marimba, glockenspiel, snare drum, tenor drum, bass drum, tom-tom, cymbals, maracas, claves, wood-block, triangle and (if used) wind-machine. Other instruments required are 2 flutes (both doubling piccolo), 2 oboes, 2 clarinets and bass clarinet, 2 bassoons and double-bassoon, 3 trumpets, 3 trombones, piano, harp and strings.

The sound of 'gentle breathing' is required to be heard – whether by the wind-machine, by amplification of real breathing, or by other means. The presence of the 'breathing' sound at the beginning, intermittently, and at the end has a significance for the symphony. Tippett called it a 'birth-to-death' piece and intended certain effects of 'shaking' or trilling to symbolize the transformation produced by cellular growth.

The listener finds in the single continuous movement a kind of re-combination of standard symphonic components. The structure, buttressed by three spaced-out statements of a chord slowly built by the six horns, presents an exposition of the main material, a slow movement, a scherzo, then a recapitulation. Subsidiary episodes are inserted on the way, one being based on a fantasia for strings by the English composer Orlando Gibbons (1583–1625).

After the initial 'birth image', in which slowly pivoting chords are suggestive of breathing or other steady body-rhythms, there is a momentary pause. The composer then presents three orchestral groups with identification in the score – brass ('power'), strings ('vigour') and woodwind ('lyric grace'), roles which are to be pursued later. Now the six horns, exposed alone, build up their chord, based on a low E flat – a poetic outburst answered by woodwind, solo viola, piano and harp. Soon, ushered in by a kettledrum roll, cellos and double-basses begin a fast continuation, leading eventually to a new building-up of the horn chord, this time pitched a tone higher.

The equivalent of a slow movement follows, in which the piano and other instruments seem to improvise meditatively. A meandering melody on the oboe passes to the english horn. Sudden drum strokes end the idyll and introduce a new, stormy interlude: its climax leads to a massive trilling followed by a dramatic pause.

The scherzo section follows, with light, brief figures – marked 'flying' in the score. Later, with the same verbal indication, strings alone soar aloft in Tippett's version of the Gibbons fantasia. After other instruments have invaded, the built-up horn chord again occurs, at a still higher pitch. Now begins the symphony's final section, serving as a sort of recapitulation and farewell and soon recalling the earlier characterization of brass, strings and woodwind in their 'roles'. Violent and peaceful moments, apparently un-reconciled, are juxtaposed. Slow-pivoting chords like those of the opening are allowed to end the symphony, on harmonies that sound softly but stay unresolved, questioning.

Concerto for Double String Orchestra

> Allegro con brio
> Andante cantabile
> Allegro molto
> Duration: 22–23 minutes

This work, along with the oratorio *A Child of Our Time*, was mainly responsible for establishing the composer's reputation. Its first performance was given in London on 21 April 1940, with the composer conducting. It revives one of the baroque uses of the word 'concerto', a work in which one instrumental group is contrasted and combined with another. Here, however, it is not a small group opposed to a larger: two equally balanced orchestras of conventional string disposition (1st and 2nd violins, violas, cellos, double-basses) are used. A violin and cello emerge as soloists in the second movement.

Parts of this work have a strong modal feeling (i.e. a basis not corresponding to either the conventional major or minor), but the notes A, D, C come to establish themselves as key-centres for the three movements. The 'blue notes' of jazz seem to have influenced the bitter-sweet clashes of notes in the soulful, singing melody of the slow middle movement; but the sharp, syncopated accents of the two outer movements perhaps derive from the composer's interest in sixteenth-century music rather than from jazz.

In the first movement the two orchestras engage in athletic contest. Sometimes a rumba beat (with accents on first, fourth and seventh quavers of a 4/4 bar) jolts the expected rhythm. The opening material makes a later return in a reinforced statement.

After a few introductory bars the second movement presents an eloquently appealing melody on a solo violin, then on all the first violins. (There is now less opposition between orchestras.) After animated development, a solo cello recalls the melody in quietness.

Opposition between the orchestras re-establishes itself in the finale, and so do clashes of rhythmical accent: the opening time signature is a simultaneous 3/4 and 6/8. The orchestras unite in a powerful theme with downward movement; then the cellos of both orchestras deliver a quieter theme. Later in the movement both these themes return and lead to a joyous surprise: what seems a new, swinging tune (actually evolved from the main theme of the second movement) takes over, providing a rich-sounding and confident finish.

VAUGHAN WILLIAMS

1872–1958

Ralph Vaughan Williams lived to be very much the grand old man of English music: the colleague of his youthful years, Gustav Holst, had died twenty-four years before him. He remained active into his eighties, his last (ninth) symphony receiving its premiere a few months before his death. Although he wrote in many media, with a series of operas of which the last (1951) was *Pilgrim's Progress*, his chief esteem came through choral music and symphonies – these two types achieving a fusion in the *Sea Symphony* (first performed 1910) to words by Walt Whitman.

In youth a collector of English folksong, Vaughan Williams made some use of it in his orchestral music and also of a strain of 'English pastoral' individually derived by him from modal scale patterns and other archaic materials. The early composition usually referred to as the *Tallis Fantasia* (see below) powerfully pondered on these archaic roots and won a wide and durable international acceptance – while the symphonies, from the mellow *London Symphony* to the harsh no.6 and beyond, were little heard outside Britain.

A *Romance* for harmonica (mouth-organ) and strings, (1951) and a tuba concerto (1954) are among his later works.

A London Symphony

> Lento – Allegro risoluto
> Lento
> Scherzo (Nocturne)
> Andante con moto – Maestoso alla marcia – Lento
> Duration: 41–46 minutes

The composer was at pains to deny that this was a 'descriptive' piece. But he admitted that the reminiscence of the Westminster Chimes (those of Big Ben) in the first and last movements, and of a lavender-seller's street cry in the second movement, could be taken as 'local colour'. The first performance, conducted by Geoffrey Toye, took place in London on 27 March 1914; the composer later revised it three times and notably shortened it until arriving at a definitive version in 1934. The orchestration allowed for the omission of certain woodwind and brass instruments and for their parts to be 'cued' in by others – but this reflects the expected deficiencies of strength in British orchestras of the time, not an alternative artistic conception. A harp ('doubled if possible') is used as well as triple woodwind, 4 horns, 2 cornets *and* 2 trumpets, 3 trombones and tuba, kettledrums plus other assorted percussion (including 'jingles') which requires two players.

In conforming with the composer's practice, the symphony was not given a key-label. But it is in G major – the first and last movements being in that key, the mysterious second movement starting and finishing ambiguously, the third in D minor. The first movement begins with a veiled, slow introduction: through the mist the chimes of the half-hour are heard on the unexpected tones of a harp playing with the special effect of 'harmonics' (see p. 373). The extroverted main section then begins – a noisy, discordant theme of teeming activity prominent at first. A more jaunty vein, which brings in the triangle, portrays the holiday mood traditionally associated with Hampstead Heath: a cornet tune rings out. After musical development, both those moods re-emerge in altered form and with a happy ending.

The second movement, with a solo on the english horn emerging from the misty sound of muted strings, is meditative. The composer allowed an association with the quiet of a square in bygone Bloomsbury. A new tune arrives on a solo viola and leads to an imitation of a lavender-seller's call (at first on a piccolo). An emotional climax arises and subsides, leaving to the solo viola the quiet ending of the movement.

Most musical nocturnes are quiet and slow. This symphony's third movement is a night-piece with a different image. First comes a scurrying section which is literally repeated. The horns enter forcibly, but the scurrying soon returns. A more lively contrast ensues: a street-tune and perhaps the suggestion of a mouth-organ (from the horns). Again comes the scurrying theme: it fades, with a solo violin and a bassoon persisting.

The finale in its passionate opening music recalls the mood of the opening of the symphony. A march follows, and a mighty climax with a tam-tam stroke. The Westminster chimes are again heard (the third quarter, now), followed by a section marked 'Epilogue' – said to symbolize the ceaseless, unhurried Thames, and ending on quiet string chords.

Fantasia on a Theme by Thomas Tallis

Duration: 14–18 minutes

Though said on the title-page to be for 'double stringed orchestra', Vaughan Williams's work is in fact for three and not two bodies of players. As well as a larger (main) orchestra and a smaller (9 players), a string quartet is formed from the principal players of the respective sections.

Thomas Tallis (c. 1505–1585), one of the most distinguished composers of the Tudor period, contributed nine tunes to a collection of metrical psalms published in 1567. One of these ('Why fumeth in sight') is the tune borrowed by Vaughan Williams for his *Fantasia* – a term implying the free flow of ideas without adherence to a recognized formal pattern. The first performance, conducted by the composer at the Three Choirs Festival in Gloucester on 6 September 1910, was followed by two revisions before the work reached its definitive form.

The music is solemn but at the same time passionate, the unusually rich string palette enlarging on the grave strains of Tallis's tune. That richness of sound is typified by the opening (united orchestra). Shortly, beneath a *tremolo* on a single note from first violins, the theme (in an antique modal cast not quite corresponding to G minor) is heard in full, then with greater animation repeated. The two orchestras now take on separate roles (the smaller orchestra is muted); then the solo viola meditates in rhapsodic manner, joined by the first violin and afterwards by the rest of the solo quartet. The fantasy of musical ideas proceeds, leading to a hushed final recurrence of the tune and to a major-chord ending which gives yet a further archaic effect (a *Picardy third*: see p. 378).

VERDI

1813–1901

To rank among the three or four of the world's most durable composers of opera is sufficient fame for Giuseppe Verdi. Finding his first success with *Nabucco* in 1842 at Milan, he developed a powerful style which underwent considerable changes before his line of operatic tragedies finished in 1887 with the Shakespearean *Otello*: Shakespearean comedy in the form of *Falstaff* ended his operatic career six years later. The chorus of Hebrew slaves from *Nabucco* and the grand march from *Aida* are frequent concert excerpts, but promoters are otherwise hard pressed to find anything apart from the famous *Requiem* and the so-called *Four Sacred Pieces* – a group of separate, ill-fitting numbers for various vocal and instrumental performers.

So why not raid the overtures, as in the case of Rossini and so many other celebrated composers of opera? But Rossini's custom (like that of his contemporaries) was to write overtures in an extended formal pattern which made them satisfactorily self-contained. Verdi, some half a century later, rarely did so, preferring to equip most of his mature operas with no more than a short prelude. In composing *Otello* and *Falstaff*, he plunged into the first vocal number without even that. The example that follows is an exception.

Overture, The Force of Destiny

Duration: 7–8 minutes

It was a sign of Verdi's world fame that *La Forza del Destino* was first produced in St Petersburg on 10 November 1862. Three 'hammer-blows' which open the overture, and are repeated, suggest the hand of Fate which blindly takes control of the characters – a pistol-shot killing the heroine's father unintentionally, later a strange coincidence of encounters in Spain and Italy. Those hammer-blows, on the note E, become the emphatic notes in the main melody which follows immediately in A minor. The hammer-blows return, and other melodies from the opera are heard. The one which dominates the final part of the overture (and ends it, in E major) is sung by the heroine as she begs the Father Guardian of a monastery for refuge in her sorrow.

VIVALDI

1678–1741

'The red priest', as he was called from the colour of his hair, was born in Venice, worked mostly there, but spent his last years in Vienna at the Austrian emperor's court. The general public of today, which has made *The Four Seasons* into a best-seller on records, knows little of Vivaldi's large output of opera and other vocal works. His stature and originality made him a composer whom Bach found worth adapting. (See the note on the last of the works examined below.)

Though a priest, Vivaldi's life was that of a working musician, some fifteen years being spent as music instructor in a Venetian hospice for orphan girls. (The Italian term *conservatorio*, used for an institute with such a role of safeguarding or preserving, gave rise to the French/English term *conservatoire/conservatory* in its musical sense.) The three-movement concerto form, fast–slow–fast, was Vivaldi's favourite but not exclusive orchestral form. Most of the concertos, but not all, have solos for violin, cello, or (more rarely) other instruments; and although some concertos carry descriptive or playful titles, most do not.

Of Vivaldi's works, which today are estimated at more than 750, only a selection was published in his lifetime; but these works still remain the best known. As well as the set from which *The Four Seasons* comes, they include a set of 12 concertos called *L'estro armonico* (harmonious spirit), another set of 12 called *La Stravaganza* (extravagant fancy), and another set of 12 called *La Cetra* (the lyre).

Vivaldi's strings are in the modern grouping of first violins, second violins, violas, cellos and double-basses. But the cellos, with the double-basses which reinforce them an octave lower, have the specific job of providing (almost continuously) the bass of the harmony which gives music of this period its sense of secure progress. The bass line is also played by a keyboard instrument (harpsichord or organ), the keyboard-player also sounding the harmony in right-hand chords. See the note on *continuo*, p. 370.

The concertos

The word *concerto* had a very generalized significance in Vivaldi's time. Of more than 500 concertos ascribed to him, over sixty are for string orchestra without soloists; conversely, over twenty are works for a small group of soloists without orchestra. But most are works in which one or more soloists are contrasted with a string-orchestral background; and most of these (about 230) are for violin and orchestra. The violin was Vivaldi's own instrument and he belongs to the school of major Italian composers exploiting the instrument's exceptional range, penetration and expressive powers.

With very few exceptions, Vivaldi's concertos are in three movements, fast–slow–fast. An opening fast movement generally observes ritornello form (see p. 11); that part of the musical material which recurs in different keys (the ritornello) is entrusted to the orchestra, while the soloist's material springs out of it and extends or contrasts with it, using a soloist's greater technical skill. A final fast movement may be in this form too; a central slow movement is generally simple in structure, with the soloist commanding pathos by song-like expression.

Concertos for violin and string orchestra, opus 8, nos. 1–4 (The Four Seasons)

Duration: 40 minutes

Vivaldi's celebrated set of twelve concertos, opus 8, was published not later than 1725 with a dedication to a Bohemian nobleman, Count Wenzeslaus von Morzin, whose orchestra may have already performed them. The set bears a rather enigmatic Italian title, *Il cimento dell'armonia e dell'invenzione*, translated as *The rivalry between harmony and invention*. Best known are the first four of the set, collectively called *The Four Seasons* – all in different keys and all adhering to the structure described above with occasional surprises for reasons of picturesque description.

As will be seen, some of the headings of individual movements plainly indicate that the music is intended to be descriptive. Moreover, each concerto is prefaced by a sonnet, with more detailed description; the lines are also placed in the printed score at various points of the music itself. But the sonnets were written to 'demonstrate' the music, not the other way round.

The contrasts between movements, and the contrast of the solo violin and the orchestra within movements, achieve a lively variety of tone and pace. Whether with energy, agility, or deep sentiment, the soloist must dominate. The pictorial touches lend a humorous sauce to the music but are not its essence.

No.1 in E major, 'Spring'

> Allegro
> Largo e pianissimo sempre
> Pastoral dance: Allegro

In the first movement the chirruping birds are soon heard, with the solo violin prominent. Thunder makes a brief disturbance. The soloist is silent in the restful slow movement, in which the loudly emphasized notes of the violas are supposed to represent the dog barking while his master, the goatherd, sleeps. In the dance-style finale, the solo violin exhibits the skill of playing on two strings simultaneously (double-stopping).

No.2 in G minor, 'Summer'

> Allegro non molto
> Adagio
> Stormy summer weather: Presto

The opening movement, at first in 3/8 time and suggesting 'tiredness from the heat', is interrupted by a vigorous 4/4: under the solo violin's repeated notes, the cuckoo's call is suggested in the downward phrases in a solo cello's theme. The opening strain resumes, but gentle breezes turn into a sudden storm which prompts the shepherd to complain (solo violin). In the slow movement the solo violin spins out a smooth melody: the shepherd sleeps, but apparently not without worry over the weather! The storms of the finale justify his anxiety.

No.3 in F major, 'Autumn'

> Country people's song and dance: Allegro
> Sleeping drunkards: Adagio
> The hunt: Allegro

Rejoicing in the harvest occupies the first movement, one tipsy reveller falling over (descent from the solo violin's highest notes). In the slow movement, representing sleep after revelry, the solo violin is silent. The finale is one of the most celebrated of musical hunting scenes, with imitation of hunting-horn calls and, later, rapidly running figures as the prey tries to escape but is caught and killed.

No.4 in F minor, 'Winter'

> Allegro non molto
> Adagio
> Walking on the ice: Allegro

Shivering, stamping of feet and chattering of teeth are suggested by both orchestra and soloist in the first movement with its rapid repetitions of notes. The change of key to the second movement (E flat) suits the change of atmosphere: the violin's song is of fireside repose. The finale goes outdoors again: walking on the ice seems to bring a fall, and a later suggestion of stability is brushed aside as the scurrying violin represents the blustery winds.

WAGNER

1813–83

From his own day until now, Richard Wagner's music has been as much relished in the concert-hall as in the theatre. His chain of highly successful operas, from *The Flying Dutchman* to *Parsifal*, yielded overtures and purely orchestral extracts – often with an appreciable pictorial content, such as 'Siegfried's journey down the Rhine' from *Götterdämmerung* and the 'Good Friday Music' from *Parsifal*. In some of his works from *Tristan und Isolde* onwards (1865) occur other passages which, although using voices, are almost self-sufficient without them and lend themselves to orchestral performance.

In earlier works such as *The Flying Dutchman* and *Tannhäuser* Wagner based part of his appeal on the traditional force of catchy tunes with regular construction and emphatic choruses – and likewise later in *The Mastersingers*. Elsewhere, he captivates by an urgency of interleaving themes both vocal and orchestral, conveyed in rich sound. In order to achieve this richness he vastly enlarged the orchestra, often requiring reinforcements of the existing woodwind and brass instruments and (in the four operas of *The Ring*) introducing a new family of 'Wagner tubas' which were played by horn-players but produced a special, darker tone.

Quite a different sound-world is inhabited by the *Siegfried Idyll*, conceived for a domestic and not a theatrical occasion; along with the set of songs to poems by Mathilde Wesendonck, it is Wagner's only well-known non-operatic work.

Overture, The Flying Dutchman

Duration: 10 minutes

Wagner was himself the conductor when *The Flying Dutchman* (*Der fliegende Holländer*) was produced at Dresden in 1843. Its story is that of the accursed sea-wanderer who can be redeemed only by love.

Not only has the opera itself remained popular; the overture is admired for its depiction of sea-storm and the dramatic contrast of emotions. The piccolo in addition to two flutes, and the english horn in addition to two oboes, lend a special extension to the woodwind colours. A standard orchestral complement of 2 clarinets, 2 bassoons, 4 horns, 2 trumpets, 3 trombones and tuba is used, with kettledrums and strings.

The opening *tremolo* of strings is a classic summoning of agitation – agitation of the elements of nature and of our minds as well. (The device had been most effectively used by Weber – see p. 362 – and was to form a favourite symphonic opening of Bruckner's.) Here, the heavy bass theme below represents the Dutchman himself (in D minor) and will be encountered in the ˏopera when his ship approaches. The storm rages, then subsides to a moment of stillness. A slow, earnest theme is heard in F major: it represents the heroine, Senta, and her role in redeeming the Dutchman.

The mood changes. Woodwind and brass deliver a light tune which is the dance of the sailors *not* from the Dutchman's ship. More use of the Dutchman's and Senta's themes leads to a climax, a dramatic pause, and a change to a joyful D major which embraces both those themes. This D-major section either proceeds shortly and with uninterrupted lively pace to its end or (a revision on the composer's part, usually adopted in concert performances) has a drawn-out cadence suggesting the opera's final moments – Senta's self-sacrifice, the redemption of the Dutchman, and the unity of the lovers in death.

Prelude, The Mastersingers

Duration: 9–10 minutes

Compared to the prelude to *Tristan and Isolde*, which sets the mood for the opening scene and moves directly into it, the music which welcomes the audience to a performance of *The Mastersingers* is an overture of the old-fashioned kind. It is a long work in which a number of different tunes from the opera are organized into a formal, sonata-like scheme with an assertive conclusion. In stage performances there is a modified ending which goes straight to the opening chorus, but none the less the overture has been rounded off in feeling and in key – C major, the key which, in the opera, is chosen by Wagner to represent rightness, authority and the joy of song.

The opening is taken from the processional music of the master-singers' guild. Under the guild's aegis, in the final scene, the contest of song takes place by which the young knight Walther wins the hand of Eva – after an exposure of the would-be cheating of his odious rival, Beckmesser. This C-major music over, the orchestra passes to less weighty, more fleeting themes, prominent among them a motive derived from the crowd's mockery of Beckmesser (recognizable if one fits the words of the libretto in English trans-lation: 'Surely she'll refuse him'). A return to C major presents an imposing contrapuntal web in which the tuba has perhaps its greatest-ever moment of orchestral glory, playing the Master-singers' theme and finishing with an unaccustomed trill.

A triangle (decorating the joyful final bars), harp and piccolo are also added to an otherwise standard medium-sized orchestra, with double woodwind, 4 horns, 2 trumpets, 3 trombones, kettledrums and strings.

Prelude and Love–Death, Tristan and Isolde

Duration: 17–18 minutes

The opera *Tristan and Isolde*, produced in Munich under Hans von Bülow's baton in 1865, is a revolutionary work – not merely in the harmonies which baffled even such a contemporary as Berlioz, but in a libretto (the composer's own, as usual) which identifies love with oblivion and even with death. Of the two ill-fated, adulterous lovers, Tristan allows himself to be killed in a sword-fight; Isolde expires on his body, singing of abandoning herself to waves or clouds: 'Unconscious – highest joy!' This, the end of the opera, is known as Isolde's *Liebestod*, for which 'love–death' is an English equivalent.

The opera's prelude is composed of surging themes to be realized in the couple's passionate love; it is linked (not by the composer, but as a practicable concert piece) with the Love–Death, where the earlier, surging music is recalled within a context of an ecstatic fulfilment. The notes of Isolde's vocal part being almost completely doubled by various instruments of the orchestra, the music may be performed purely orchestrally with only the smallest adjustment. The orchestration includes triple woodwind (including bass clarinet and english horn) and harp.

The famous opening to the prelude, very quiet, presents two short phrases, the first on the cellos, the second on the woodwind; they alternate and are transformed. The music, in an indeterminate key at first, seems to settle in A major. After a stormy climax the music again becomes soft and fragmented, the prelude ending on two *pizzicato* notes low on cellos and double-basses.

The 'Love–Death' music begins immediately: through trembling strings, a bass clarinet and then an ordinary clarinet give out the smooth theme which corresponds to Isolde's description of her dead lover: 'Mild and gentle, see how he smiles!'. Isolde's thoughts recapture their passionate love. The music attains its goal in B major and fades: the harp ceases its flow and only a few seconds before the end the second (woodwind) phrase of the prelude is breathed again as a last farewell.

Siegfried Idyll

Duration: 17–18 minutes

Christmas Day was the birthday of Wagner's wife (and former mistress) Cosima. Early on that day in 1870, at their home near Lucerne in Switzerland, Wagner surprised her with a performance by seventeen musicians of this new work. Their son Siegfried, born before their marriage during the previous year, had been named after the heroic character of *The Ring*. Wagner was on the point of finishing the third opera of that cycle, actually entitled *Siegfried*. From that opera comes most of the thematic material of this instrumental work – hence the name given on publication. The original manuscript, however, gives the title as *Tribschen Idyll* (after the name of their villa).

The music is slow and tender throughout. A single flute, 1 oboe, 2 clarinets, 1 bassoon, two horns and a single trumpet (tellingly reserved for the climax) are used, plus strings. The opening theme (strings) is associated with the 'eternal womanhood' of Brünnhilde, the warrior–heroine. Later the oboe announces another theme derived from an old German lullaby. The strings put on mutes, and against twittering violins the woodwind announce a theme identified with the name of 'glorious Siegfried'. The trumpet joins in a joyful assertion, and the 'eternal womanhood' theme softly closes the work.

WALTON

1902–83

Although older than Benjamin Britten, William Walton in his later years tended to be overshadowed by Britten's many-sided brilliance and by the younger man's greater flair for the theatre. But in the dozen years from about 1929 Walton's output of orchestral and choral work was such as to fear no comparison. Earlier, he had shown himself as the brilliant and mildly shocking composer of *Façade*, which was to find life in three different forms.

Elgar's legacy of the grand gesture is sometimes detectable, particularly in the coronation march *Crown Imperial* (1937). But a thoroughly individual voice spoke in Walton's First Symphony, the Viola Concerto of 1929 and the Violin Concerto of 1939 (commissioned by Heifetz). The cantata *Belshazzar's Feast* (1931), in which the biblical story is reinterpreted in Osbert Sitwell's text, showed orchestral as well as choral skill. (Two extra brass groups, sometimes misleadingly referred to as two brass bands, reinforce the climaxes.) Among Walton's wartime film scores, that for *Henry V* yielded some effective concert extracts. A new batch of sizeable orchestral works composed after the Second World War included the Cello Concerto and the Second Symphony.

Symphony No.1

> Allegro assai
> Presto con malizia
> Andante con malinconia
> Maestoso – Brioso ed ardentemente – Vivacissimo – Maestoso
> Duration: 40–45 minutes

Walton had difficulty in completing his first symphony and permitted the first three movements to be given, without the intended finale, under the conductorship of Sir Hamilton Harty in London on not minutes!) is 12, 11, 11, 6 and 33. Composed in Vienna in 1913, they were not heard until 22 June 1926 at Zurich, when the composer himself conducted. The scoring treats all the instrumentalists as soloists – a string quartet replaces the usual orchestral string section and the unique, strange-sounding ensemble includes harmonium, guitar, mandolin and celesta along with flute (doubling piccolo), oboe, clarinet (doubling high clarinet in E flat), bass clarinet, horn, trumpet, trombone, harp and percussion (including xylophone, glockenspiel and sheep bells).

The sheep bells seem to indicate an impressionist approach – a depiction of a country scene. There can be, in this short duration, no thematic development – indeed no themes. The succession of changing tone colours, almost note by note, occupies the listener's attention.

GLOSSARY

Technical terms used in the text are explained here, and so are such terms used by composers as directions for performance – e.g., *andante, presto, scherzando*. Where the word is not English, the origin (French, German, Italian, Latin, Russian) is given. The English equivalents given are not comprehensive, but are confined to those relevant to this book.

ad lib (Lat., ad libitum) at discretion, i.e. at the discretion of the performer.

adagio (Ital.) slow.

affettuoso (Ital.) with feeling.

agitato (Ital.) agitated.

alla (Ital.) in the style of (like French 'à la').

allargando (Ital.) becoming slower.

allegretto (Ital.) not quite so lively as allegro.

allegro (Ital.) lively; term also often indicating the principal (faster) main, section of a movement which begins with a slow introduction.

amoroso (Ital.) lovingly.

andante (Ital.) fairly slow.

andantino (Ital.) (usually) not quite so slow as andante.

anima (Ital.) spirit; *see* con.

animato (Ital.) animated.

arabesque (Fr., Eng.) a decorative phrase.

arpeggio (Ital.) harp–like, i.e. (of a chord) played with the notes successively, usually from the bass up, not with all notes simultaneously struck.

baroque term used to indicate the prevalent style of Western music approximately 1600–1750.

bass either the lowest (male) voice or the lowest-pitched note of a harmonized passage of music.

bass drum a large shallow drum of low but indefinite pitch.

basset-clarinet modern name for a clarinet built slightly longer to produce lower notes (see p. 246).

basset-horn instrument of the clarinet family of lower pitch than standard clarinet but not so low as bass clarinet: used by Mozart, e.g. in his opera *The Magic Flute*. The basset-clarinet is something else: see preceding entry.

bassoon bass woodwind instrument played with a double reed.

ben, bene (Ital.) well, very.

bitonality the use of two keys ('tonalities') together.

bongos (bongo drums) small Afro–Cuban single-headed drums which are joined together horizontally and played with the fingers and other parts of the hand.

bourrée, old dance-movement in quick double time, beginning with an up-beat.

brass that section of an orchestra comprising instruments made of brass or similar metal – regularly, horns, trumpets, trombones, tuba.

brio (Ital.) spirit, liveliness: **con brio**, with spirit.

BWV, German initials used to number Bach's works (Bach–Werke–Verzeichnis – Bach Work Index).

cadenza (Ital.) a soloist's elaboration, especially in a concerto at a designated point towards the end of a movement.

camera (Ital.) chamber, room; **da camera**, (music) for performance by a small orchestra – or, sometimes, for performance in a hall as distinct from a church.

canon composition (or part of a composition), for several 'voices' (*see* voice) where one follows the other, repeating the melody.

cantabile (Ital.) in a singing style, i.e. smooth and expressive.

canzona, canzone (Ital.) song, especially one of simple or popular character, not elaborate as in an opera.

capo (Ital.) head, beginning; *da capo* (abbr. D.C.), instruction to go back to the beginning and repeat the music to a specified point.

celesta (pronounced as English word; it is not Italian) instrument looking like a small upright piano but having hammers striking metal bars giving bell-like sound.

cello (abbreviation of Ital. *violoncello*), bowed four-stringed instrument, one of the family of which the principal member is the violin; pitched lower than the viola, higher than double-bass.

chaconne piece in which one phrase, generally in the bass-line, repeats itself below changing upper parts.

chamber orchestra twentieth-century term for an orchestra smaller than normal symphonic size (usually with reduced-size string section and no trombones or tuba).

chorale (mock-German word; German *Choral*) hymn.

chord a simultaneous sounding of several notes.

chromatic using (prominently) the 'sharps and flats' outside the prevailing scale.

clarinet woodwind instrument with single reed and normally a wooden (exceptionally a metal) body, in use since mid-eighteenth century. In this book and most other references, the word normally refers to the standard-sized instrument in B flat or A; of other existent sizes, the most frequently met are the higher-pitched instrument in E flat and the bass clarinet. *See also* basset-horn.

classic(al), classicism terms identifying a reserved, stable style, especially that of the 'Vienna classics' (Haydn, Mozart, Beethoven).

claves (Span.), two short cylindrical hardwood sticks struck together as an instrument of percussion – originally a Latin-American dance-band instrument.

clavier any keyboard instrument, or the keyboard itself.

clef distinguishing mark at the beginning of a stave fixing which line represents which note.

coda (Ital.) an 'extra' section (literally 'tail') at the end of a movement.

col, coll', colla, colle (Ital.) with the (*see* con). *For* col legno *see* legno.

come (Ital.) like, as.

comodo (Ital.) easy (i.e. at an easy pace).

compass the stretch of a singer's or instrumentalist's range from lowest to highest.

con (Ital.) with; con anima, with spirit.

concertante (Ital.) performing together as partners; or 'like a concerto' in the term *sinfonia concertante* (but see p.251).

concertino either the small group of soloists in a *concerto grosso*, or (twentieth-century) a little concerto.

concerto (Ital.) see p.10.

concerto grosso (Ital.) a (baroque) piece in which a large group of instrumentalists is contrasted with a smaller; or the term for the larger group itself.

concord a chord which seems at rest, without the need to be 'resolved' on another chord.

continuo (Ital., abbr. of *basso continuo*) a type of accompaniment (current particularly c. 1600–1750) played from a bass-line, most commonly on a keyboard instrument. From the bass-notes, the player worked out the correct harmonies, sometimes aided by numerical shorthand indications provided by the composer.

contrabassoon *see* double-bassoon.

cor anglais *see* english horn.

counterpoint the simultaneous combination of melodies.

courante (Fr.) old French dance in triple time.

crescendo (Ital.) becoming louder.

crotales (also called 'ancient cymbals') small metal discs struck by a beater: unlike the regular (and larger) cymbals, they are tuned to definite pitch.

cymbal percussion instrument consisting of a plate of metal which is usually either struck with drumstick (single stroke or roll) or clashed against another cymbal. *See also* crotales.

da (Ital.) from; *see* capo.

de (Fr.) of, from.

descant an upper line of melody above the principal melody.

development the composer's process of proceeding from themes by splitting them, combining them, changing their inner elements, etc.; hence the *development section* of a symphonic movement, following an initial statement of themes.

di (Ital.) of.

diminuendo (Ital.) becoming softer.

divertimento (Ital.) short piece, supposedly of an entertaining kind, in several movements.

divisi (Ital.) 'divided', e.g. of a section of the orchestra when its members are split so that some play an upper and some a lower line.

dolce (Ital.) gently, sweetly.

dolente (Ital.) mournfully.

dominant note of the scale standing a perfect fifth above the keynote (as G is above C), which has a particularly close relation to the keynote in normal (tonal) harmony.

dopo (Ital.) after.

doppio (Ital.) double; **doppio movimento**, at twice the (preceding) speed.

double (as verb) an expression denoting the capability of the player of one instrument to switch to another instrument – 'flute doubling piccolo'.

double-bass the largest and lowest bowed stringed instrument of the orchestra.

double-bassoon (also known as contrabassoon) largest and lowest instrument of the orchestral woodwind, approximately an octave below the bassoon.

double-stopping on a bowed instrument, the act of playing on two strings simultaneously, necessitating the placing of fingers separately to 'stop' both strings. Similarly **triple-stopping, quadruple stopping**.

e (Ital.) and.

ein, eine (Ger.) one.

english horn, woodwind instrument of oboe type, but standing a fifth lower than the oboe. More usually in Britain called cor anglais; but the translated form english horn is more sensible, is accepted American usage, and corresponds also to use in other languages – Italian *corno inglese*, etc.

entr'acte (Fr.) piece played between the acts of a play.

exposition the first main section of a movement, in which the principal themes are presented before being subject to development.

et (Fr., Lat.) and.

family colloquial expression for a broad grouping of instruments, e.g. the woodwind family.

fanfare a musical figure, often on brass instruments and related to the characteristic calls of a bugle or natural trumpet, intended to summon attention like a signal to action.

fantasy a free musical form, not in a set pattern.

figure an identifiable, recognizable group of notes.

finale (Ital.) last movement of a musical work, or the last number in each act of an opera.

fine (Ital.) end.

florid ornate; a **florid** melody, one in which many supplementary notes are heard as well as the main notes.

flourish same as fanfare.

flute general name for various types of woodwind instruments without reeds, particularly the cross-blown instrument which is one of the standard higher-pitched orchestral woodwind instruments. The alto flute, slightly lower, but held the same way, is occasionally used by twentieth-century composers.

forte, fortissimo (Ital.) loud, very loud.

fugue music in which successive entries of a melody follow each other at different pitches, creating an overlapping effect.

fuoco (Ital.) fire; **con fuoco**, with fire, ardently.

für (Ger.) for.

galant (Fr., Ger.) courtly, polite – a term of style applied historically to a simple graceful music in the mid-eighteenth century (roughly between Bach's and Mozart's styles)

gavotte old dance in 4/4 time, with two beats before the first bar.

giusto (Ital.) exact; **tempo giusto**, strict time.

glissando (mock-Ital.) sliding; applied to continuous upward or downward sliding of pitch on stringed instruments or trombones, etc., but on the harp to a continuous sweep up or down the strings.

glockenspiel (Ger., play of bells) percussion instrument of tuned metal bars giving small bell-like sound: played with keyboard or (more usually) small hammers held in hand.

gong general name for a large circular disc struck with mallet as percussion instrument; tuned specimens are found, or untuned (among which is the tam-tam).

grave (Ital.) slow.

grazia, grazioso (Ital.) grace, graceful(ly).

habanera Latin-American dance (from Havana, Cuba) in characteristic rhythm later associated with the tango.

hairpins colloquial expression for marks of increasing (<) and decreasing (>) loudness.

harmonic (as noun) one of the pure constituent tones of a normal musical sound; a string-player's *harmonics* are high, pure notes achieved by setting only part of the string in vibration.

harp plucked stringed instrument of ancient origin; the modern orchestral model is the double-action harp, with pedals.

Hob. abbreviation for (Antony van) Hoboken, whose classificatory catalogue is used to number and identify Haydn's works.

horn type of wind instrument descended from primitive use of an animal's horn for blowing through. The term now applies especially to the coiled brass orchestral instrument which was developed (particularly in France, whence the name French horn) from the earlier hunting horn or hand-horn. See also english horn.

il (Ital.) the (masculine).

interval the 'distance' between notes in a scale, in a chord, etc; so a major second, e.g. from C to D, is less than a major third, C to E.

invert to turn upside-down, e.g. to subject a theme to a transformation in which upward movement is replaced by an exactly similar downward movement, and vice versa.

janissary music type of music with cymbals and triangle incorporated into certain works by Mozart and others in imitation of Turkish military bands.

jig old dance normally in 6/8 time; the French *gigue* and Italian *giga* correspond to it.

K. abbreviation for Köchel's index giving numerical order to Mozart's works.

kettledrum cauldron-shaped drum originally from the Orient, and originally smaller and more delicate sounding than now; in modern form, tuned to a definite pitch, normally by handles on the rim, or (twentieth-century) by pedals. Timpani is a synonym for the plural form.

key (1) hand-operated lever, as on the keyboard of a piano; (2) an ordering of the notes of the scale, the major and minor keys being the prevalent such orders in most Western music.

khorovod (Rus.) round-dance.

la (Fr., Ital., Sp.) the (feminine).

largo slow, broad.

largamente broadly, grandly.

le (Fr.) the (masculine).

leader British term for the person who heads the first violin section of an orchestra and is the orchestra's chief liaison with the conductor. In North American usage 'leader' means conductor and 'concert-master' corresponds to British 'leader'.

legato (Ital.) smoothly.

leggero, leggeramente (Ital.; also in older spelling *leggiero*, etc.) light(ly).

legno (Ital.,) wood; **col legno**, instruction to string-players to reverse their bows so that the wood of the bow hits the string.

leicht (Ger.) light(ly).

lent, lento (Fr., Ital.) slow.

les (Fr.) the (plural),

licenza (Ital.) liberty; **con alcuna licenza**, with some freedom.

Lied (Ger.) song.

ma (Ital.) but.

maestoso (Ital.) majestically.

major *see* key.

maracas (Span.) a pair of gourd rattles, shaken (in Latin-American popular music and occasionally in orchestral use) to produce a 'shuffling' sound.

marcia (Ital.) march.

marimba a type of xylophone (developed from Latin-American models) having a range lower than the standard instrument.

martenot abbreviated form of ondes Martenot: see p.235.

marziale (Ital.) martial, in military or march style.

menuet (Fr.) minuet.

mesto (Ital.) sad.

minor *see* key.

minuetto (Ital.) minuet.

mit (Ger.) with.

modal *see* mode.

mode an ordering of the notes of the scale; thus 'major mode' is sometimes used for 'major key'. But since there are alternative orderings which historically preceded the major/minor systems, the terms *mode* and *modal* often refer to the *non*-major/minor orderings found for example in folk-music.

molto much, very.

morendo (Ital.) dying away.

mosso (Ital.) with movement.

motif, motiv, motive (Fr., Ger., Eng.) (1) a theme, especially one which symbolizes something non-musical e.g. a character in an opera; (2) a *smaller* group than a theme, being the smallest group of notes that can be identified as a unit.

motto, motto theme a theme which pervades a work, perhaps appearing in more than one movement.

movement the main division of a longer work such as a symphony or concerto (in essence or origin considered to be centred on a single speed, fast or slow, and thus contrasted with other movements).

movimento (Ital.) not *movement* in the above form, but *motion*.

mute a device placed on instruments (especially those of strings and brass) to quieten or otherwise alter the sound-quality.

natural (of a wind instrument) having no valves and therefore confined to a simple series of notes such as those obtained by blowing through an animal's horn, etc.; hence natural trumpet.

nocturne a piece suggestive of night.

non (Fr., Ital.) no, not.

notation the writing down of music, or a system of such writing.

note, (1) the written symbol for a single musical sound; (2) the simple musical sound itself.

number an item of music, especially in stage works ('the act has five numbers').

obbligato (Ital.) term denoting a prominent accompanying instrument ('voice with flute obbligato').

oboe woodwind instrument blown through a double reed; the **oboe d'amore** was a variant instrument of slightly lower range, used in Bach's time. *See also* english horn.

octave an interval of 8 notes (counting both extremities), e.g. C to the next C up or down. So a melody *in octaves* means the same melody simultaneously performed an octave apart, e.g. when sung by both women's and men's voices.

ondes Martenot an electronic instrument played from a keyboard; *see* p.235.

open (of a note) not modified by the player's hand, e.g. **open strings** on a violin, not **stopped**.

opus (Lat.) a work; term used, with digits following, to number a work in the composer's supposed sequence of composition or publication.

ostinato (Ital.) a short figure many times repeated, usually in the bass.

overture *see* p.14.

part in musical contexts not usually a section or division of a work, but a layer or strand given to a particular performer or performers: 'the clarinet part', 'the vocal parts'.

partita (Ital.) a suite.

pasodoble (Sp.) twentieth-century Spanish dance in quick 2/4 time.

passage a short section of music, especially one which has a transitional or subsidiary function.

pastiche (Fr.) a piece written in the style of some other composer or period.

pastoral suggestive (e.g. by imitative sounds) of the countryside.

pause a halting of the music at a designated note or rest.

pavan, pavane (Eng., Fr.) slow, stately dance dating from the sixteenth century or earlier.

pedal (1) foot-operated lever, as on piano or harp; (2) a sustained low note as the bass of harmony.

pentatonic (Gk.) five-note; particularly, the *pentatonic scale*, re-producible on the black notes of the piano.

pesante (Ital.) heavy, heavily.

piacere (Ital.) pleasure, used in phrase *a piacere*, with freedom of expression.

piacevole (Ital.) pleasantly.

piangendo (Ital.) weeping.

pianissimo, *see* piano.

piano (Ital., pronounced *pi-ah-no* to distinguish it from instrument) soft; **pianissimo**, very soft.

picardy third the interval of a major third – as part of a final major chord in a minor-key piece.

piccolo small flute pitched an octave above the standard flute.

pitch the property according to which notes appear to be 'high' or 'low'.

più (Ital.) more; **più allegro**, faster.

piuttosto (Ital.) rather, somewhat.

pizzicato (Ital.) plucked (the manner of plucking a string on a violin, etc. by hand, instead of bowing it).

poco (Ital.) a little; **un poco adagio**, rather slow.

poi (Ital.) then, next.

polytonality the use of several keys ('tonalities') together.

portamento (Ital.) the expressive effect of sliding between two notes instead of making a clear jump to the second one.

prelude (1) a piece preceding a play or opera, as an alternative sometimes preferred in the nineteenth and twentieth centuries to *overture*; (2) an 'introductory' piece in some other sense (see the Debussy example, p.136); (3) an independent short piece, e.g. Chopin's for piano.

prestissimo (Ital.) *see* presto.

presto (Ital.) fast; **prestissimo**, very fast.

quasi (Ital.) approximately, like, in the manner of.

rallentando (Ital.) becoming slower.

recapitulation not a literal repetition (*see* repeat) but that part of a movement which restates the opening material in a new, more unified way.

recitative type of vocal utterance in which music makes an approximation to speech-rhythm; hence, an instrumental utterance resembling this.

repeat a literal repetition, especially of a large section of music; **repeat mark**, a written indication for such a procedure.

rest a gap of silence notated by a number of beats, while the pace continues (not a pause).

rhapsody *see* p.14.

ritardando (Ital.) becoming slower.

ritenuto (Ital.) held back.

ritornello (Ital.) *see* p.14.

rococo historical term to denote much the same as *galant*.

romantic(ism) historical term for an early nineteenth-century style supposedly more individual and expansive than previous classicism; hence applied also to later music sharing this characteristic.

rondo form of movement in which the main theme periodically returns in the same key.

rubato (Ital.) 'robbed', i.e. a feature of performance in which the music is briefly speeded up or slowed down without losing basic pulse.

saraband, sarabande (Eng., Fr.) old dance in slow 3/2 time.

saxophone name of a family of wind instruments having a reed resembling a clarinet's – and therefore classified among the wind, not brass, despite a metal body.

scherzando *see* scherzo.

scherzo (Ital.) a lively, humorous movement, usually as third movement of a symphony and in 3/4 time; **scherzando** or

scherzoso, humorously – a direction not necessarily confined to movements designated scherzo.

semitone *see* tone.

serenade in Viennese classical and some later music, a work in several movements designed for social entertainment.

sforzando, sforzato (Ital.) suddenly accented.

siciliana (Ital.) a dance, or a piece evocative of it, in gently swaying 6/8 or 12/8 time.

side-drum *see* snare-drum.

sinfonia (Ital.) the term from which the English *symphony* is derived.

sinfonietta twentieth-century term made up as a diminutive of the preceding (but not itself an Italian word) to mean a little symphony or a little symphony orchestra.

snare drum, small drum slung slightly to one side when marching – hence alternative British (not US) name, side-drum; used in the orchestra, military band, dance band, etc. The lower skin is in contact with gut strings, or wires (called snares), which add a rattling effect to the tone and can be disengaged at will.

soave (Ital.) sweet(ly).

sonata-form *see* p.12.

sostenuto (Ital.) sustained, prolonged.

spirito spirit; liveliness; **spiritoso**, lively, sprightly.

staccato (Ital.) detached, short – said of the manner in which a performer sounds a note with a sharp attack and then quits it immediately.

stop (1) **stopped notes**, notes on the horn modified by the player's pushing the hand into the bell; (2) **to stop**, of string-playing, to shorten the length of the vibrating string by the placing of the finger – hence **double-stopping** (on two strings) etc.

stringendo (Ital.) tightening, accelerating.

strings name given to that section of the orchestra comprising the stringed instruments played with a bow – violins (normally divided into first and second), violas, cellos, double-basses. The harp, though strung, is conventionally not included.

subject a musical unit identifiable in the structure of a work, e.g. first and second subjects as the contrasting elements in sonata-form.

suite (Fr.) *see* p. 14.

symphonic poem *see* p. 14.

symphony *see* p. 14.

syncopation the placing of a strong accent on a normally weak beat.

tam-tam a form of large gong not tuned to definite pitch.

temple block hollowed-out wooden block approximately shaped like a human head — a percussion instrument of oriental origin, usually in several sizes to give different pitches.

tempo (Ital.) a basic speed ('the tempo becomes faster').

theme (1) an identifiable group of notes, important in the structure of a work; (2) a self-contained section of music subject to a set of later changes ('theme and variations').

toccata (Ital.) a brilliant show-piece, especially one for keyboard (or an orchestral imitation).

tombeau (Fr. tomb) a work dedicated to someone's memory.

tom-tom, name given in the West to certain kinds of African and oriental drums; those used in jazz bands and occasionally in the orchestra are usually in sets of two or more, tuned to different pitches and struck with sticks.

tone (1) a pure sound at a certain pitch ('a note on the violin may be acoustically analysed as comprising several tones'); (2) North American equivalent for 'note' in a phrase like 'this chord is made up of three tones'; (3) the *interval* comprising two steps (semitones) of the conventional scale, e.g. from C to D.

tone poem *see* p. 14.

transpose to write down or perform music at a pitch other than the pitch originally notated. Thus 'transposing instruments', e.g. horn or clarinet, are those which sound notes at a pitch higher or lower than the written notes which the player reads.

treble term used to denote higher-pitched instruments or parts, opposite to bass.

tremolo (Ital.) a trembling – hence, a musical effect (e.g. the rapid back-and-forth of a string-player's bow) designed to suggest this physical effect. Hence **tremolando**, the action of performing thus.

triangle three-cornered metal-framed percussion instrument, struck with a metal stick, tuned to a high but indefinite pitch.

trill a repeated rapid articulation of a note in alternation with the next (higher or lower) note.

trio (1) a threesome; (2) the central section of a minuet, etc; *see* p. 13.

trombone (from Ital., literally 'large trumpet') type of brass instrument generally possessing a slide which serves to vary the effective length of the tube, thus making a different series of notes available. In today's orchestral use, the indication 'three trombones' generally means two tenor trombones and one bass. Sizes smaller (higher) and larger (lower) also exist.

troppo too much, chiefly in the phrase **non troppo**, not too much.

trumpet metal wind-instrument, cylindrically bored, regularly appearing in the orchestra from the seventeenth century. The basic modern form (from mid-nineteenth century) has three valves. The standard size in today's orchestra is that in B flat or C; smaller (higher) and larger (lower) instruments are occasionally specified.

tuba type of bass brass valved instrument made in several sizes and shapes; since its invention (1835) it has become the normal lowest brass instrument of the orchestra. On its own, the word generally means a standard-sized **bass tuba**; the smaller **tenor tuba** is more usually called (in Britain) euphonium. See also Wagner tuba.

tubular bells a set of metal tubes struck with a hammer and tuned to the notes of a scale.

tutti (Ital.) all, especially the orchestra as distinct from soloist in a concerto, etc.

twelve-note system of musical composition associated with Schoenberg and his school, in which all 12 notes (corresponding to the 7 white and 5 black on the piano), are treated as equal, instead of being related through their place in major or minor keys.

un, una, uno (Ital.) one.

und (Ger.) and.

unison a simultaneous sounding of a note by more than one performer. (The term is extended to denote a sounding in octaves).

valve mechanism on the horn, trumpet, etc. to alter the length of the tube and thus to make a new series of notes accessible.

veloce (Ital.) fast.

vibraphone percussion instrument on which metal bars (laid out on the pattern of a piano keyboard) are struck with small padded beaters held in both hands; the sound is electronically vibrated.

Viennese Classics, Viennese School the musical style and personages associated with Haydn, Mozart and Beethoven; the term **Second Viennese School** is applied (less often) to Schoenberg, Berg and Webern.

viola bowed stringed instrument, a lower-pitched relative of the violin, in pitch between a violin and a cello.

violin bowed four-stringed instrument, the principal (and highest) member of the family of instruments (called the violin family) which came into general use in the late seventeenth century. The other regular orchestral members are the viola, cello and double-bass.

violoncello *see* cello.

virtuoso (Ital.) a highly skilled performer.

vivace (Ital.) lively.

vivo (Ital.) lively.

voice term often used in instrumental contexts to indicate a single line or part.

Wagner tuba type of instrument in two sizes (tenor and bass) devised by Wagner for his cycle of operas, *The Ring*, and occasionally used orchestrally by other composers. The sound is in between horn tone and true tuba tone and the instruments are entrusted to horn-players.

whip percussion instrument in which two sticks of wood, hinged at the top, are slapped together.

whole-tone scale, the scale which has no semitones, e.g. C,D,E, F sharp, G sharp, A sharp, C.

wind-machine, a large rotating roller covered and placed in such a way as to simulate wind – originally devised for theatres, and occasionally used by composers for special effect.

woodwind that section of an orchestra comprising instruments which have a single tube with a key-mechanism to select the note sounded, and are generally made of wood – though flutes are often made of metal and saxophones always are. Flutes, oboes, clarinets and bassoons are basic to the orchestra; their 'extensions' (e.g. piccolo as the higher instrument of the flute family and double-bassoon as the lower-pitched relative of the bassoon) are increasingly found in the orchestral repertory written since 1800.

xylophone percussion instrument consisting of tuned wooden bars (hence the name, from Greek for 'wood' and 'sound'), arranged in order as on a piano keyboard and struck with small hard-headed sticks.

INDEX

INDEX

Bold type indicates a principal discussion of the work or the composer